Women Navigating Globalization

NEW MILLENNIUM BOOKS IN INTERNATIONAL STUDIES

SERIES EDITORS

Eric Selbin, Southwestern University
Vicki Golich, Metropolitan State College of Denver

FOUNDING EDITOR

Deborah J. Gerner, University of Kansas

NEW MILLENNIUM BOOKS issue out of the unique position of the global system at the beginning of a new millennium in which our understandings about war, peace, terrorism, identity, sovereignty, security, and sustainability—whether economic, environmental, or ethical—are likely to be challenged. In the new millennium of international relations, new theories, new actors, and new policies and processes are all bound to be engaged. Books in the series are of three types: compact core texts, supplementary texts, and readers.

EDITORIAL BOARD

Titles in the Series

Global Backlash edited by Robin Broad
Globalization and Belonging by Sheila Croucher
Women Navigating Globalization by Jana Everett and Sue Ellen M. Charlton
The Global New Deal, 2nd ed., by William F. Felice
The Information Revolution and World Politics by Elizabeth C. Hanson
Sword & Salve by Peter J. Hoffman and Thomas G. Weiss
International Law in the 21st Century by Christopher C. Joyner
Elusive Security by Laura Neack
The New Foreign Policy, 3rd ed., by Laura Neack
International Negotiation in a Complex World, 3rd ed., by Brigid Starkey, Mark A. Boyer, and Jonathan Wilkenfeld
Global Politics as if People Mattered, 2nd ed., by Mary Ann Tétreault and Ronnie D. Lipschutz
Military-Civilian Interactions, 2nd ed., by Thomas G. Weiss

Women Navigating Globalization

Feminist Approaches to Development

Jana Everett and Sue Ellen M. Charlton

ROWMAN & LITTLEFIELD
Lanham • *Boulder* • *New York* • *Toronto* • *Plymouth, UK*

Published by Rowman & Littlefield
4501 Forbes Boulevard, Suite 200, Lanham, Maryland 20706
www.rowman.com

10 Thornbury Road, Plymouth PL6 7PP, United Kingdom

British Library Cataloguing in Publication Information Available

Library of Congress Cataloging-in-Publication Data

Everett, Jana Matson.
    Women navigating globalization : feminist approaches to development / Jana Everett and Sue Ellen M. Charlton.
        pages cm. — (New millennium books in international studies)
    Includes index.
    ISBN 978-1-4422-2576-3 (cloth : alk. paper) — ISBN 978-1-4422-2577-0 (pbk. : alk. paper) — ISBN 978-1-4422-2578-7 (electronic) 1. Women in development. I. Charlton, Sue Ellen M. II. Title.
    HQ1240.E927 2014
    305.4—dc23
                                                                    2013030896

Contents

Illustrations

FIGURES

PHOTOS

TABLES

Preface

Commentators in the United States may proclaim that feminism is dead, but today around the world provocative performances demonstrate the energy, passion, and creativity of young women who believe that a woman's struggle to control her body is far from over. In 2013, Femen, a group that began in Ukraine, staged a topless protest in Paris over the threatened stoning of a young woman in Algeria and has used the same tactic to protest sex tourism. Groups in India, Brazil, Israel, and Britain have staged marches in solidarity with SlutWalks, which started in Canada after the police recommended that women, in order to stay safe, not dress like sluts. In India, the Gulabi (pink) Gang beats up men who abuse women.

In different parts of the world and in different communities, women challenge versions of feminism that associate little or no dress with freedom, arguing instead that their integrity and identity require veiling and conservative dress. This challenge represents an equally important subversion of the global culture that exploits voyeurism of the female body as part of consumer marketing. Meanwhile, others argue forcefully that the central issues for women's movements must be global poverty and gender equity.

These debates are part of the evidence that feminism remains a vital force with plenty of unfinished business in the work of creating a world where all women are valued, respected, empowered, and enjoy equal access with their male counterparts to resources. Our goal in writing this book is to contribute to this vision by approaching contemporary globalization and development through the lens of feminist analysis. We believe that *without* feminist analysis, our understanding of both development and globalization is incomplete. The result is flawed or distorted policies that fail to improve the lives of millions of people around the globe.

This is a collaborative book in every way. During the long gestation of this project, we met frequently at a coffee shop halfway between our respective homes in Denver and Fort Collins to discuss drafts of chapters and to catch up on each other's lives. We tried out the material in our college classes and incorporated student feedback. Our goal has been to create an accessible book that reflects a feminist perspective on women, globalization, and development, influenced by our own backgrounds in comparative politics, international relations, and international experiences. We are indebted to friends and colleagues from India, China, Japan, France, and many other countries. We especially appreciate the counsel of friends who told us more than once that we were "missing the point." We have also learned that, despite our similar backgrounds and professional disciplines, we approach issues and writing differently, with the result that this is a true labor of negotiation.

Inevitably, some topics are inadequately explained, given the restrictions on manuscript length as well as our time, energy, and expertise. Several omissions merit mention. Although we do not subscribe to heteronormativity, we have not been able to incorporate the recent work on sexual identity, transgender, or intersex identities as they relate to development. Little is included on the significant social movements of indigenous women. Coverage of the various world regions is uneven, the result both of our own level of expertise and the availability of research. The various facets of contemporary militarism demand greater assessment. Our focus on four case studies means that many equally important topics have been deferred, but we hope that our analytical approach foregrounding structure and agency and levels of analysis will assist readers in studying other topics.

We also recognize some important limitations of feminist analysis as an intellectual project. Our understanding of feminism and of social relations more generally comes from our own lives as white American women who grew up in the mid-twentieth century. We operate within a Western worldview, and we acknowledge our difficulty in grasping how we might perceive social reality within a different worldview. Too often, Western feminists have felt entitled to give advice to other women about the obstacles to and the route toward a fulfilling life. Although our goals are analytical and not prescriptive, we acknowledge the limitations of our analysis.

Many people contributed to this project, and we are deeply grateful to them all. Foremost are our students, who read, questioned, and suggested. We are both indebted to our respective political science departments and universities for their resources: the University of Colorado Denver and Colorado State University. Jana is grateful for the support from the American Institute of Indian Studies and Fulbright programs, which enabled her to conduct research in India; to the many Indian citizens who have taught her so much; and especially to Mira Savara for providing both hospitality and insight. Sue Ellen recognizes that she could never have completed this project without both institutional support and the ongoing friendship and support of her feminist colleagues at home and abroad.

Every intensive writing endeavor demands forbearance from friends and family. The changes in our respective families remind us of what is really important in our lives—and those of women the world over. One could add that these changes remind us of how long we have collaborated. Over the time this project has taken,

Jana's daughter Carson married Scott; both completed their PhDs; and have two fine sons, Aaden and Isaac, whom she visits as often as she can. Sue Ellen is lucky to have many family members close by, enabling her to attend birthdays, school concerts, and graduations. Above all, she is grateful to Jim Boyd, whose patience and support have expanded with the years.

Books are always collaborative projects, and we especially appreciate the expertise and advice of Susan McEachern, who showed remarkable patience with our manuscript. The comments of anonymous reviewers, as well as the professionalism of the Rowman & Littlefield production staff, have been invaluable.

1

Feminism and Development in a Global World

Observers of global news reports in 2012 could easily wonder how much progress women had made in improving their lives around the globe. Some stories received wide coverage in the media and were followed closely on the Internet. Egyptian women voted for a new constitution that would restrict their legal rights, seeing it as a step toward democracy. An Indian college student was gang-raped on a bus, beaten with an iron rod, and subsequently died. Six teachers and administrators in Newtown, Connecticut, lost their lives as they tried to protect young children in a mass shooting at an elementary school.

Other stories received more limited coverage. Management consultants touted women as the third largest emerging economy after China and India.[1] Some celebrated a domestic workers' convention ratified by members of the International Labour Organization.[2] North Korean women found that their roles as breadwinners gave them more power in a restrictive, patriarchal society.[3]

In different ways, stories such as these illustrate the ways in which globalization operates as a multifaceted and often disjunctive process, resulting in consequences that are frequently unpredictable, uneven, or contradictory. To illustrate, in the North Korean example, the repressive central government has rejected an open market-based economy, seemingly isolating the country from the worldwide surge of economic globalization. Nonetheless, a combination of food shortages and financial desperation has driven some women to sneak into China, which has long been an ardent player in global economics. Women are also the main traders in the private markets that have sprung up in spite of government restrictions. Some evidence suggests that women are at the forefront of what civil disobedience exists in North Korea. In the midst of these indications of improvements in the life chances of women, however, some research shows that domestic violence—widespread throughout the world—has now increased in North Korea.[4]

1

These examples raise questions about the nature and meaning of globalization, its impact on development and on gender relations. Globalization encompasses both political-economic and sociocultural dimensions.[5] Many dimensions of globalization are irrefutable, including the tidal wave of market economics and consumer cultures. At the same time, a variety of political, social, and intellectual movements challenge and disrupt the dominant conditions of globalization. Feminist thought and action have been at the forefront of these disruptive processes, with some notable consequences. For example, feminists have been important in efforts to redefine development from the conventional measures of economic growth as measured by GDP to general measures of well-being. Feminist thought and action also disrupt the idea that globalization is solely a top-down process. Women in local and household settings through their struggles have capacities to resist, work around and through, or even redirect women's development.[6]

In this book we investigate some of women's struggles within and against globalization. We chose our case studies precisely to demonstrate the variation in the context of globalization and development in a variety of settings. Globalization is, by definition, a universal process, but it manifests itself in different ways from society to society. The principles of a neoliberal political economy may be adopted with enthusiasm or reluctance by governments pursuing rapid development. Consumer cultures are ubiquitous, but adapt to and are penetrated by traditional local customs. Western secularism competes with resurgent religions. Both the advocates and opponents of gender equity make use of transnational organizations and new information communication technologies.

WHY A FEMINIST APPROACH?

This is a feminist book, which means simply that the authors care deeply about gender equality: equal rights and opportunities for women and men, respect accorded to women and men of all cultures and classes, and access to resources for all. We recognize, however, that there are *many* feminist approaches; that is, there are multiple *feminisms*. One of the most important achievements of the United Nations world conferences on women, which are explained in chapter 2, was the space provided for competing feminist voices from numerous cultural and political perspectives. As Western feminists, we make no claim to speak for all women in the world. At the same time, we do not dismiss Western perspectives as too ethnocentric or too imperialistic as to be irrelevant to the debates about global developments. The most we can expect is *reflexivity*—that is, to be conscious of where we stand in our own history and culture, and how this stance influences our approach.

The question remains: What can feminist analyses contribute to our study of globalization and development? We maintain that *without* feminist analysis, our understanding of both development and globalization is incomplete. The result is flawed or distorted policies that fail to improve the lives of millions of people around the globe. Put differently, we ask what is missing when gender is not included in research and policy on these topics.

Sensitive to multiple feminist lenses, we endeavor to understand the global structures and processes that impede or support the empowerment of women. The context is globalization as it evolved through the late twentieth century into the early twenty-first century, and the processes are those we call "development." We ask what the connections are between these and gender roles in today's world. In the discussion that follows, we introduce the terms *globalization, development,* and *gender,* and explain our decision to use "women" in the title of the book. We distinguish between structure and agency, as well as levels of analysis, concepts that are central to our approach and that are applied to the discussions in subsequent chapters. Taken together, we argue for a feminist analysis of the following questions:

1. How do the forces of globalization, particularly neoliberal globalization, shape development strategies?
2. Given the nature of neoliberal globalization, how do development strategies affect poor women, in particular?
3. What are the constraints and opportunities available to women in the twenty-first century as a result of these development strategies and the multifaceted nature of globalization?
4. What individual and collective strategies have women used to improve their lives under globalization? How successful have they been?

Guided by these questions and using several case studies, in the concluding chapter we return to the feminist aspirations articulated over the past half century: the transformation of global structures and processes and the empowerment of women.

GLOBALIZATION AND DEVELOPMENT

The chapters that follow emphasize the political economy of globalization, especially what we call *neoliberal globalization*. Neoliberal is the word used to describe particular features of the structures that have come to dominate the global economy since the 1980s. The origins of the term are more fully explained in chapter 3, but the central characteristic of neoliberalism is an acceptance of the basic principles of market capitalism in a country's internal and external economic policies. In practical terms, neoliberal policies mean that few countries are able to isolate themselves from the structures of global production, finance and investment, and labor allocations. The assets, competitiveness, and flexibility of individuals, countries, and corporations determine whether they are winners or losers in this system of global competitiveness.

The *liberal* in neoliberalism derives historically from the structures and practices of economic and political openness and competitiveness that emerged in Europe in

the eighteenth and nineteenth centuries. These became central to the political economies that are found today in Western, industrialized countries such as the United
States. At its origins, liberalism stood in opposition to the tyranny of monarchs; as
a philosophical principle, it provided support for civil rights such as free speech, the
rule of law, and competitive political processes.[7] A liberal economy was one in which
government interference in economic processes was minimized. By the late twentieth century, the liberal norms of earlier decades took on new meanings in a global
economy dominated by Western, industrialized countries, particularly the United
States, and by the international organizations that they largely controlled, such as the
World Bank. Hence the prefix "neo" was added to liberalism to signify the changed
global context that emerged during this period.

The historical political and economic processes that came to characterize contemporary globalization, and particularly neoliberalism, are critical to understanding development and its implications for gender equality. Development itself is a
historical process: It describes what has happened in the past and what is expected
in the future. But it is also a concept or worldview that defines what it means to be
modern. More is said about this concept and debate over modernity in chapter 3, but
by the late twentieth century it was hard, if not impossible, to separate the idea of
development from its roots in the European and American liberal societies of earlier
decades. Most policy makers, for example, have seen a "developed country" as one
with increasing levels of industrialization and urbanization, labor efficiency (to produce surpluses for sale), private property rights, and growing consumption of goods
and services by the general population. Although most Westerners take these changes
for granted, they also acknowledge that environmental degradation and bad working conditions for most laborers have long been accepted as a historical by-product
of development for most countries before living conditions improve. For women,
the consequences of development policies have often been uneven or contradictory,
with the result that many feminists have contested the very meaning of the concept.

Governments and international organizations took the position that these changes
could best (or only) be achieved through the application of capitalist economic principles and openness to global market forces. The policies of the dominant players in
the international system, including international organizations and Western governments, linked the worldview of market capitalism to their lending and investment
policies. When implemented at the national level, these policies inevitably influenced the direction of development. To illustrate, a lender might demand the reduction of government programs as a strategy to shrink government debt. The resulting
cutbacks in services would affect some segments of the population more than others.
The results varied by country, region, and culture, but typically the poor and women
would be negatively affected because they lacked the resources to take advantage of
the more open, competitive markets. In many instances, therefore, the processes of
development might be very uneven in different regions and among different classes
of the same country. Feminist approaches have been essential in illuminating the
uneven impact of globalization and its implications for development policies.

Why should women so often tend to be poorer and particularly ill-placed to compete in a modern economy? Do development policies invariably hurt women as much as (or more) than men? Under what conditions do women and the poor tend to benefit from development in the global economy? The easy answer to the first question is the dominant worldwide pattern of female subordination to men, which most feminist theories emphasize in their analyses of power structures at all levels of society. The nature of this subordination has changed throughout history, has multiple roots, and varies from one region to another. For example, despite the introduction of formal legal equality in many countries over the past half century, in most African countries and about half the countries in Asia, women's access to land and other types of property is limited by existing statutory and customary laws.[8]

The short answer to the second question is "no"; development policies do not invariably hurt women despite the evidence that women and girls have often been disadvantaged by these policies. This raises the third question of the patterns and the variability in the benefits and costs of development policies, and which segments of society reap more benefits or pay more costs. In the four case studies at the core of this book, both the patterns and the variations in these patterns are illustrated for different parts of the world. In the next section, we explain the analytical tools that frame our discussions in these case studies. We distinguish between the roles of structure and agency, as well as between levels of analysis.

STRUCTURE AND AGENCY

In the simplest sense, structure refers to the social, political, economic, and ideological forces that set the historical context for our lives. Individuals, groups, even governments, operate in this context. These forces do not necessarily direct our actions on a day-to-day basis, but they constitute a reality that offers opportunities, as well as setting constraints. Structural forces are varied; they change over time, but usually very slowly. The kinds of forces that are relevant for most of us include ideas (such as democracy, human rights, or free markets), natural resources and technology, and institutions (including state structures).[9]

Chapter 3 notes the importance of some of these structures as they have evolved in the modern era, and particularly in the past half century. One illustration is the fundamental *idea* of development and the related assumption that development entails material progress, for which both individuals and governments should strive. Another dominant idea, one that has emerged partly as a consequence of development thinking but is of more recent origin, is that all human beings have rights, and that practices common two centuries ago (such as slavery) are incompatible with modernization.

Just as we are conditioned by ideas, we are also circumscribed by *natural resources and technology*. Water is a natural resource, and its availability or unavailability frames the way we "do" development. Potable water is seen as an attribute of modernity, particularly as modern chemistry and engineering deliver it to us. Central to the notion of development is that humans can transform their material and natural surroundings through technology; but just as globalization has provided an abundance of resources for some, others have seen their natural resources, including water, depleted or taken from their control.

The precise meaning of the term *institution* is evasive, but for our purposes it means a durable organization, law, or custom with widespread acknowledgment and acceptance. The nation-state is one such institution, as are specific governments. Legal systems, marriage (in both custom and law), private property, dowry, and slavery are also institutions. These institutions change through time or even disappear, but they structure the lives of those people who live within their bonds. Since the middle of the twentieth century, many global institutions have become familiar and closely linked to policies of development and gender: The United Nations and the World Bank are two such examples. These global institutions do not have the immediate impact on our lives that our government and laws do, but they do influence the context of development for many people. Similarly, financial institutions (banks, credit, stock markets) are central to people's lives, even as many of us do not understand their precise functioning.

Taken together, ideas, natural resources and technology, and institutions form the structural context for our lives. In the words of Anthony Payne, "This is emphatically not to be understood as a cage. . . . It is properly conceived as the source of both opportunities *and* constraints, as being both enabling *and* binding, as permitting agency *within* bonds."[10]

If structure sets context for our lives, then *agency* is what we can and will make of it. Put differently, human beings are both objects (as suggested by the discussion of structures) and subjects of history. In the instance of gender relations, ideas, material conditions, and institutions all shape the roles and actions of men and women. But people in turn can alter the conditions and expectations of gender roles. For example, in central Europe and southern Europe, as well as parts of East Asia—notably Japan—fertility rates have declined dramatically in the past twenty years. Scholars have identified a variety of factors as responsible for the demographic shift: longer life expectancy, lower infant mortality, and the incompatibility of motherhood and employment. The incompatibility is a result of inflexible labor markets, insufficient public services (such as day care), and a highly asymmetric division of labor in the home. All of these reflect structural arrangements. As a consequence, women, exercising agency, marry later or not at all, and have fewer children.[11] But men may change their ideas about gender roles and do more in the household, and women may change ideas about combining motherhood and employment. Over time, these women and men change structures (such as governments and private business) and public policies—for example, regarding the provision of day-care facilities.

The United States is unique for its philosophical and cultural emphasis on individual agency, and Americans often underestimate the importance of structure (or believe that people can easily escape its constraints). However, for many people in the world, agency is best viewed within the close confines of a family or community network, where opportunities for individual expression of agency are more difficult. A widespread premise in much recent thinking about development is that the expansion of individual capability (and human capabilities more generally) should be the dominant goal of development strategies and projects. This surely would mean guaranteeing a minimum standard of living, although a continual expansion of material wealth is not necessarily part of enhancing human capability. The underlying assumption of capabilities enhancement is that greater capability leads to more opportunity to exercise agency, either to exploit the advantages of an existing structure, to push or change that structure, or even move beyond its boundaries. The main risk in this type of thinking is that it underestimates the power that structures have over our lives. We will see this dilemma in the case studies in chapters 4–7.

Any effort to understand contemporary globalization, the development policies that operate in the context of globalization, their impact on ordinary citizens, and our ability to contend with or change these policies requires this distinction between structure and agency. Most writers on these topics privilege one or the other, despite the importance of understanding both and the interactions between them. These interactions are essential to understanding gender relations and the status of women. Although we cannot determine the precise historical origins of female subordination, we do understand that the secondary status of women is imbedded in structures across the globe. Certainly differences exist in the degree and nature of subordination, but its central features are universally recognizable, from the relatively few females in positions of economic and political power to the violence perpetrated against girls and women. Feminist research and theory have explored both the historical patterns of discrimination and its specific manifestations. How has it varied by time and place, and how have the structures of class, culture, and race influenced these variations? How have the processes of development and globalization altered these structures? Later chapters in this book provide illustrations of both the similar and the dissimilar features of structural subordination.

Individual and Collective Agency

We acknowledge the constraints that the structures of gender subordination impose on girls and women. At the same time, we cannot ignore the abundant research on the importance of agency, the ability of people individually and collectively to adapt to, influence, resist, or change the dominant structures. Agency is the inspiration for all feminist movements, indeed, all social and political movements, through time and across space, although agency has been expressed in many different forms. In the United States alone, feminist agency has been found in individual letters, diaries, speeches, essays, and books. It has been inspired by religion and by unbridled secularism. It has manifested itself in small consciousness-raising discussions and huge public protests. Many who have rejected the label of feminism nonetheless have fought for gender equality.

Both individual agency and collective agency have been expressed in opposition to gender equality in the United States and across the globe. Most often, the opposition has been grounded in cultural or religious justifications, and the pattern has been to argue in favor of maintaining the "natural" differences and divisions between male and female. Indeed, these differences are found in a school of feminist thought that we call "difference feminism" that, however, has not been premised on the inherent inferiority of girls and women (see chapter 2). Ironically—given the historical roots of Western feminism in liberalism—many who subscribe to the basic tenets of liberalism have used economic or political justifications for specific policies that hinder gender equality. Opposition to policies or laws that are designed to assure equal pay for comparable work is an example. This opposition is frequently justified by reference to the imperatives of economic efficiency or the smooth operation of the competitive marketplace.

Elsewhere around the globe, agency has taken the form of opposition to colonialism and racism, both silent and noisy protests against military governments, peace marches, and environmental activism—the list is long and diverse. Agency may be expressed quietly within the arena of the family, or it may be expressed publicly. Gradually, some structures have been altered; many have not. Often we do not recognize the changes except in retrospect. An example would be the changes in the United States over the past century that made rape, including marital rape, a public issue. The transformation of rape from private to public issue has required a combination of legal, political, social, and cultural changes—many of these the result of feminist organizing. Nonetheless, as noted above, agency has also been expressed in opposition to these kinds of changes. For example, buried in our history books are the arguments used to defeat the hard-fought efforts of the past century to amend the US Constitution to include an "equal rights amendment" (ERA), which reads as follows:

Section 1. *Equality of rights under the law shall not be denied or abridged by the United States or by any State on account of sex.*
Section 2. *The Congress shall have the power to enforce, by appropriate legislation, the provisions of this article.*
Section 3. *This amendment shall take effect two years after the date of ratification.*

Although the ERA received congressional approval in 1972, and numerous states ratified it during the 1970s, it failed in 1982, not having obtained the necessary ratifications by three-fourths of the states. The best-known opponent was Phyllis Schlafly, a conservative Republican who spearheaded a lobbying campaign with her STOP ERA movement; but opposition was also widespread among conservative evangelical Christians, Roman Catholics, Mormons, and Orthodox Jews, as well as important segments of the business community.[12]

The defeat of the ERA is a good example of effective collective agency expressed in opposition to what many Americans thought was a principle of gender equality.

The ERA opponents, in contrast, often viewed the ERA as a movement to erase "inherent" differences between females and males, arguing for example that unisex toilets in public facilities would be one of the pernicious outcomes of an equal rights amendment.

LEVELS OF ANALYSIS

The structures referred to in the preceding section operate on different levels. Some are intimate (family, dowry); some more distant (village or town, ecosystem, language group); some national, the most obvious being state structure and laws; and increasingly, many are international or global. Although some are discrete and localized, most are interconnected: One might escape the confines of a particular marriage, but it is difficult (nearly impossible in some societies) to escape the institution of marriage and the property laws and customs that accompany it. An individual may not have much money but is still likely to be affected by a financial crisis that begins in another country. Thus agency is never *purely* individual; to expand agency requires first understanding the levels of networks within which it exists, a point that becomes clearer as we examine particular instances of gender and development.

Scholars in different academic disciplines typically use the term *levels* to refer to institutions that are central to their specializations. For example, sociologists may think of the family or household as local, whereas political scientists use "local level" primarily to refer to administrative or government units, such as towns and cities. Thus different academic lenses introduce greater complexity into a topic that is, by its nature, already complex. Therefore, in discussing gender and development, three central realities about levels as a tool of analysis must be borne in mind: first, social, political, economic, and cultural institutions overlap at every level; second, no level is entirely independent of another level—to a degree, one level is always influenced by another; and third, rarely is a precise boundary between levels discernible.

Our discussions of levels of analysis will refer to local, regional, national, and international, defining as appropriate both the geographical scope and the type of institution (see figure 1.1). The word "international" is better suited to this type of analysis because numerous institutions that are important for development and gender are international without being global. A case in point is the European Union (EU), which, although international is not global. Nonetheless, its laws regarding gender equity, labor practices, human trafficking, and such are vital to understanding gender relations in the EU member countries. The essential point in using levels as a tool of analysis is worth repeating: Empowering individuals, or enhancing their agency, requires changes in attitudes, norms, policies, and laws at every level. The two-way arrow reminds us that influence flows in both directions: it may be top-down or bottom-up, or a mixture of these.

To illustrate the nature of overlap between types of institutions, the interrelationships of influence between levels, and the imprecise boundaries of levels, consider

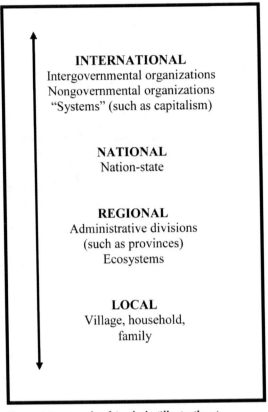

Figure 1.1. Levels of Analysis (Illustrations)

the example of families. Although it is easy to accept families as defining a local level, we recognize that they are formed by structures at more distant levels: Laws governing marriage and child custody are determined by regional or national governments or by religious institutions that are national, even transnational. In the absence of laws, regional or national custom will define what constitutes a marriage and also the rights that exist within that marriage. Global cultural trends often influence patterns of consumption within the family. Many families are not confined to a single geographical location: Kin may be in different regions or even different parts of the world. As a result of these factors, it would be misleading to say that a family is strictly a social institution, found in a limited geographical area, and insulated from wider influences.

The term *domestic structures* encompasses both the household (in which members co-reside under a single roof) and family (where members are tied by kinship relations).[13] In many societies, hierarchy structures domestic relations, with males typically having more status and power. But these relationships may be affected by age or physical condition. In other societies, relationships may be relatively egalitarian between male and female, but hierarchical by age. In situations where divorce is common or cohabitation between single individuals is frequent, the configuration of a domestic unit is quite different, with gender relations variable and often determined by personality and skills. The domestic unit headed by a single parent, for example, is widespread; although associated with divorced parents in North America or Europe, in much of the world it is often the result of migration or death of one parent.

Amartya Sen has argued that all households show features of both cooperation and conflict. In order to understand how households carry out the functions of production, consumption, and distribution, it is important to understand what Sen has called "social technology." Sen expands the narrow view of technology, which refers to the mechanical, chemical, or biological processes used in making a good, by including the social organization that permits the use of specific techniques of production. The social technology of the household is characterized by gender divisions in patterns of work, which are part of a larger social context. This larger context, in turn, is defined by both cooperative and conflictual behavior. Adding to the total well-being of the household requires cooperation, whereas allocating the components of that well-being (goods, health care, leisure time, etc.) entails conflict.[14]

Research on household structures and dynamics illuminates the ways in which the term "local" is multifaceted: It encompasses the individual; her kin relations; physical and social space (such as a family compound); and the cultural, economic, and ideological structures that determine her life. At the same time, the point made earlier about the interrelationships between levels and the lack of precise boundaries is seen in the case of the families and households. For example, the norms and practices of households that are patriarchal and patrilineal are widely spread throughout South Asia, so they may be considered at least regional and perhaps international in scope. If an important goal of development is to enhance personal agency, this goal requires first understanding the variability of local contexts, and second, the interconnectedness of this context with broader environments. This understanding, in turn, requires a levels-of-analysis approach.

If research has illuminated the importance and diversity of structural contexts at different levels, the relationships between the levels are not always clear. Yet these relationships are central to understanding the complexities of globalization, gender, and development. By the twenty-first century, *empowerment* had achieved widespread acceptance as a shorthand term for the process of enhanced agency, particularly for women. Agency assumes enhanced capabilities, as noted above, but the emphasis on *process* means that women should have a role in defining and securing the desired change.[15] Process, in turn, entails enhanced participation in public or civic life, which the World Bank has called "voice."[16] Political rights are most often secured at the national level, but they can only be put into operation pursuant to changes (in culture, for example) at the regional and local levels. To illustrate, legal or constitutional changes in a national parliament may guarantee women the right to own property, but religious norms, social customs, or family dynamics may prevent her access to this resource. In societies where the ability to hold *and use* property, particularly land, is linked to participation in public life, women are thus shut out because changes at the national level have not altered reality at the intermediate and local levels.

In the example just cited, we see the interrelationships of agency and structure as they operate across levels. The example also illustrates the multidimensionality of the process of empowerment, which requires changes in overlapping spheres of structure and action—social, economic, religious, and political. The 1995 Beijing *Platform for Action*, adopted by the Fourth UN World Conference on Women, explicitly recognized both the multidimensionality of the empowerment process and the need for action at all levels. For example, chapter 4-D of the *Platform* addresses violence against women from the international level in the context of war, at the national level through violence "perpetuated or condoned by the State," to the household, including the neglect or abuse of girls and women. To address widespread violence against women, the *Platform* then calls for a variety of measures: better data and statistics, reformed media images, education of men and women at all levels, formal condemnation by governments and international organizations, and the provision of local community services.[17] In countries where regional political or administrative units are important, such as the federal government systems of India, Canada, or the United States, changes in provincial or state laws are also relevant.

The next section distinguishes between the terms *sex* and *gender*, and introduces some of the reasons for the debate over the use of "male" and "female" as categories that are fixed in nature. Feminist thinking and research on these topics is central to our understanding of the secondary status of women and girls, as well as the variety of strategies available for policies of empowerment.

SEX, GENDER, WOMEN:
FEMINIST RESEARCH AND THEORY

Feminist research and theory have wrestled with the question of the degree to which the basic categories of "female" and "male" are biologically or socially constructed. Most, but not all, feminists have adhered to the distinctions between the terms sex and gender that enjoy international acceptance, emphasizing what is deemed to be socially determined as opposed to what is inherent in humans.[18] The word "sex" denotes the physiological and biological characteristics that distinguish male and female. The most widely recognized of the male-female differences are found in the reproductive systems. Examples of commonly known attributes include menstruation, unique to females; and testicles, unique to men.

The word "gender" generally refers to socially and culturally constructed norms of masculine and feminine, including roles, behavior, and status. Much feminist research has focused on the origins and evolution of these distinctions in an effort to confront what might be called biological determinism—that is, the assumption of a natural and inescapable inevitability to the categories of male and female. Feminists have long argued that this kind of determinist thinking sustains a hierarchical order in which girls and women are always subordinate. How we think about sex and gender is therefore central to our analysis of what *might* change and what *should* change.

Some scholars, however, have challenged this sex/gender paradigm, arguing variously that our understanding of "sex" is not grounded in scientifically observable distinctions but is itself a socially constructed category. Others have argued for biology as logically inherent in gender distinctions. Some have pointed out that not until relatively late in Western history did the dualism found in both sex and gender distinctions come to dominate our thinking and, therefore, our expectations.[19] We know that historically, ancient cultures may have offered more space for imagining the complexity of human characteristics. To illustrate, stories and figures of the Indian deity Ardhanarishvara are believed to date back two thousand years. A bisexual image, Ardhanarishvara combines the physical characteristics and symbols of Shiva and Parvati to represent the unity of male and female elements in the universe (see photo 1.1). Our knowledge of the origin of such images, as well as how and why they have changed over time, is, however, sparse.

Feminist research continues to probe the nature of sexuality, sexual identification, and sexual orientation, including gay and lesbian, bisexual, and transgendered populations. Once viewed as social and biological aberrations to be dismissed or shunned, research increasingly explores issues specific to these and other minority populations. This kind of research has encouraged an ongoing deconstruction of concepts such as female, male, man, and woman, with the result that it is more and more difficult to make unchallenged generalizations about what is universally valid about such categories. Ironically, research that deconstructs analytical categories in turn raises questions about the viability of the central political aims that define feminists as men and women who seek to end the oppression of women. If the category of women is itself contestable, then what unifies women to the degree that feminists can make claims on their behalf?

Despite this dilemma, we have chosen to use the term *women* throughout this book. To most readers, the nuances of feminist debates may appear arcane, and the prevailing distinctions between women and men retain sufficient validity to make them central references. More to the point, the data that this book draws on heavily employ the traditional distinctions and make a clear case for the assertion that women *as a group* are disadvantaged almost universally. To understand the reasons for this hierarchy of disadvantage, however, requires knowledge of *gender relations* in comparative contexts and how these contexts have been influenced by globalization. Thus our choice is to use the research that illuminates the *context* of gender relations while not masking our theoretical and political concerns primarily for the status of women and the structures that maintain their secondary status.

The dynamic conditions of globalization have produced new barriers and opportunities for women and men around the world. Sometimes, the same phenomenon may be seen as either advantageous or disadvantageous depending on one's lens.

Photo 1.1.   Statue of Ardhanarishvara, the Male/Female Hindu Figure. Photo courtesy of James W. Boyd

To illustrate, what has become known as the "global care chain" makes available income-earning opportunities for women who otherwise might have no source of income. Thus a Filipina leaves home to work as a maid or nanny in Hong Kong or elsewhere in Asia. The cost to her is that she leaves her children in the care of her parents or other relatives; moreover, she often finds herself subject to economic or sexual exploitation in another country. However, she assumes these risks as preferable to fewer or no income-earning opportunities at home. In addition, her job provides new freedom to another mother who is now able to become a banker or university professor while the Filipina helps with housework and child care.[20] In this example, class as well as nationality or ethnicity is important in determining who benefits from the care chain.[21]

In this same illustration, we have the case of a relatively new global structure (the care chain) that is characterized by a particular type of international migration and set of economic relations. It has national consequences, as remittances from Filipinos abroad are a critical source of income for the Philippines. It reflects class and often ethnic or racial hierarchies, and clearly has important implications for families and communities in both the sending and the receiving countries.[22] The structure is very dynamic, as a change in international political or economic conditions (e.g., a depression or revolution in the receiving country) may lead to a sudden plunge in employment opportunities. Feminist research has illuminated these patterns and their impact on "hidden" migrants, as well as gender relations in both the sending and receiving countries.[23]

Understanding these dynamic conditions, we have chosen to focus on broad patterns that illustrate the interrelationships between local, national, and global structures of contemporary globalization. The critical patterns are those of particular relevance to development as it influences gender relations and the status of women. What, in turn, are the options for women to improve their life conditions, both individually and collectively?

GRASSROOTS TO GLOBAL: ORGANIZING FOR SURVIVAL AND CHANGE

The case of the Filipina maids and the global care chain illustrates an important feature of two contemporary demographic patterns. First, the number of female migrants has been increasing; by 2010 nearly half of all international migrants were women. In some instances, the migration reflects the improvement in women's educational levels and economic opportunities. In other cases, however, the migration reflects the absence of opportunities at home or a desperate need to escape civil conflict or environmental catastrophe.

Second, the number of female-headed households has also increased. Often the absence is the result of the migration of one parent to another country.[24] Many instances, however, involve never-married, divorced, separated, and widowed parents. Across the world, the percentage of households headed by a single woman varies considerably, ranging from 10 percent in Jordan to almost half of families in Namibia, Swaziland, and Ukraine.[25] These figures, however, mask regional, race, and ethnic differences. For example, the 2010 US Census indicated that approximately 13 percent of US households were headed by a single female, but the percentage was as high as 30 percent for African Americans.[26] Although there are exceptions, female-headed households are more likely to be poor than households with two parents or a household headed by a single male. This is the pattern in the United States, as well as in Latin America and most of Europe. The implications for the well-being of parents and children, as well as broader patterns of national and regional development, are obvious.

The pattern of rapidly changing family structures is found in most societies, and as a result women often find themselves as the sole source of support for themselves and their children. Whether they migrate from farm to city, from one part of their country to another, or to another country, they are generally physically and economically more vulnerable than men. It is this vulnerability and its relationship to globalization and development that informs our choice of case studies in chapters 4 to 7.

No attempt has been made in this book to analyze every issue or describe every situation around the globe. Our concern has been to provide analytical tools to help readers make sense of the divergent realities confronting women and men and their children in different situations that illustrate the impact of globalization and the attendant policies of development. We combine the broad scenario with specific examples of the interrelationships that have come to dominate our lives.

The second chapter addresses the characteristics of a feminist approach to studying development and globalization. In keeping with our assertion of multiple feminisms, it lays out some of the most important tensions in feminist theory. For example, why do some feminists reject the argument that fundamental differences exist between women and men, an argument they see as furthering the hierarchical ordering of male and female? Others assert the importance of the essential male-female distinction as central to understanding both subordination and the potential for equality. Still other feminists focus primarily on the debate over the importance of class and race, as well as gender, in our thinking about development, whereas some are committed to "deconstructing" terms such as gender and development.

Chapter 2 also explains the way in which "women in development" reached the global political agenda, why this "WID" movement was criticized by advocates of a "GAD" (gender and development) approach, and the recent rise to prominence of the concept of "care work." Finally, the chapter examines the importance of the United Nations system in fostering a globalized women's movement.

Chapter 3, titled "Development, Globalization, and Power," places both development and globalization in historical perspective. It focuses on the debates over the meaning of development and dissent from the dominant modernization theories, and why these are important for women. The challenges to development are found at two levels: first, those who criticize the way in which development is conceptualized; and second, the challenges to specific development regimes and policies. In both instances, gender has generally been overlooked as an important factor in understanding development.

The second half of chapter 3 explains the way in which globalization has developed and changed, particularly in the post–World War II world. Since the 1980s, neoliberalism has become a central feature of globalization, but it is not the only important dimension. Globalization is more than economics, and it is important to understand the political, technological, and social dimensions of globalization, as well as its economic aspects. The chapter closes with the debate on globalization and gender.

Chapters 4–7 consist of four case studies that cover the topics of human trafficking, water, work, and health. Each chapter summarizes the fundamental issues of the case, the role that structure and agency play in determining the options available to women, and how a levels-of-analysis approach accounts for the complexity of the issues. The global politics of the cases are illustrated, showing the overlapping institutions, movements, and governments that are part of the context for the problems that poor people, in particular, face. The diversity of positions feminists take as they struggle with the issues is illustrated through the organizations they form and the policies they propose. The cases were chosen both for their intrinsic importance and to demonstrate the diversity of issues, feminist analysis, and organizations that play a role in development.

The best-known case for its gender politics is that of the international trafficking of humans. Chapter 4 lays out the global context of trafficking, particularly sex trafficking. It explains why, despite near-universal revulsion over the practice, so little progress has been made in combating it. Using the cases of trafficked women from two very different countries (Russia and Bangladesh), we analyze the mixture of structural factors and individual agency that contribute to trafficking. The chapter emphasizes the feminist debate over both the source of trafficking and proposed policies to address it.

The case analyzed in chapter 5 is as well known as trafficking, although not for its gender implications. Despite research that goes back several decades examining the unique and shared responsibilities of women and men in water management, until recently policy makers have tended to see water as gender neutral. We focus on water in chapter 5 because no development is possible without it and because development demands enormous quantities of it. Structural changes—geographical, economic, and political—influence both the quantity and quality of water, and in turn the ability of countries to develop and families to prosper. Drought and inadequate infrastructure in the tiny Himalayan country of Bhutan means less hydroelectric power for India, where rapid development has escalated demands for electric power. Massive blackouts result, plunging half the country into sweltering darkness. Factories and trains stop, there is no air conditioning, and housewives cook by candlelight.[27]

In probing the importance of water for poor women, we again examine two individuals, one a farmer in Peru and the other an urban worker in Johannesburg, South Africa. Both are single household heads and both struggle with inadequate access to water. The governments of Peru and South Africa have been influenced by neoliberal policies, which are seen in their approach to water. The case of water also illustrates the complexity of global politics, with United Nations agencies, professional organizations, and multinational corporations all players in the business of water. Unlike the case of sex trafficking, no clearly identifiable fault line appears in feminist thinking about water. Most feminists have concentrated on influencing the policy making of water management from the local to the international level. The primary disagreement exists between those who see water in terms of its economic or market value and those who see access to water as a human right.

In contrast to water, scholars have never questioned the inescapable gender dimensions of work, the topic of chapter 6. In view of the vast scope of the subject, chapter 6 concentrates on describing the global structures of work and the major changes that have taken place in the nature of work during recent decades. The consolidation of global neoliberalism has affected nearly every income-generating opportunity for both men and women, from white-collar jobs to manufacturing, agriculture, and informal sector labor. Global players—for example, those in the United Nations system—emphasize decent standards for work; but policies of structural adjustment by national governments, as well as the practice of outsourcing work to other countries, have frequently diminished work opportunities in some countries and labor standards in others.

The chapter explains that microfinance has been promoted as a strategy that improves income-earning possibilities for the poor, notably women. In recent years, however, controversial studies have suggested that microfinance is often inadequate as a poverty-reduction strategy and at worst may be exploitive in its lending conditions. Feminists fall on both sides of the debate about microfinance.

In addition to the discussion of microfinance, chapter 6 examines two organizations in the workplace that illustrate very different working contexts and strategies for poverty alleviation. One is an organization for agricultural workers in the grape industry of northeast Brazil, a region that has been deeply influenced by national and international open-market approaches to development. The other organization is found in India, and it has earned international admiration for its work over the past four decades among informal-sector women workers. In contrasting ways, the two organizations reflect the potential for collective action designed to improve conditions and income in the workplace.

The fourth case study confronts the issue of health, which, like work, affects women and men of every class and ethnicity. Health is, of course, intimately related to working conditions and very often to water. For some health conditions, major gender differences are few, whereas for others, sex and gender are *the* determining factor. Nowhere is this more obvious than in reproductive health. Pregnancy and childbearing are the dominant realities for women around the world; although prenatal care and childbirth have received a great deal of global attention in the past half century, they remain one of the greatest health risks for poor women. Consequently, chapter 7 pays particular attention to this dimension of health.

Feminists have succeeded in broadening definitions of reproductive health to include the controversial issues of birth control and abortion, and in placing violence against women on the policy agendas of international agencies and national governments. In many ways, their strategies illustrate the effectiveness of collective agency expressed through lobbying, fund-raising, and other political channels. The two case studies profiled in chapter 7 emphasize the importance of networking at both the national and international levels in order to initiate policy changes that address the health issues specific to women.

During the first decade of the twenty-first century, health-sector reform became a significant political agenda in Chile. The role of the then health minister, Michelle Bachelet, illustrates the importance of having a government "insider" to initiate policy reform. The Chilean case also shows the way in which an international organization, in this instance the Pan American Health Organization, can push for greater civil society involvement. The second case study in chapter 7 also features an international organization, the African Union, which was pushed by a coalition of regional women's organizations to adopt a Women's Rights Protocol to the African Charter on Human and Peoples' Rights.

Despite these measures of progress, reproductive health issues still divide many feminists, pregnancy and childbirth present unacceptably high risks in too many places, and violence against women is still a universal reality. Persistent inequities throughout the world remind us that the goals of gender equality are far from realized in the realms of health as in the areas of work, water, and trafficking. Chapter 8 takes a closer look at what seems to be most effective in the quest for gender equality. What constitutes successful agency under conditions of development and globalization?

The case studies featured in chapters 4–7 were chosen because they illustrate the role of agency from the individual to the international levels in countries committed to development and subject to the pressures of globalization. Trafficked individuals may be trapped in transnational trafficking structures but respond in different ways. Poor women, one rural and the other urban, in Peru and South Africa confront the structures of neoliberal water policies by drawing, again in different ways, on the community resources that are available to them. In this way, they straddle individual and collective agency; one appeals to a traditional water users' association, and the other joins a new street demonstration. In chapter 6, the collective organizations are formal and clearly defined: a labor union in Brazil and a labor union turned development organization in India. Finally, as noted above, in chapter 7 the cases of Chile and the African Union shift the lens to different levels and types of organizational strategies, ones that engage government officials, international organizations, and civil society advocacy groups.

As noted earlier, we designed our case studies to illustrate the contradictory effects of globalization, the unequal aspects of development policies, and the spaces available for the exercise of individual and collective agency. Under these conditions, we have learned that successful agency and organizational strategies in pursuit of gender equality are variable. Feminist researchers have compiled numerous studies of what seems to work best under which circumstances, although we are far from having a single blueprint that defines effectiveness. A few principles seem to stand out, however, and these are explored further in chapter 8. Individual agency may lead to escape from repression or adapting and using it for personal benefit, but it seldom changes structures without collective support. This collective support may be informal (such as a network of women) or formal, and the examples range from the local to the national and international levels. For national policy changes, government support is essential and best realized by a combination of insider and outsider pressure. International policy statements and programs may gradually produce real movement toward gender equality or may disappear into oblivion. Their success depends on the degree of support from both governments and advocacy groups. In the end, these are matters of political strategies.

NOTES

1. Marion Bowman, "Capitalism's Bright 'Third Billion' Future?" openDemocracy, December 7, 2012, http://www.opendemocracy.net/print/69777.

2. Nisha Varia, "A Victory against Modern Day Slavery," openDemocracy, December 1, 2012, http://www.opendemocracy.net/print/69654.

3. Tania Branigan, "Women in North Korea: 'Men Can't Earn Enough Money So It's Our Job Now,'" http://www.guardian.co.uk/world/2012/dec/11/women-north-korea-men-jobs.

4. Report by Louisa Lim, http://www.npr.org/2012/12/28/168193827/out-of-desperation-north-korean-women-become-breadwinners.

5. Marianne H. Marchand, "Reconceptualising 'Gender and Development' in an Era of Globalisation," *Millennium: Journal of International Studies* 25, no. 3 (1995): 577–603; and "The Future of Gender and Development after 9/11: Insights from Postcolonial Feminism and Transnationalism," *Third World Quarterly* 30, no. 5 (2009): 921–35.

6. Saskia Sassen, "Local Actors in Global Politics," *Current Sociology* 52, no. 4 (2004): 649–70; and Sassen, "Countergeographies of Globalization: The Feminization of Survival," in Linda E. Lucas, ed., *Unpacking Globalization: Markets, Gender, and Work* (New York: Lexington Books, 2007), 21–34.

7. Western feminist thought has roots in early political liberalism. See, for example, Mary Wollstonecraft, *A Vindication of the Rights of Women* (1792). Wollstonecraft (1759–1793) was a British advocate of equal rights for women and, more broadly, all citizens.

8. United Nations, Statistics Division, *The World's Women 2010: Trends and Statistics*, chap. 8, "Poverty," available at http://unstats.un.org. Beginning in 1990, and every five years thereafter, the United Nations Statistics Division issues a report detailing the differences in the status of women and men in population, health, education, work, decision making, violence against women, environment, and economic participation and poverty.

9. We have been influenced by the conceptualizations of political economists and critical theorists, notably Robert Cox, Sandra Whitworth, and Anthony Payne. See Robert W. Cox, "Social Forces, States and World Orders: Beyond International Relations Theory," *Millennium: Journal of International Studies* 10, no. 2 (1981): 126–55; Sandra Whitworth, *Feminism and International Relations: Towards a Political Economy of Gender in Interstate and Non-Governmental Institutions* (New York: St. Martin's Press, 1994); and Anthony Payne, *The Global Politics of Unequal Development* (New York: Palgrave Macmillan, 2005).

10. Payne, *Global Politics*, 19.

11. For recent data on Japan and other countries, see the Population Reference Bureau's *World Population Data Sheet*, issued annually, at http://www.prb.org.

12. Donald T. Critchlow and Cynthia L. Stachecki, "The Equal Rights Amendment Reconsidered: Politics, Policy, and Social Mobilization in a Democracy," *Journal of Policy History* 20, no. 1 (2008): 157–76. Critchlow and Stachecki detail the mobilization of the (highly effective) collective agency of the ERA opposition.

13. Joy Deshmukh-Ranadive, "Gender, Power, and Empowerment: An Analysis of Household and Family Dynamics," in Deepa Narayan, ed., *Measuring Empowerment: Cross-Disciplinary Perspectives* (Washington, DC: World Bank, 2005), 104.

14. Amartya K. Sen, "Gender and Cooperative Conflicts," in Irene Tinker, ed., *Persistent Inequalities: Women and World Development* (New York: Oxford University Press, 1990), 129–30.

15. Anju Malhotra and Sidney Ruth Schuler, "Women's Empowerment as a Variable in International Development," in Narayan, *Measuring Empowerment*, 72.

16. Andrew D. Mason and Elizabeth M. King, *Engendering Development through Gender Equality in Rights, Resources, and Voice* (Washington, DC: World Bank, 2001).

17. For the text of the *Platform for Action*, see http://www.un.org/womenwatch/daw/beijing/platform/index.html.

18. See, for example, the World Health Organization distinction at http://www.who.int/gender/whatisgender/en.

19. An extensive discussion of this and other elements of feminist theory is found in Mari Mikkola, "Feminist Perspectives on Sex and Gender," *The Stanford Encyclopedia of Philosophy*, Winter 2011, at http://plato.stanford.edu/archives/win2011/entries/feminism-gender.

20. We recognize that in numerous instances the employer is not earning her own income, but the household support simply enables her to pursue a more active social life.

21. For examples of the global care chain in the United States, see Ashwin Sheshgiri et al., "The Other Mothers of Manhattan," *New York Times Magazine*, July 15, 2012, 26–33, 50. The article features nannies from Mexico, Guyana, Jamaica, St. Lucia, Trinidad, and New Jersey working in New York City.

22. See Julien Brygo, "Filipino Maids for Export," *Le Monde diplomatique* English edition, October 12, 2011, at http://mondediplo.com/2011/10/12maids. In most years, the World Bank reports that overseas remittances (from both women and men) account for about 10 percent of the Philippines gross domestic product.

23. Cynthia Enloe was one of the first to highlight the role of nannies and maids, including Filipinas, in the global care chain. See her *Bananas, Beaches, and Bases: Making Feminist Sense of International Politics* (Berkeley and Los Angeles: University of California Press, 1990), chap. 8. See also *Global Woman: Nannies, Maids and Sex Workers in the New Economy*, ed. Barbara Ehrenreich and Arlie Russell Hochschild (New York: Henry Holt, 2004).

24. About one-third of all international migration occurs between developing countries ("south-south" migration), one-third from south to north, one-quarter between countries of the north and a small percentage (6 percent) from north to south. United Nations, Department of Economic and Social Affairs, Population Division, "Migrants by Origin and Destination: The Role of South-South Migration," *Population Facts* (No. 2012/3), June 2012, at http://www.un.org/esa/population/publications/popfacts/popfacts_2012-3_South-South_migration.pdf.

25. The figures vary by year. The examples cited above are from 2007. More recent data follow the same varied trends—for example, Colombia with 34 percent of households headed by a single female. See the World Bank's database at http://databank.worldbank.org.

26. US Census Bureau, "Households and Families: 2010" (2010 Census Briefs), issued April 2012, 7–8.

27. A scenario similar to this occurred in August 2012. Although India does import hydro-electric power from Bhutan, the blackout resulted from a combination of inadequate electric grids (weak infrastructure), generally inadequate energy sources (coal, gas, nuclear, as well as water), and political bungling.

2

Navigating Globalization:
Feminist Approaches to Development

The time was early September 1995, and the place was Huairou, a suburb of Beijing, China. A delegation of West African women, in identical dresses, plopped their boom box on the concrete, turned up the music, and began to dance with joy. Hesitant, we stood and watched. Suddenly, one of the dancers grabbed a shy, young Japanese woman. "Come, dance with us!" One by one, we did, tangled with purses, umbrellas, and tote bags, while imagining the old American pop song Helen Reddy sang in the 1970s: "I am woman, hear me roar."

More than thirty thousand women and men from every country in the world had gathered to celebrate, network, plan, and lobby the Fourth United Nations World Conference on Women that, with its official representatives of governments and international organizations, was meeting in central Beijing. The Huairou gathering was called the NGO (nongovernmental organization) Forum, and it overlapped with the official UN conference. Workshops addressed every conceivable topic and every region of the globe; informal conversations continued day and night in a flea market of tables, pamphlets, and ideas. Three women from Iran, displaying pamphlets attacking the "Great Satan" (the United States), threw back their chadors to discuss women and politics with Americans. Seemingly, it was a new era tailored to fulfill the goal of the NGO Forum: "To bring together women and men to challenge, create and transform global structures and processes at all levels through the empowerment and celebration of women."[1]

Feminist theories and approaches to development aspire to create the equality, justice, and solidarity that the 1995 NGO Forum called for. But there are a multitude of feminist theories with disparate ideas on how to empower women—and these theories are in tension with each other. This chapter describes a feminist approach to development and lays out some of the most important tensions in feminist theory. It also discusses the ways in which feminist ideas in the form of

Women in Development (WID), Gender and Development (GAD), and care-work frameworks entered the development discourse. It then traces the impact of the UN system through its global women's conferences. Finally, under the heading "Political Will," the chapter reflects on the mixed outcomes of efforts to engender the development process.

CHARACTERISTICS OF A FEMINIST APPROACH

What is a feminist approach to understanding globalization, gender, and development? It is more than a specific method of research; it is a perspective or a framework that challenges what J. Ann Tickner calls "the often unseen androcentric or masculine biases in the way that knowledge has traditionally been constructed in the disciplines."[2] This framework is important to studies of globalization because, as Mary Hawkesworth observes, most studies of globalization do not refer to women, gender relations, or feminism, giving the impression that the effects of globalization are gender neutral, "gendered power relations" do not operate, and women are not contesting these power relations.[3]

In contrast to the dominant assessments of globalization, feminist scholars argue that gender is central to globalization in such aspects as the feminization of the global labor force, the differential effects of structural adjustment policies, and the creation of global care chains.[4] Catherine Eschle notes that global capitalism "disrupt[s] gender relations and produce[s] emancipatory as well as oppressive opportunities and effects for women."[5] An example of the emancipatory opportunities that globalization provides or enables is the formation of transnational feminist networks, which work to redress unequal gender relations. These opportunities have been created or facilitated by international structures such as the United Nations, and women and men now have arenas for exercising collective agency in a way not available to them a half century ago. In contrast, the destruction of local agriculture or industry that often results from globalized economic structures is oppressive when it undermines food supplies and means of livelihood.

Drawing on the work of a number of scholars, the following discussion emphasizes four dimensions of a feminist approach that captures its distinctiveness.[6] First, *theory and research* inquire into the causes of gender inequality instead of accepting male dominance and female vulnerability as normal or natural. A feminist approach seeks to identify the structures that create, maintain, and sometimes challenge gender hierarchy. For example, feminist questions investigate gendered differences in economic resources and political power, asking why women are economically disadvantaged across the globe, why only a small minority of national policy makers are women, and why the vast majority of soldiers are men. Another set of feminist questions examines the political effects of gender symbolism and the role of gender norms. For example, Tickner asks, "[H]ow do gendered structures of masculinity and femininity legitimate war and militarism for both women and men?"[7] By asking these kinds of questions, a feminist approach makes visible unexamined assumptions regarding gender that characterize theory and research on globalization, and the development policies that flow from these.

The second characteristic of a feminist approach is the *normative position* it takes that women should enjoy equal rights, respect, and access to resources, and that research and policy should advance this aim. It assumes the desirability of women's empowerment and aspires to enhance women's agency. Feminists have construed social changes that empower women in a broad variety of ways—from revolution to specific policy initiatives. As feminist thinking has evolved since the 1970s, scholars and activists have become increasingly aware of how difficult it is to translate theory and research into outcomes empowering women. Nevertheless, because they are grounded in a commitment to gender justice and equality and can frame public policies, both theory and research have the potential to help improve women's lives globally.

The third characteristic of a feminist approach to gender and development is *reflexivity*. Mary Margaret Fonow and Judith A. Cook describe "reflexivity as the tendency of feminists to reflect on, examine critically, and explore analytically the nature of the research process."[8] This includes an acknowledgment of the subjective aspect of research and theory, sensitivity to the social *and* cultural location of the researcher and power relations between researcher and subject, and accountability for the knowledge constructed. This tendency in feminist scholarship is a reaction against the mainstream assumption found in much academic work that research should be value free, a position feminists see as hiding, not eliminating, the re-searcher's personal perspective. As noted in chapter 1, our social location as Western feminists shapes our perspective, and we believe that our travels, friendships, and reading in and of the Global South have enabled us to embrace a critical feminist stance on development. At the same time, we acknowledge our shortcomings in truly understanding the life experiences of those marginalized by development. Caroline Ramazanoğlu notes that putting reflexivity into practice is extremely difficult, both because of human fallibility and because of practical problems, so reflexivity operates more as an honorable intention than an achievement.[9]

The fourth dimension of a feminist approach is the use of *gender as an analytic category*. Gender can be defined as both the socially constructed differences between the sexes and as the site of hierarchical power relations.[10] Socially constructed gender differences shape notions of appropriate behavior, attributes, and identities for both men and women; and these notions vary across cultures. Gender as a site of power refers to the asymmetrical relations of gender that are created, preserved, and trans-formed in institutions, processes, symbol systems, and interpersonal relations. Gen-der power typically involves the privileging of male characteristics while denigrating female characteristics, promoting men's interests at the cost of women's interests, and normalizing male dominance and female submission.[11] The social technology of the household, explained earlier, illustrates all of these features of socially constructed differences and hierarchical power relations.

In the 1980s, Catharine MacKinnon helped pioneer the use of gender as an analytic category in the American legal profession by examining the ways in which supposedly gender-neutral institutions, such as state structures, constitutions, and laws, actually contribute to the construction and maintenance of a gender hierarchy privileging men and male characteristics.[12] Through her use of gender as an analytic category, MacKinnon drew attention to the role of structures in women's subordination. In the past two decades, feminist scholars in many countries have forced us to rethink the "neutrality" of institutions in their own cultures.

The first two points mentioned above—asking feminist questions and having a commitment to gender justice—mean that a feminist approach to research or policy is shaped by feminist theory in ways that provide diagnoses of the factors responsible for women's subordination and offer different strategies to remedy the situation. With the emergence of feminist movements in nations around the world, we have come to appreciate that there are multiple feminisms and many feminist theories. Instead of presenting a "laundry list" of the characteristics of these multiple feminisms, we summarize three sets of clusters that illustrate the central tensions in feminist theories as the processes of globalization have exposed them.

TENSIONS IN FEMINIST THEORY

Equality versus Difference: The Equality Argument

The first set of tensions is that of equality versus difference. One important strand in feminist theory is the argument that women should have equal rights with men. The rationale for equal rights is that all human beings possess a fundamental dignity; and characteristics such as gender, class, and race are, or should be, irrelevant. This is the core of the liberal feminist perspective, which often endorses a strategy of gender neutrality. Liberal feminists identify irrational traditions as the cause of gender inequalities.

From the mid-nineteenth century to the early twentieth century, during the first wave of feminism, women in the United States, Europe, and some colonized nations campaigned for the same rights as men to participate politically, obtain an education, inherit property, and sue for divorce. Since the beginning of the second wave of feminism in the 1960s, liberal feminists have concentrated on pragmatic strategies to achieve equal rights for women: reforming laws, policies, and the education system; improving women's opportunities in the paid labor force; increasing the number of women in leadership positions; and collecting gender-disaggregated data.

Liberal feminism focuses on strategies to enlarge individual freedom, including the acquisition of basic legal and political rights. An important contemporary form of liberal feminism is the capabilities approach, developed by Amartya Sen and Martha Nussbaum.[13] This approach asserts that certain capabilities are required to enjoy a life with dignity and that these fundamental entitlements are central to achieving gender justice and human development. Sen addresses human capability generally, whereas Nussbaum enumerates those she finds essential, including life; bodily health and integrity; senses, imagination, and thought; emotions; practical reason; affiliation; play; living in relation to the natural world; and control over one's political and material environment.[14] The United Nations Development Programme's (UNDP) annual Human Development Report contains a human development index (HDI) that measures average life expectancy, literacy, and education levels across nations; this can be seen as a first step toward putting the capabilities approach into practice. Without excluding considerations of structure, the capabilities approach emphasizes human agency and proposes tools for comparisons across nations and cultures.

Difference Feminism

In contrast to the emphasis on *equality*, another important strand in feminist theory argues for recognizing the *differences* between men and women, promoting women's values and perspectives, and crafting policies that address the specific needs of women. Labeled "difference feminism," this strand is rooted in women's experiences and provides a critique of the male norms that are dominant in society.[15] For example, women's household work is rarely included in national income statistics because traditionally such statistics include only paid work.[16] In examining the gender division of labor, difference feminism emphasizes the commitment of women to social reproduction in contrast to men's historical concentration in the sphere of paid work (production). Social reproduction refers to daily household activities of cleaning, meal preparation, and care-work responsibilities for partners and across generations, from raising children to looking after aged parents and in-laws. These tasks are essential to societal health and survival for most people in most historical periods, but they have been unpaid and consequently devalued. Thus one important result of the focus on social reproduction has been to highlight the invisibility and necessity of much of women's work.

Ecofeminism presents a very different illustration: It links men's domination of women to economic development practices leading to a rapacious exploitation of nature; and it argues that women are better placed—by their intrinsic qualities as well as their often intimate dependence on natural resources such as land, forests, and water—to manage those resources in a sustainable fashion.[17]

Difference feminism has also focused on violence against girls and women, attributing the violence to the gender division of labor and the domination of men over women. In the debate on sex trafficking, explored in chapter 4, difference feminists assume that the exploitation of women results primarily from male sexual dominance and lust. Some difference feminists have also presented women's perspectives as superior to those of men, arguing that women are more nurturing and peace loving. They have maintained that putting women in leadership positions will result in a more peaceful world or better environmental stewardship.

Difference feminism has been criticized for essentialism, the implication that natural or innate differences exist between men and women. In the past, essentialist perspectives on gender differences have supported discrimination against women. An example of the way in which the emphasis on women's essential nature results in discrimination is protective legislation in the workplace that limits the times and hours women can work or the kinds of jobs they can hold on the assumption that inherent sex and gender differences limit what they can and should do outside the home. The result of such legislation is to restrict women's economic opportunities.

Emerging in the 1990s, the "women's rights are human rights" movement represents a creative way of combining elements of equality and difference. Promoting the human rights of women both affirms women's equality with men and expands the concept of human rights violations from harms caused by state action to include harms caused by family members and social, economic, and political practices that are grounded in gender differences. The origins of this movement date to the early United Nations emphasis on human rights in the 1940s and the perspectives embodied in the Commission on the Status of Women from the same era. The adoption of the Convention on the Elimination of All Forms of Discrimination against Women (CEDAW) in 1979 reflected an initial fusion of human rights and women's rights, but the number of reservations expressed at the time of its adoption illustrated the persistence of tension between equality and difference perspectives. Another important accomplishment for the women's rights as human rights movement was the passage by the UN General Assembly in 1993 of the Declaration on the Elimination of Violence Against Women, which addressed gender violence in both public and private spheres.

Gender-exclusive Focus versus Gender-plus Focus: Diversity Feminism

The second tension in feminist theory addresses the extent to which gender is the only important factor in understanding the subordination of women. In this respect, feminist theories range along a continuum. At one end is an almost exclusive focus on women's oppression as women and at the other end is an inclusive approach to the multiplicity of hierarchies constraining women in addition to gender, such as race or ethnicity, class, and national origin. Although equality and difference feminism are dissimilar in many ways, they both tend to focus exclusively on gender. Since the 1960s, several feminist approaches have been calling attention to the ways in which many women are constrained by class and race, as well as by gender hierarchy. These approaches all argue that any meaningful feminist strategy for development must involve transforming economic structures to reduce inequality.

In the 1970s socialist feminists were among the earliest diversity feminists. With theoretical roots in the Marxist emphasis on economic and social structures, they called for the overthrow of patriarchy and capitalism, identifying both male domination and the economic system as structures requiring transformation.[18] At the first UN Women's Conference in Mexico City, Western feminists talked about women's rights, whereas women from the Global South spoke of economic and military repression. In the words of Domitila Barrios de Chungara, a Bolivian tin miner's wife and activist, "The first and main task isn't to fight against our *compañeros*, but with them to change the system we live in for another, in which men and women will have the right to live, to work, to organize."[19]

This broader, inclusive conception of feminism was also a central theme in the document put together by the DAWN network of Third World Feminists for the 1985 UN Women's Conference in Nairobi: "We want a world where inequality, based on class, gender and race is absent from every country and from the relationships among countries."[20] In the twenty-first century, the emphases on economic structure, class, and gender equality reemerged in the debate over water privatization, as explained in chapter 5.

Feminists espousing a more inclusive approach criticize both equality and difference feminists for presenting universal claims about women's oppression and liberation. Women of color in the United States and women from the Global South argue that there is great diversity among women and that the universal feminist projects have too often represented an imposition of white, Western, middle-class values on the rest of the world, reproducing "Western hegemony in the name of promoting the advancement of women."[21] These critics are often called diversity feminists, and they call for a politics of location that "pluralize[s] and particularize[s] the meaning of 'women,'" theorizing "how the social constructions of race, class, and sexuality profoundly alter the status of gender."[22] They argue that a diversity of women's voices, as well as organizations and policies that address the intersectionality of multiple forms of oppression (race, class, culture, and sexuality), are needed to enhance women's agency among subjugated groups.[23] Diversity feminists envision many feminisms growing out of historically specific locations instead of a single global feminist vision. Durbar, an Indian organization representing women who have been trafficked, discussed in chapter 4, illustrates the practical implications of diversity feminism.

Both ends of the gender-exclusive and gender-plus continuum can be problematic. As noted above, an exclusive focus on gender equality has tended to benefit elite women without addressing the needs of working-class and poor women. However, it has also been the case that the inclusive approaches found in diversity feminism and the formation of broad coalitions based on class and race may submerge gender issues and even consign female activists to secondary roles.

Deconstructionism

The third set of tensions is between "articulating women's voice and deconstructing gender."[24] The feminist theories described above have been concerned with women's demand for recognition and the efforts to end men's domination. Deconstruction feminism takes a very different approach: It argues that to alter the male/female power relations, it is necessary to question and deconstruct the categories of "male" and "female" in order to undermine the power structures inherent in the discourse of gender.

Deconstruction feminism emerges out of poststructuralist theory, which asserts that cultural discourses constitute social reality and human subjectivity, and offers tools for analyzing these discourses. Here the emphasis is on structures of thought.

A deconstructive approach is useful in calling attention to what is omitted and marginalized in the categories and concepts we use. For example, as mentioned above, feminist scholars examining security issues question why the concept of national security in political science is associated with military strength, whereas broad dimensions of human security, particularly issues of development, are not considered relevant.

A poststructuralist approach takes a skeptical stance toward universalizing theories of progress, development, and liberation, arguing that in practice they advance the interests of their authors and are exclusionary and oppressive to others. Feminists have used this approach to critique development theories to reveal how they marginalize women. A deconstructionist approach also enables feminists to look critically at their own political projects, which may reflect the interests of some women and not others. Deconstruction feminists criticize general concepts, such as "the Third World woman," arguing that they silence dissident voices and obscure underlying power relations. The backward, poor, and vulnerable Third World woman is conceptualized as the opposite of the modern, affluent, and liberated Western woman. From a deconstructive perspective, this binary opposition legitimizes a hierarchical relationship in which the Western feminist rescues the Third World woman whose own knowledge is made invisible.

One of the most important values of deconstruction feminism is the way in which it clarifies that the effort to categorize a messy, fragmented reality into neat packages of intellectual constructs may advance our understanding, but it also leaves out, silences, and obscures certain aspects of that reality. For example, a difference feminist construction of women as peaceful does not fit the cases of women leaders such as prime ministers Golda Meir (Israel, in office 1969–1974), Indira Gandhi (India, 1966–1977 and 1980–1984), or Margaret Thatcher (Britain, 1979–1990). All three were heads of government when their countries fought wars. Deconstruction feminism also reminds us that we carry assumptions arising from a Western (or Asian, or Middle Eastern) worldview. This is essential when we study other cultures.

A limitation of deconstruction feminism is that it neglects the role of material conditions—institutions, resources, and laws—with its focus on discourse. The major weakness of this approach, however, is that "critique is privileged over action."[25] Liberal, difference, and diversity feminisms are better guides to political action because each incorporates goals and strategies, whereas deconstruction feminism remains suspicious of general principles. In deconstructing the category "woman," deconstruction feminism may, in Kathy Ferguson's words, "rob women of the capacity for resistance and struggle that their own women's voice can provide."[26]

Ferguson contends that deconstruction feminism and the other feminist perspectives need each other because deconstruction feminism keeps the others honest while the others provide direction. She states, "Rather than thinking of the tensions . . . as contradictions that we must resolve, we might better approach them as riddles that we must engage."[27] We think Ferguson's point applies to the three sets of tensions in feminist theory examined above. Instead of resolving the tensions or choosing one or another tendency, we recommend holding the different strands in tension with each other. The advantage of this strategy will be seen in chapter 4, where the analysis of trafficking and the proposed policies to address it illustrate both the tensions in feminist theory and the efforts to resolve them.

In sum, we all make certain assumptions about the way reality operates. These assumptions condition the way we think about or "frame" problems and, consequently, the policy solutions we propose to address them. The significance of a feminist approach is that it guides our assumptions with a commitment to gender justice; it has produced a wealth of research on the contexts and relations of gender injustice; and as a result, it has exposed as critical for understanding globalization and development the relations of power and gender hierarchy embedded in structures and processes that most people have long considered gender neutral. By recasting assumptions, understanding, and therefore policy proposals, a feminist approach points us in the direction of greater gender justice.

Despite these accomplishments, feminist theory, research, and movements have too often fallen short of producing real improvements in the lives of poor women. In part, this is due to the overarching power of the ideological, economic, cultural, and political structures within which we live. But it is also clear that feminists are often at odds over their diagnosis of the problems and the policies needed to address them. These disagreements reflect the tensions explained above; many of them are inherent in debates over the nature of globalization and development.

The above section on tensions in feminist theories takes an analytical approach to the subject, presenting a conceptual overview of theories that developed unevenly over time. The next two sections discuss how these tensions played out in feminist efforts to engender development practice and the emergence of global women's advocacy networks out of a series of UN women's conferences. Here a historical approach is taken, looking at processes that unfold over time.

THE POLITICS OF WID AND GAD

Beginning in the 1960s, development practitioners, scholars, and policy makers sought to address the gender gap in development thinking and practice. The first phase of gender awareness came to be labeled "women in development" (WID) in the 1970s. A second phase followed, becoming more common in the late 1980s. This second phase, known as gender and development (GAD), was largely a response to the first and sought to address the perceived shortcomings in both theory and practice that characterized WID.[28] Both the WID and the GAD approaches mirrored the larger debates within the development communities over the meaning of development, the barriers to economic growth, who gained and who lost from development projects, and even the right of those in the "first" or industrialized world to define the problems of poor, predominantly agricultural countries.

The WID field resulted initially from the realization that development as practiced through the 1960s had "left out" women and in fact had often disadvantaged them. In response, WID drew on liberal feminist theory to argue that women should be integrated into development programs by emphasizing their productive roles.[29] In contrast, GAD argued that women had always been a part of development, but they were in subordinate relationships based on gender, class, race, and nationality. GAD's theoretical heritage was more mixed, reflecting mainly diversity feminism with its attention to multiple social hierarchies, but adding some elements of difference feminism in a focus on reproduction as well as production (see table 2.1).

The discussion that follows summarizes the WID-GAD trajectory and debates, then reviews the international organizing that transformed much of our thinking about the role of women specifically and gender more generally in development processes. The trajectory of the 1960s–1990s was not a tidy, linear chronology. At times it was unruly, marked by both contradictory and overlapping ideas and movements. Organizations came and went; government ministries committed themselves to "integrating women into development" or to "engendering development," only to minimize or even abandon their commitments a few years later. Activists, policy makers, and scholars all wanted to be heard; but because they were connected to development issues in different ways, their views on what should and could be done also differed.[30]

Table 2.1. Comparison of Women in Development and Gender and Development

	WID (Women in Development)	GAD (Gender and Development)
Origins	1970s; American influence (academics, practitioners)	Late 1980s, counterpoint to WID; global influences
Theory	Liberal economics and modernization theories: women disadvantaged by development policies of 1950s and 1960s (liberal feminism)	Class analyses and dependency approaches; criticized basic assumptions of economic liberalism (diversity feminism)
Emphasis; policies	Call to integrate women into development programs through policy changes; emphasized women's productive roles (instrumental view)	Argued women always part of development; questioned some assumptions of development; emphasized household, gender relations, issues of class, race, and ethnicity
Contribution	Did not challenge existing social structures; emphasized the status of women and specific issues such as income generation and education	Called attention to the "private sphere" and need to examine intra-household relations and the structure of power; women viewed as agents, not passive recipients of development

One of the earliest moves toward integrating women into development came from Sweden. In 1963, the Swedish parliament first proposed the use of foreign aid funds to improve women's access to training and education; and by 1968, Sweden had suggested to the United Nations a long-range program for the advancement of women.[31] In the United States, an amendment to the 1973 Foreign Assistance Act required the US Agency for International Development (USAID) to promote the integration of women into development programs funded by the US government.

These early WID initiatives were grounded in a growing awareness of gender as a factor in the division of labor. Danish economist Ester Boserup did more than any scholar of her generation to criticize the omission of women's roles in the vast literature on economic change. In the preface to her 1970 book, *Woman's Role in Economic Development*, Boserup wrote: "Economic and social development unavoidably entails the disintegration of the division of labour among the two sexes traditionally established in the village. With modernization of agriculture and with migration to the towns, a new sex pattern of productive work must emerge, for better or worse."[32] Boserup addressed numerous topics that would later receive more detailed analysis from scholars and development workers, such as the division of labor in traditional agriculture, the impact of colonialism on women's labor, export-sector work, migration, and the significance of education.

Boserup's analytical approach, though innovative for its time, was nonetheless grounded in the dominant economic assumptions that characterized most thinking about development in the 1960s and 1970s. She assumed that modernization is an economic phenomenon defined by rural-to-urban migration, wage work, manufacturing, capital accumulation, and increasingly complex technologies. Although sensitive to cultural differences, she tended to see them as a barrier that would give way before a unique development model,[33] and she emphasized women largely in isolation from their social relationships with men.

In contrast, subsequent gender and development (GAD) approaches emphasized gender *relationships*, the multiple ways in which women and men relate to each other. For example, these approaches were more attentive to the interplay of productive and reproductive activities, the latter including all of the tasks implied in creating, maintaining, and protecting the family and household, broadly interpreted. These approaches also led analysts to consider the origins of female subordination in patriarchal family and social relations, as well as in forms of economic production. Taken together, gender and development approaches generally were more sensitive to *intra*-national class and ethnic differences than we see in the work of Boserup and early women-in-development analyses.

In addition to gender relations, the productive-reproductive dynamic, and the role of intra-national differences, GAD approaches drew attention directly to structural issues that differentiated national economies. They moved our thinking more clearly in the direction of understanding a country's position in the international economic system. In this move, the GAD approaches were indebted to changes in development thinking more broadly, including those explained in chapter 3. Although the gender and development and women in development approaches emphasized different factors, both were primarily concerned with individual nation-states. Only in the 1990s did the structures and forces of globalization fundamentally alter our thinking about women/gender and development. The emergence of a renewed focus on care work, particularly in a global context, was one of the most important feminist contributions at the end of the twentieth century and beginning of the twenty-first century; and it represented a new phase in linking gender and development in the global economy.

CARE WORK

Understanding the reality of the multitude of reproductive and productive responsibilities confronting most women, feminists have always responded with contrasting analyses and policy recommendations. For example, during the peak of industrialization in Europe and North America, nineteenth- and early-twentieth-century socialist feminists typically called for liberating women from "housework" by encouraging paid labor and, in some instances, communalizing household and family tasks. Their primary goal was to insist that women, like men, belong in the public sphere. Liberal and difference feminists, led by economists, have worked to highlight the significance of reproductive activities by attaching a monetary value to tasks such as cooking, transporting, child care, cleaning, and so forth. Both of these approaches have been deeply influenced by a view of development as primarily economic. In contrast, more recent thinking about development reassesses the importance of social reproduction and the way we understand it.

Mainstream theories of development have long ignored or diminished the significance of reproductive labor in assessing policy strategies or outcomes. But by the 1990s, partly in response to the added burden on women of some neoliberal economic policies, one strain of feminist thought turned WID on its head, emphasizing the centrality in the development process of what is now widely referred to as "women's care work." Care work refers to the disproportionate efforts of women doing housework, dependent care, and meeting psychological needs of family members. It also includes the work of housemaids, nannies, and other service workers from across town or from another country performing these tasks for pay.

Feminist analysis of care work shows the influence of difference feminism and the interest of GAD writers in intra-household relations. Joan Tronto offers an expansive definition of care work, which she describes as "a species activity that includes everything that we do to maintain, continue, and repair our world so that we can live in it as well as possible. That world includes our bodies, ourselves, and our environment, all of which we seek to interweave in a complex, life-sustaining web."[34] Care work does not fit neatly into frameworks of development as it straddles existing categories such as instrumental tasks and affective labor, unpaid and paid work, public and private sphere, economy and family.

The economic and political dimensions of development theories have taken for granted the massive time and effort women invest in care work, with the result that this work has been largely invisible in crafting and implementing development policies. To illustrate, it is estimated that as much as 70 percent of the hours spent on care work are contributed by women.[35] Kate Bedford notes that "the dominant models of growth overlook the enormous value of these activities disproportionately done by women" and "overburdened women by failing to take into account unpaid household labor."[36] Feminist scholars argue that this situation has been exacerbated under neoliberal globalization because public services that benefit the poor are typically one of the first areas cut when government budgets shrink. At the same time, women face increased pressures and opportunities to enter the paid labor force. Development strategies fail to consider that "any person's public existence floats upon this enormous amount of care work and reproductive labor that has come before and transformed a human infant into a capable citizen."[37]

To address these issues, feminist scholars have advocated both fundamental changes in thinking about care work and development, and some practical policy reforms. Mahon and Robinson argue that we need to deconstruct the autonomy/dependence dichotomy and see interdependence as "a defining feature of social life instead of thinking of independent men and dependent women."[38] Because care work contributes so broadly to the development of human capabilities, both public policy support and the active participation of men in family care should occur. Scholars note a tension between "a wish to support and value care and to liberate women from the confines of caregiving so as to enable their more active presence in the public sphere."[39] In part, this tension reflects cultural differences. For example, Western women tend to see care work as a burden, whereas Caribbean women tend to emphasize the importance of this work.[40] All of these approaches, however, show the impact of conceptualizing development in the context of gender relations.

The three types of policy interventions that have been made in the area of care have to do with increasing time (paid care leaves), resources (cash transfers), and services (child care).[41] Although most feminist scholars advocate a larger state role in care work, Bedford reports that a World Bank program in Ecuador involved a privatized solution instead of a public program, encouraging men to engage in care work as an alternative to supporting child-care services, a strategy that many feminists would applaud.[42] In general, feminist scholars and practitioners alike advocate improvements in remuneration and rights for paid care workers, both of which require a change in political thinking about the importance of care work and its centrality in development.

INTERNATIONAL DYNAMICS: THE UNITED NATIONS SYSTEM

Although most people think of globalization purely in economic terms, the political structures and activities of international organizations are central to the global order in the twenty-first century. The most familiar of these is the United Nations, established in 1945. Debates about development and gender have been deeply influenced by the United Nations system, its organizations, its conferences and covenants. From the creation of the Commission on the Status of Women in 1946 in the immediate aftermath of World War II, to the drafting and signing of the Convention on the Elimination of All Forms of Discrimination against Women (CEDAW), to the international conferences on women, population, human rights, and the environment, the United Nations is central to the story of gender and development.

The United Nations Charter, signed in 1945, affirmed "faith in fundamental human rights" and also "the equal rights of men and women." From its earliest months of operation, issues of women's rights were highlighted in the activities of the General Assembly and the Commission on the Status of Women. The Commission undertook to study a variety of barriers to gender equality, including legal and political inequalities (such as the absence of female suffrage), and by the 1950s had turned its attention to a central contradiction that persists to the present: The goal of guaranteeing universal human rights and gender equality inevitably challenges deeply imbedded customs and cultural practices in many societies. In 1954, the General Assembly adopted a resolution calling on its member states to "take all appropriate measures" with a view to abolishing "customs, ancient laws and practices" relating to marriage and the family that subject women to conditions that are inconsistent with the Universal Declaration of Human Rights.[43]

The fact that more than a half century later this tension between the long-standing goals of gender equality and the reality of cultural differences persists could be interpreted as simply another failure to implement the UN declarations. This conclusion, however, belies the considerable progress that has been made in uncovering, defining, and placing on the international political agenda laws and practices that degrade many women. Part of this history has been to link the rights emphasized by the Commission on the Status of Women in its early decades directly to development, with the result that by the beginning of the twenty-first century, the convergence between issues of development and of gender equality was widely accepted.

This historical convergence has been a laborious process, but as we will see in future chapters, points of consensus have been growing. Much of the consensus that has emerged has been the result of the Commission on the Status of Women and four UN conferences on women along with the nongovernmental (NGO) gatherings that accompanied them. The conferences led to what one participant has called a "feminist methodology" of globalizing frameworks around economics, the environment and rights, and a process of feminist consciousness-raising. The process starts with testifying to local or individual experiences, moves to a negotiation of differences, and finally to the effort to articulate a general position that synthesizes the diversity of experience.[44]

The first United National Conference on Women was set to mark the beginning of the United Nations Decade for Women (1976–1985). Held in Mexico City, the conference celebrated International Women's Year (IWY, 1975) with the theme

Figure 2.1.   International Women's Year (IWY) Logo

"Equality, Development, Peace." The IWY logo, a dove of peace incorporating the symbols for women and equality, was ubiquitous (see figure 2.1). Like the succeeding three conferences, the Mexico City meeting drew thousands of participants to the parallel NGO gathering. The issues debated at Mexico City reflected a potpourri of causes and international cleavages. In retrospect, four long-term legacies of the IWY conference were especially significant. First, both the official conference and the parallel meetings generated a momentum for women's movements around the globe and established a mandate for government initiatives to address issues of gender equality. Second, the gatherings exposed the differences that existed between the women's rights advocates from Europe and North America, many of whom were ignorant of the economic realities of much of the world, and the participants from Latin America, Asia, and Africa. Third, IWY encouraged research and theory about the reality of gender inequality and its link to development processes around the globe. To illustrate, scholars and activists concerned with food production popularized the phrase, "the farmer . . . she . . ." to counteract ignorance of gender roles in agriculture, especially in sub-Saharan Africa (see figure 2.2). Finally—and perhaps most important—the conference mobilized grassroots organizations and established multiple feminist agendas around the world.

Each of the three succeeding UN conferences had its own dynamics, and by the Fourth UN Conference on Women, in 1995, more than thirty thousand people converged on Beijing (see table 2.2). During the period between the first and fourth conferences, government organizations and policy statements, research findings, data gathering, and NGOs proliferated around the globe. All of these were—or, at least, professed to be—devoted to the advancement of women. Women and men seemed to be organizing everywhere, and many United Nations forums that were not created with the primary intent of addressing gender issues were pressured by activists to

Figure 2.2. Cartoon Emphasizing Women's Roles in Sub-Saharan Agriculture. Original drawing courtesy of Jaquelyn Bonnema

include gender in their deliberations on development—for example, the conferences on the environment (Rio de Janeiro, 1992), population (Cairo, 1994), and social development (Copenhagen, 1995).

One of the first concrete accomplishments of this frenzy of organizing was the drafting, adoption (by the UN General Assembly in 1979), and ratification of CEDAW. The story of CEDAW illustrates both the strengths and weaknesses of this global activity. As noted in the discussion on equality and difference perspectives in feminism, the negotiation of the Convention and the reservations expressed at the time of its adoption exposed the deep-seated cleavages that still persist over demands for gender equality.[45] Although the overwhelming majority of UN member governments subsequently ratified the document, the signatories included many countries that have become notorious for their egregious violation of human rights generally and women's rights specifically.[46]

Despite large areas of consensus, the controversies over CEDAW, male-female equality, and the cultural "appropriateness" of human rights definitions viewed as Western-dominated are with us in the twenty-first century. Much of the controversy may be traced to the rejection by many people of the secularist bias in development, which is explained in chapter 3.

Despite its detractors, CEDAW remains a benchmark in the ongoing process of defining and establishing global legitimacy for human rights. It does represent a

Table 2.2. United Nations Women's Conferences, 1975–1995

Date	Location (Secretary General)	Themes	Parallel NGO Meeting[a]
1975	Mexico City–IWY (Helvi Sipala, Finland)	WID emphasis: education, health, employment, peace, human rights; call for research data; North-South differences become apparent	IWY Tribune, approximately 6,000 participants
1980	Copenhagen: "Mid-Decade Conference" (Lucille Mair, Jamaica)	Five-year progress review; GAD emphasis on causes of inequality; tension over cultural differences; international political conflicts influence Conference—e.g., Israel-Palestine; emphasis on women's organizations	Forum, approximately 7,200 participants
1985	Nairobi (Leticia Shahani, Philippines)	International economic issues—debt reduction, strategic adjustment (SAPs); new focus on violence, pornography; increasing racial, cultural diversity; "Forward-Looking Strategies" agenda	Forum '85, DAWN founded,[b] approximately 15,000 participants
1995	Beijing (Gertrude Mongella, Tanzania)	Targeted issues of international and domestic violence; debates over reproductive freedoms; concern about women's declining economic situation (impact of SAPs)	NGO Forum, approximately 30,000 participants

[a] The nongovernmental meetings that overlapped the formal intergovernmental UN conferences were known by different names. Attendance figures are approximate: most participants registered, but many did not; and numbers for attendance vary considerably.

[b] Development Alternatives with Women for a New Era. Founded in India, DAWN refers both to the platform document prepared for the Forum and the organization of those, primarily from developing countries in the South, who criticized the dominant growth model of modernization.

process of international consultation and debate, and for many advocates of gender equality in numerous countries, the Convention serves as a tool to pressure their governments.[47] Put differently, the Convention is central to the effort to publicize and give legitimacy to gender equality. It is ironic, however, that the effervescence of *political* globalization that generated the adoption of CEDAW, along with the energy and optimism reflected in the UN conferences, was diminished in many ways by the *economic* forces of globalization at the end of the twentieth century.

One of the central lessons to emerge from the experience of the UN system during the second half of the twentieth century is that conferences and policy agendas *always* reflect the international political and economic contexts within which they take place. For example, hostilities between Israel, Palestinians, and representatives of

Arab states percolated through many of the sessions at the four UN conferences on women. In March 2012 UN officials proposed convening a Fifth UN World Conference on Women (5th WCW) in 2015. Feminist reactions were mixed given the lack of prior, systematic consultation with civil society groups or UN Women and inadequate funding for UN Women and women's rights organizations. But those supporting the convening of the 5th WCW saw it as an opportunity to raise consciousness and perhaps generate the kind of networking among women worldwide that had emerged during the earlier conferences.

POLITICAL WILL

If one takes a long view and compares the early twenty-first century with the middle of the twentieth century, it is hard not to be impressed by the enormous progress made in placing issues of gender and development on policy agendas from the local to the global level. It is a rare person, and certainly not one knowledgeable about the realities of development, who argues today that development processes are gender neutral. Furthermore, in much of the world, domestic and international laws and conventions now deem violence against women to be morally and legally unacceptable. Fifty years ago, safe houses didn't exist, few knew what "genital mutilation" meant, and military sexual slavery was not a subject of international legal discourse.

We have made enormous strides simply in *counting* women, girls, and their activities. Statistics disaggregated by gender were rare fifty years ago; they are now common. As a consequence of the United Nations conferences on women, both donors and recipients of development assistance systematically introduced criteria for including gender issues in their development strategies. New tools for gender equity, such as "gender budgeting," have made their way into some government practices, making it possible to assess the differential impact of public budgets on women and men. Thus even the most arcane of government activities, drawing up an annual budget, now may be subjected to gender analysis.

Feminist activities seeking to alter development practices are astonishingly diverse in their approaches and the levels at which they work. They range from the scholars who explore household structures or international migration patterns, to bureaucrats who argue with colleagues on a daily basis in order to chip away at institutional gender bias. They include high-profile lawyers and politicians who argue on behalf of rape victims caught in war zones, to local NGOs helping those victims put their lives back together. They are as diverse as the languages, cultures, and religions they represent, and it is perhaps surprising that they agree at all on key policy agendas.

Despite this energy, the life conditions of most women and men around the world today look little better—and often they are worse—than in the mid-twentieth century. Income gaps have grown in many countries, including in rich countries such as the United States. Environmental degradation and its cost to the poor, who are least able to pay the price, have accelerated. Some of the most heinous war crimes—such as the systematic use of rape to demoralize enemy populations—have occurred on a widespread basis, ruining the lives of their victims. AIDS and other infectious diseases continue to destroy families. What are we to make of what seems to be a massive failure on all fronts?

Central to this failure, we argue, is a lack of political will. Much of what has been accomplished has been transformed into technical or bureaucratic procedures that have been "routinized"—another form to fill out, another box to check off. In this sense, "gender mainstreaming," the process of including references to gender issues in development strategies, has been successful. However, it has not been transformative in terms of the lives of those supposedly benefiting from these strategies. Ines Smyth argues that, in fact, the word "gender" has helped to neutralize the specific commitment to women's conditions by making it easier to think of development more as a technical matter and less as a political matter.[48] It also helps mask the fear that NGOs and international institutions have of the word "feminist," which is linked to a political project that directly threatens existing power arrangements at all levels. Finally, notes Smyth, the recognition of cultural diversity has increasingly been deployed to avoid "interference" in local, regional, and national structural arrangements. "One cannot fail to note a discrepancy here. Development organizations . . . express reluctance to impose what are considered Northern cultural values on gender; at the same time, they appear fairly unconcerned about exporting Northern views and practices on how best to grow crops, dispense credit, manage an organization or communicate with people."[49]

The persistence of gender injustice and inequality is thus the result of a variety of real problems. Bureaucracies have their own internal organizations, cultures, and priorities; maintenance of the bureaucratic structure itself takes precedence over any policy initiative that threatens that structure. Overturning patriarchal structures and altering repressive cultures by definition threatens existing power arrangements and consequently is rejected by those in power. Efforts at change will be resisted and may be co-opted, subverted, or simply eliminated by destroying the individuals or organizations pressing for change.

In recent years, these kinds of debates over development and globalization have led to a rethinking of the connections between gender and development and how we might better address the inequalities between women and men that lead to female subordination. Acceptance is growing that empowerment ultimately occurs as a result of fundamental changes occurring in the communities within which women and men live, and these communities range from the domestic unit to the nation-state. Feminists increasingly argue in favor of positioning women as full participants in the community, enabling them to claim equality and demanding accountability from those who hold power. Anne Marie Goetz describes this as "inclusive citizenship," and prescribes practical steps to achieve this, including legal pluralism (recognizing customary dispute resolution as well as formal law), linking customary law to international human rights norms, and using collective action to assert citizenship claims that give women voice in their communities.[50]

Feminists now pursue both inclusionary and transformative approaches to achieve gender equality.[51] Inclusionary approaches require engagement with the state and international organizations, seeking women's representation in positions of power, as well as laws and public policies responsive to the needs of women. Transformative approaches involve confrontations with the state and challenges to cultural norms to achieve a redistribution of economic, social, and political power. Both of these approaches are apparent in efforts to improve women's access to water discussed in chapter 5.

It is important to stress that the approaches are not mutually exclusive. Feminist strategies may draw on both simultaneously or sequentially. For example, in December 2012, a young Indian woman boarded a bus with her boyfriend in New Delhi. He was beaten, while she was gang-raped and so badly injured that she subsequently died. Massive protests followed in Delhi and other Indian cities; both women and men accused the police and government officials of indifference. Feminists, joined by a variety of grassroots activists, aired complaints about a culture that tolerates—even encourages—discrimination and violence against women.

Meanwhile, dozens of people representing women's and human rights groups testified before the government committee established to recommend changes to the criminal justice system and submitted nearly eighty thousand recommendations to the committee.[52] Feminists critiqued the committee report, as well as the legislation adopted by parliament to implement some of the recommended reforms, such as broadening the definition of rape and criminalizing stalking. Other goals were sidelined in the spurt of reform, but feminists recognized that legislation alone would not stem the pervasive cultural tolerance of violence against women. Nonetheless they were in the forefront of engaging the government deliberative process, even as they confronted the police, organized demonstrations, and called for cultural awareness of the problems facing Indian women.

The India example reminds us that any successful strategy must be multidisciplinary, multipronged, and ultimately political. This should not be construed as an argument for rejecting gender mainstreaming in development agencies, or accumulating statistical data. Nor is it an argument for the supremacy of one feminist theory over another, for—as noted earlier—it pays to hold the theories in tension with one another. One does not abandon the effort to enhance individual autonomy because one acknowledges the constraints imposed by a global neoliberal economic system, a repressive state, or corrupt village politics. One can be self-conscious and "reflexive" about one's personal cultural lenses, even while refusing to accept them as an insuperable barrier to cross-cultural dialogue or a global human rights agenda.

The next chapter provides more in-depth discussion of the background and central issues of what development is—and is not. It clarifies the importance of bringing a feminist perspective into debates and practice, especially in the era of neoliberal globalization. In the subsequent four chapters, we describe promising strategies for addressing four very different kinds of problems that are widespread in the world. Each represents a different cluster of development issues and requires multiple strategies across all levels. Each reveals the multiple dimensions of globalization. Finally, each reflects the constraints imposed by structures, but also the opportunities that may be available for enhancing agency.

NOTES

1. Quoted on the front piece of the NGO Forum *Schedule of Activities*.
2. J. Ann Tickner, "Feminism Meets International Relations: Some Methodological Issues," in *Feminist Methodologies for International Relations*, ed. Brooke Ackerly, Maria Stern, and Jacqui True (Cambridge: Cambridge University Press, 2006), 20.
3. Mary E. Hawkesworth, *Globalization and Feminist Activism* (Lanham, MD: Rowman & Littlefield, 2006), 3.
4. See Hawkesworth, *Globalization and Feminist Activism*; Catherine Eschle, "Feminist Studies of Globalisation: Beyond Gender, Beyond Economism?," *Global Society* 18, no. 2 (2004): 97–125; and Valentine M. Moghadam, *Globalizing Women: Transnational Feminist Networks* (Baltimore: Johns Hopkins University Press, 2005). The term "global care chain" refers to the globalization of reproductive activities that rely on labor migration from other countries. The hiring of nurses and nannies is an example.
5. Eschle, "Feminist Studies of Globalisation," 121.
6. Sandra Harding, ed., *Feminism and Methodology* (Milton Keynes: Open University Press, 1987); Mary Margaret Fonow and Judith A. Cook, eds., *Beyond Methodology: Feminist Scholarship as Lived Research* (Bloomington: Indiana University Press, 1991); Caroline Ramazanoğlu, with Janet Holland, *Feminist Methodology: Challenges and Choices* (London: Sage, 2002); Sharlene Nagy Hesse-Biber and Michelle L. Yaiser, *Feminist Perspectives on Social Research* (New York: Oxford University Press, 2004); and Tickner, "Feminism Meets International Relations."
7. J. Ann Tickner, "What Is Your Research Program? Some Feminist Answers to International Relations Methodological Questions," *International Studies Quarterly* 49, no. 1 (2005): 5.
8. Mary Margaret Fonow and Judith A. Cook, "Feminist Methodology: New Applications in the Academy and Public Policy," *Signs: Journal of Women in Culture and Society* 30, no. 4 (2005): 2218.
9. Ramazanoğlu, *Feminist Methodology*, 119.
10. Joan Wallach Scott, "Gender, a Useful Category for Historical Analysis," *American Historical Review* 91, no. 5 (1986): 1053–75.
11. We acknowledge that this could mean privileging female power, but rarely has this been the case throughout history.
12. Catharine MacKinnon, *Toward a Feminist Theory of the State* (Cambridge, MA: Harvard University Press, 1989). See also her influential article, "Feminism, Marxism, Method and the State: Toward Feminist Jurisprudence," *Signs: Journal of Women in Culture and Society* 8, no. 4 (1983): 635–58.
13. Amartya Sen, *Development as Freedom* (New York: Knopf, 1999); and Martha Nussbaum *Women and Human Development: The Capabilities Approach* (Cambridge, UK: Cambridge University Press, 2000).
14. Nussbaum, *Women and Human Development*, 78–80.

15. Mary Dietz, "Current Controversies in Feminist Theory," *Annual Review of Political Science* 6 (2003): 399–431, identifies three divergent perspectives in current discussions of feminist theory: difference, diversity, and deconstruction feminism.

16. Marilyn Waring, former member of the New Zealand parliament, was one of the first to argue this in her 1988 book, *Counting for Nothing: What Men Value and What Women Are Worth*, 2nd ed. (Toronto: University of Toronto Press, 1999); and Lourdes Benería, *Gender, Globalization and Development: Economics as if All People Mattered* (New York: Routledge, 2003).

17. As in the case of other feminisms, there are numerous versions of ecofeminism. One example is the well-known writer and political activist Vandana Shiva. See *Staying Alive: Women, Ecology and Development* (New York and London: Zed Books, 1988) in which she introduces her argument about "maldevelopment" as "the death of the feminine principle."

18. Nancy Fraser, "Feminism, Capitalism and the Cunning of History," *New Left Review* 56 (2009): 97–117.

19. Domitila Barrios de Chungara and Moema Viezzer, *Let Me Speak? Testimony of Domitila, a Woman of the Bolivian Mines*, ed. and trans. Victoria Ortiz (New York: Monthly Review Press, 1978), 199, quoted in Jayati Lal et al., "Recasting Global Feminisms: Toward a Comparative, Historical Approach to Women's Activism and Feminist Scholarship," *Feminist Studies* 36, no. 1 (2010): 13–14.

20. DAWN stands for Development Alternatives with Women for a New Era, and the platform document was published as a book by Gita Sen and Caren Grown, *Development, Crises, and Alternative Visions: Third World Women's Perspectives* (New York: Monthly Review Press, 1987), 80.

21. Jill Steans, "Debating Women's Human Rights as a 'Universal' Feminist Project: Defending Women's Human Rights as a Political Tool," *Review of International Studies* 33, no. 1 (2007): 15.

22. Dietz, "Current Controversies," 408.

23. For a discussion of intersectionality, see S. Laurel Weldon, "The Structure of Intersectionality: A Comparative Politics of Gender," *Politics and Gender* 2, no. 2 (2006): 235–48.

24. Kathy E. Ferguson, "Interpretation and Genealogy in Feminism," *Signs: Journal of Women in Culture and Society* 16, no. 2 (1991): 322.

25. Jane S. Jaquette and Kathleen Staudt, "Women, Gender and Development," in *Women and Gender Equity in Development Theory and Practice: Institutions, Resources, and Mobilization*, ed. Jane S. Jaquette and Gale Summerfield (Durham, NC: Duke University Press, 2006), 37–38.

26. Ferguson, "Interpretation and Genealogy, 337.

27. Ferguson, "Interpretation and Genealogy, 339.

28. Some scholars identified a third "school" called "women and development" (WAD), which also emerged as a critique of WID and was influenced by dependency theory. See Nalini Visvanathan, "Introduction to Part 1," in *The Women, Gender and Development Reader*, ed. Visvanathan et al. (London: Zed Books, 1997), 21–22.

29. Naila Kabeer, *Reversed Realities: Gender Hierarchies in Development Thought* (London: Verso, 1994), 27.

30. Irene Tinker, "The Making of a Field: Advocates, Practitioners, and Scholars," in *Persistent Inequalities: Women and World Development*, ed. Tinker (New York: Oxford University Press, 1990), 27–53.

31. Josette L. Murphy, *Gender Issues in World Bank Lending* (Washington, DC: World Bank, 1995).

32. Ester Boserup, *Woman's Role in Economic Development* (New York: St. Martin's Press, 1970), 5.

33. See the critique by Lourdes Benería and Gita Sen, "Accumulation, Reproduction and Women's Role in Economic Development: Boserup Revisited," in Visvanathan, *Women, Gender and Development Reader*, 42–51.

34. Berenice Fisher and Joan Tronto, "Toward a Feminist Theory of Caring," in *Circles of Caring*, ed. E. Abel and M. Nelson (Albany: SUNY Press, 1990), 36–54, quoted in Joan Tronto, "Vicious Circles of Privatized Caring," in *Socializing Care*, ed. Maurice Hamington and Dorothy C. Miller (Lanham, MD: Rowman & Littlefield, 2006), 5.

35. Ofelia Schutte, "Dependence, Work, Women, and the Global Economy," in *The Subject of Care: Feminist Perspectives on Dependency*, ed. Eva Feder Kittay and Ellen K. Feder (Lanham, MD: Rowman & Littlefield, 2002), 142.

36. Kate Bedford, "Loving to Straighten Out Development: Sexuality and 'Ethnodevelopment' in the World Bank's Ecuadorian Lending," *Feminist Legal Studies* 13, no. 3 (2005): 298. See also her *Developing Partnerships: Gender, Sexuality and the Reformed World Bank* (Minneapolis: University of Minnesota Press, 2009). One of Bedford's critiques is the heteronormativity of development theory and practice (that all sexual/marital partners are composed of men and women).

37. Tronto, "Vicious Circles of Privatized Caring," 4.

38. Rianne Mahon and Fiona Robinson, "Conclusion: Integrating the Ethics and Social Politics of Care," in *Feminist Ethics and Social Policy: Towards a New Global Political Economy of Care*, ed. Mahon and Robinson (Vancouver: UBC Press, 2011), 181.

39. Shahra Razavi, "The Political and Social Economy of Care in a Development Context: Conceptual Issues, Research Questions and Policy Options," Gender and Development Programme Paper No. 3 (Geneva: UN Research Institute for Social Development, 2007), 2.

40. Schutte, "Dependence, Work, Women, and the Global Economy," 144.

41. Shahra Razavi, "Rethinking Care in a Development Context: An Introduction," *Development and Change* 42, no. 4 (2011): 873–903.

42. Bedford, *Developing Partnerships*.

43. The text of the resolution, adopted December 17, 1954, may be found in Department of Public Information, United Nations, *The United Nations and the Advancement of Women: 1945–1995* (New York: United Nations, 1995), 157.

44. Peggy Antrobus, *The Global Women's Movement: Origins, Issues and Strategies* (London and New York: Zed Books, 2004), 19.

45. The final vote on the document was 130 governments in favor, with 11 abstentions. However, nearly 40 countries had expressed reservations on specific provisions. *United Nations and the Advancement of Women*, 41.

46. As of this writing, the United States Senate has not ratified the Convention.

47. See the case studies in Nancy A. Naples and Manisha Desai, eds., *Women's Activism and Globalisation: Linking Local Struggles and Transnational Politics* (New York: Routledge, 2002).

48. Ines Smyth, "NGOs in a Post-Feminist Era," in Marilyn Porter and Ellen Judd, eds., *Feminists Doing Development: A Practical Critique* (New York and London: Zed Books, 1999), 17–28.

49. Smyth, "NGOs in a Post-Feminist Era," 26.

50. Anne Marie Goetz, "Gender Justice, Citizenship and Entitlements: Core Concepts, Central Debates and New Directions for Research," in *Gender Justice, Citizenship and Development*, ed. Maitrayee Mukhopadhyay and Navsharan Singh (New Delhi: Zubaan, Imprint of Kali for Women, and Ottawa: International Development Research Center, 2007), 15–57.

51. Shireen Hassim, "Terms of Engagement: South African Challenges," *Feminist Africa* 4 (2005), http://www.feministafrica.org/index.php/terms-of-engagement.

52. Committee on Amendments to Criminal Law, *Report*, Justice J. S. Verma, chairman, January 23, 2013, http://dkmahant.files.wordpress.com/2013/01/justice-verma-committee -report-dushyant.pdf; Padmalatha Ravi, "Anti-Rape Law: Can India Get It Right?," *India Together*, March 15, 2013, http://www.indiatogether.org/2013/mar/law-rape.htm.

3

Development, Globalization, and Power

[Western] civilization takes note neither of morality nor of religion.

—M. K. Gandhi, *Hind Swaraj*[1]

The word "development" is used so often and in so many contexts that most people assume they know what it means. For policy makers and scholars, it refers at a minimum to structural changes that lead to economic growth. It assumes that economic growth, in turn, will produce greater wealth (for both individuals and nations) as well as greater power. It is no surprise, then, that governments universally pursue development.

However, both the concept of development and the way it is pursued are widely contested. The first goal of this chapter is to explain why so much controversy persists over development and how this controversy has been exacerbated by globalization. The second goal is to show why the notion of development, as it is variously interpreted, is critical to gender relations and the role of women as both subjects and objects of development. Put differently, why don't feminists all assume that development is a good thing?

THE IDEA OF DEVELOPMENT:
PROGRESS AND POWER

Chapter 1 noted that, in order to understand the widespread acceptance of development as both a worldview and a policy objective, we need to recognize its lineage in the historical experiences of Western Europe from the eighteenth to the twentieth century.

European Roots of Development Thought and Practice

Tribes, civilizations, nation-states—societies have always changed. They might grow in land and population size and wealth, or become smaller and poorer. For most of recorded history, however, none of these changes had been interpreted as "development" as we use the term today. What altered this pattern and led to modern conceptions of purposeful economic and social progress were the dramatic structural shifts that occurred in Europe.

The first major change, in the eighteenth century, was the European Enlightenment, the intellectual movement that affirmed the power of human reason and the human ability to control nature and thereby influence the course of history. The affirmation of human reason and control over nature seemed borne out by subsequent changes: the rise of science, technology, industrialization, and urbanization, which together restructured European societies over the course of two centuries. Simultaneously, powerful ideas and intellectual movements assumed political forms that characterize our thinking in the twenty-first century. For example, ideologies of nationalism helped create nation-states; democracy took form in legislatures, political parties, and elections; and liberalism led to market economies and restrictions on absolutist states. During the same era, capitalism, as well as its historical response, socialism, molded government and popular beliefs about the way economic and social systems should operate. Capitalism and liberalism paired in the conviction that wealth should be owned and controlled by private individuals or companies, with minimum government influence. By the end of the nineteenth century, however, socialist intellectuals and political activists challenged these values by calling for a range of policy changes, from greater government intervention in the economy (for example, to protect workers) to outright destruction of the capitalist order. In many ways, the debate over capitalist structures and the role of government is at the core of contemporary disputes over development, and these disputes extend to feminist arguments about the best way to improve the lives of women.

The ideas and movements that dominated the nineteenth and twentieth centuries shared a common element, a conception of history grounded in the belief of human progress. Life could and would get better; entrepreneurs, governments, labor unions—all had a role in generating progress. God, monarchs, and nature continued to exist, but they no longer circumscribed human beliefs about the future in the same way they had in the past. Out of these beliefs emerged three fundamental characteristics of the modern language, or discourse, of development. The first is the assumption that *development means linear progress* and continued improvements in human well-being. The second is that *development doesn't just happen; it is a social and government affair and a source of legitimacy* for government regimes. It is hard to imagine a nation-state today that does not pledge itself to development, however specific policies are articulated. The key issues are how to "develop" and who benefits from different policies—issues that dominate domestic politics in the United States, as well as the rest of the world.

The third characteristic of the development worldview is *secularism*, which has been so imbedded in the dominant approaches to development that it was scarcely acknowledged until the late twentieth century. Like the other characteristics of thinking about and "doing" development, secularism reflects the course of European and North American history since the Enlightenment. At the core of this history has been the assertion that public and private spheres can and should be separate. Religious conviction is properly a matter of individual faith and behavior—an assertion that colored all thinking about development even when it was violated in practice—for example, by government regulation of religious institutions.

Despite the overarching acceptance of the development worldview, dissenters raised questions about notions of progress and the best ways to assure human well-being. Although most of these early dissenters are generally now ignored, or even mocked, the issues they raised can still be found in today's questions about the meaning and historical trajectory of development.

DISSENT AND DEBATE

Since the nineteenth century, dissenters have fallen into two broad categories. There are those who challenge the fundamental conceptualization of development that emerged from the Western historical experience. A second type of dissenter has accepted the dominant paradigm, which adheres to the primary objectives of modernization: economic growth, efficient labor allocation, greater use of technology, increased consumption, and so forth. This second type of dissenter, however, has criticized particular development regimes, strategies, and policies, even while adhering to the ideal of a modern society that has characterized the European and North American experience. The lines between the two categories are often fuzzy, but many of the criticisms summarized here resonate with millions of people throughout the world, including feminists.

A Flawed, Imperialistic Paradigm of Development

At its core, the criticism of the prevailing development worldview is grounded in the reality that this worldview emerged from a particular historical experience, that of the European countries in the modern era. The critique has multiple strains, two of which dominate and are frequently intertwined. One strain emphasizes the destruction of traditional values and forms of social cohesion that accompany the norms of development. Is this really progress? What is lost when traditional societies are destroyed? Those who question the fundamental assumptions of the development worldview argue that this worldview is grounded in a cultural discourse that privileges a material entity—the economy—and understands humans primarily as producers and consumers. Other dimensions of human reality, including the spiritual, are diminished, overlooked, or simply dismissed.

The second strain criticizing the dominant construction of development emphasizes its lineage in a hierarchy of power that is historically inseparable from Western
imperialism. These critics point out that the socioeconomic-political systems of
development are the result of Western domination of the global order. The material
view of human nature and social relations that is central to development derives from
this order. Consequently, the assumptions of rational, disciplined, self-interested
humans may be understood as both *reflecting* and also *creating* development.[2]

The critique of this dominant worldview was not unknown in Europe, but its
most pervasive expression has come in those countries subjected to European imperialism. This is not surprising, because as much as development has been about
economic growth, it has also been about nation-state power. European governments
fostered development internally through policies designed to enhance government
power and externally through their quest for raw materials, outlets for manufactured
goods, and spheres of power.

An early example of the merging of cultural defense with the rejection of European domination was Mohandas ("Mahatma") Gandhi's 1910 book, *Hind Swaraj*,
or *Indian Home Rule*.[3] In his writing, Gandhi challenged the basic assumptions of
the Western European idea of civilization and development, including its rational-
ist or secularist bias, its eagerness for more and more complex technologies, and
nation-state centralization. All of these criticisms, of course, were launched in the
framework of his overarching attack on British colonialism in India.

Although largely forgotten today, Gandhi's approach foreshadowed the debate
that began to emerge in the late twentieth century about the role of religion in development and, more broadly, the secularist assumptions that have long dominated
development approaches. Much of this newer debate was stimulated by the emergence of popular religious movements and their more active role in politics. The case
of Islam, in particular, forced rethinking of many formerly widespread assumptions.
As an example, large-scale Muslim immigration to Europe raised questions about
France as a *secular* nation-state, with some politicians loudly proclaiming that it
had always been a *Christian* nation. From Turkey to North Africa, and southeast to
Indonesia, countries with majority Muslim populations pursued policies that eroded
distinctions between public and private, and affirmed Islam as central to the identity
of the nation-state.[4] Simultaneously, development approaches seen as consistent
with Islamic values and law became more prominent. By the twenty-first century,
this challenge to the basic tenets of traditional development thinking promised to
be the most durable.[5]

The feminist dilemma with this critique reflects the tensions in feminist thought
discussed in the previous chapter. Diversity feminists privilege the multiple perspectives of different life circumstances, including race, class, and culture. At the same
time, they recognize—as do liberal and difference feminists—that cultural norms are
often defined and maintained by patriarchal power structures. Liberal feminist Susan
Moller Okin exposed this tension when she asked the question, "Is Multiculturalism
Bad for Women?" One of the central points in Okin's article is the way in which

demands for the protection of the cultural integrity of minority *groups* effectively disadvantage *individuals* who may suffer under the norms of these groups.[6]

Okin's question generates additional issues that are often sidestepped in debates about culture, particularly when religion is emphasized as its defining characteristic. To what extent is culture monolithic or multifaceted? To the extent that it is multifaceted, what are the dominant and subordinate positions expressing the values that define a culture? Although few scholars are prepared to argue that cultures are monolithic, most would be equally reluctant to suggest that no common qualities are defining that culture. Sally Engle Merry proposes that we see culture as "adaptable" and "continually contested" rather than fixed or homogeneous.[7] In this way, culture may be a "rock" or a "river," with the latter recalling the insistence of diversity feminists that we keep in mind the multiplicities of class and ethnicity, for example, as well as gender.

In short, the argument that development is (or should be) secular—an assumption largely unchallenged a half century ago—is now widely contested. If one recalls that an important characteristic of the European experience was the way in which development policies were used to strengthen the (European) nation-state, today's assault on Euro-American domination, often in the name of cultural integrity, should not be surprising. Structural changes that introduce democratic procedures, such as competitive elections, may further increase the stakes in the debates over culture and religion. To illustrate, India maintains that it is a secular republic, yet it has large communities that identify primarily in terms of religion. The Indian legal system is grounded in British common law, which is secular, but it makes room for applying religious ("community") precepts in cases of personal law pertaining to marriage, divorce, inheritance, and child custody matters. In the 1980s, the Shah Bano case demonstrated the inherent tension in this system—and by extension, the conflict between group and individual rights, particularly in a democracy. Shah Bano was an elderly Muslim woman who, when divorced by her husband, won maintenance rights under Indian law. Muslim leaders protested the court decision in favor of Shah Bano, saying that it violated Muslim law, or Shari'a. In response, the government, alert to the importance of Muslim votes in key electoral constituencies, bowed to the opposition and pushed through the legislature a new law that had the effect of stripping Shah Bano of her rights. Ignored in the debate were the voices of Muslim feminists, who argued in favor of an interpretation of Islamic law that would have allowed for maintenance of rights.[8] In sum, although the debate was couched in terms of cultural rights or religion, it was grounded in issues of power—power to define the culture and power to control the government at election time.

Development, Yes, But Not Your Way

Many of the values espoused by these dissenters, ranging from preservation of nature, egalitarianism, social stability, or cultural integrity, resonate with contemporary critics of development across the world who represent diverse schools of thought. Most often, however, these critics accept the core values, such as maximizing economic productivity, of the dominant paradigm of development. Instead of challenging the core notion of development, they focus their criticism on particular development regimes and policies. They prescribe alternatives to widely held tenets such as unbridled globalization, unsustainable consumption of natural resources, or the severe social and economic dislocation and inequality that accompany most development. More will be said later in the chapter about these alternative views, but it is appropriate to note that, even as they criticize development strategies, they generally reflect their origins in European schools of thought. Two examples stand out: the preoccupation with economic inequality and anti-imperialism.

Marxism and Socialism

Beginning in the first half of the nineteenth century, social democrats and radical socialists decried the dehumanizing effects of capitalism, industrialization, and urbanization. Karl Marx emphasized the misery of the working classes, or proletariat, arguing that the structures of capitalism benefited only those who owned and controlled the means of production. Notably, he did not reject modern society or economy; his target was the way it was structured to exploit workers for the benefit of a few. In his analysis of non-European countries, he shared the prevailing European assumptions that they were, in the main, "backward."[9]

Born of European circumstances, early socialist theories were Eurocentric and, in most cases, slow to acknowledge the specific issues of women and the context of gender relations. The occasional exceptions—for example, the 1879 study by the German socialist August Bebel, *Women and Socialism*[10]—generated some interest but failed to transform socialist parties and movements until well into the twentieth century.

By the end of the nineteenth century, few Europeans denied the inequalities generated by the exuberance of capitalist growth. Greater material progress for some meant destitution for others. The ideas of Marx and other early socialists—albeit often in diluted form—inspired the formation of political parties throughout Europe, and the political debates turned to policies and strategies for modifying capitalist structures in order to ameliorate economic inequality. These debates about inequality, both domestic and international, remain with us today. One of the essential cleavages in arguments about development is how best to address this inequality. Even those who reject Euro-American influence often take their inspiration from the early analyses of European thinkers.

Anti-imperialism

The second illustration of "dissent with modernization" emerged from the spread of colonialism and imperialism. The optimism that characterized European beliefs in social and economic progress and pride in the tangible material changes of the nineteenth century were interlaced with assumptions about racial superiority. European attitudes toward the peoples and civilizations of Africa and Asia ranged from patronizing to outright racist. The late-nineteenth-century "scramble" for colonies resulted from the confluence of a number of factors: assumptions of racial superiority, competition for resources, the weaknesses of non-European states, and what became known as "Great Power" politics—the competition between the European nation-states for status, power, and territory. The first phase of imperialism, of course, could be traced back to the seventeenth century, with British and French colonies in North America, for example. But by the early twentieth century, the overwhelming majority of the Caribbean, Africa, and West, South, and Southeast Asia consisted of European or American (e.g., the Philippines) colonies.

Some writers interpreted this imperialism in the light of the power politics of the era, but in the first two decades of the twentieth century, the debate focused primarily on the relationship between capitalism and imperialism. Was domination by rich, industrialized countries over poor, agrarian (but resource-rich) societies a natural outgrowth of the concentration of wealth in capitalist economies? A number of influential thinkers argued yes.[11] This debate, of course, was linked to the debate about the source of domestic economic, social, and political inequality, and how best to address it. As noted below in the discussion of twentieth-century theories of economic dependency, these critiques of capitalist-driven development influenced thinkers decades later.

Although these nineteenth- and twentieth-century critics of the dominant European values, and indeed of European domination itself, once seemed largely consigned to historical textbooks, the views espoused reappeared in various forms in the late twentieth century. In the wake of the breakup of colonial empires and the Soviet Union, the flourishing of international organizations and nongovernmental organizations (NGOs), neoliberal policies, economic crises, and resurgent religious movements, development debates proliferated. In turning to these debates, we summarize the basic themes that are particularly relevant to gender issues.

DEVELOPMENT AGENDAS: POST–WORLD WAR II GLOBAL POLITICS

The term "agenda" refers both to intellectual and to policy priorities. In order to understand these priorities, one must appreciate the historical context of the twentieth century and particularly the events and movements of the period after World War II. *Ideas about* development and *policies of* development were then, as now, inextricably interrelated. To understand these connections, readers should visualize the international system as it existed in the late 1940s and the 1950s. In the aftermath of the war, the victorious Western states were economically and militarily predominant in the world. The United States, in particular, "was a formidable and incessant productive machine, unprecedented in history."[12]

Despite its economic (and military) power, however, the US government was pre-occupied with the real and perceived military threats posed by the Soviet Union, its East European allies, and, after 1949, the People's Republic of China. As the Cold War emerged, both scholars and policy makers in the United States were imbued with the prevailing worldview that saw the West as simultaneously victorious (thus a testimony to the superiority of its political and economic systems) and at the same time threatened by Marxist-inspired movements and communist states.

Decolonization and the Cold War

During this same postwar period, the colonial empires built up in the preceding century began to disintegrate. The Philippines became independent of the United States in 1946; the British empire in South Asia broke up with the independence of India and Pakistan in 1947, and Burma (renamed Myanmar) and Ceylon (Sri Lanka) in 1948; the Netherlands agreed to decolonize Indonesia in 1949. Although the dissolution of the French empire was more protracted, by 1950 the majority of people living in Asia were nominally independent of colonial rule. Africa and most of the rest of the world would follow in the 1950s and 1960s.

This process of decolonization is central to the story of development debates for two reasons. First, the peoples of the former colonies were overwhelmingly poor by material standards; their cultures were complex and scarcely understood in the West; their new governments were often unstable, and their economies dependent on the states that had formerly colonized them. For Westerners who were looking for ways to understand the new countries, it seemed natural that the pathway to progress for the young states should emulate that of the countries that had come to dominate the mid-twentieth century. Thus, the liberal democratic and capitalist notions of progress that emerged from the Euro-American experience created an ideology of development that, at the time, seemed to offer a way out of the poverty and instability of the former colonies.

The dominant postwar development ideology not only embodied the Euro-American notions of progress, but it was deeply conditioned by the political environment of the Cold War. This is the second reason for the centrality of decolonization in the narratives of development. The hostilities of the Cold War preoccupied policy makers directly: How could the United States, Britain, France, and other Western states forestall the spread of Soviet or Chinese influence in Asia, Africa, and Latin America? Strengthening ties with the newly decolonized countries thus became an important foreign policy objective in the wake of the global West-East competition for hegemony.

By the middle of the 1950s, the new countries were typically grouped together and labeled as the "Third World," with North America and Western Europe constituting the First, and the Soviet Union and Eastern Europe the Second. With the First and Second worlds vying for influence in the Third, understanding the nature of economic development in non-Western contexts took on some urgency. In thinking about the problems of economic and political change, European intellectuals were often influenced by Marxist understandings of economic and political change, but in the United States Marxist and neo-Marxist theorizing became significant only in the 1970s. In the 1950s and 1960s, the dominant American ideas about development, usually called modernization theory, were imbued with insights from classical Western thinkers and assumptions taken from the US experience. In the words of one later critic of this theory: "Modernization theory is essentially an academic . . . transfer of the dominant, and ideologically significant, paradigm employed in research on the American political system."[13]

Modernization and Dependency

Modernization theory was not a single, tidy theory, but a group of postulates about the nature of economic and political change and the relationship between these. One of the most famous books of the era was Walt Rostow's 1960 book *The Stages of Economic Growth*, which significantly was subtitled *A Non-Communist Manifesto*. Rostow posited an optimistic scenario in which all societies could eventually become rich, or developed, by going through five stages, from traditional society, through takeoff, to maturity. Although critics later debunked the book, it remains a classic statement of modernization theory from an economic perspective, and some of Rostow's assumptions still characterize approaches to development a half century later. For example, Rostow assumed that traditional, agrarian societies are hampered by low levels of productivity because their structures are based on "pre-Newtonian science and technology, and on pre-Newtonian attitudes towards the physical world."[14] Put differently, the kind of change that Rostow and his contemporaries envisaged required fundamental shifts in individual and collective (or cultural) viewpoints about natural and human reality and the emergence of a pragmatic, empirical, secular orientation toward life.

This sketch does not do justice to the complexity of the modernization ideas, but even in their simplistic formulation they had gained tremendous currency in Western academic and government circles by the late 1960s, just as their critics began to emerge. The critics argued that modernization theory privileged American assumptions about politics and economics, notably democracy and liberal capitalism, and overlooked the variety of ways in which societies are organized elsewhere. Some scholars within the liberal democratic tradition maintained that many of the norms dominant in modernization theories overemphasized the values of pluralism and participation at the expense of order, institution building, and cultural continuity.[15] Other critics argued that modernization theories *and* theorists were in the service of US foreign policy goals. Yet others focused on the role of the global capitalist system in undermining the ability of non-Western countries to follow the path of the rich, industrialized countries. But in general, until the 1970s and 1980s, both the mainline theorists and their critics ignored the issue of gender differences.

The critique that called attention to the international context within which nation-states confronted development challenges in the mid-twentieth century was centered in Latin America. There, scholars maintained that modernization approaches had paid insufficient attention to two important features of economic, social, and political realities in developing nations. This school has been labeled "dependency" or *dependencia* in recognition of its analytical focus. First, the dependency scholars argued that many countries played a secondary role in international trade and financial relations and were thereby condemned to relationships of "dependent development." Development in these countries is dependent on and conditioned by the economic expansion of another economy to which they are subjected. Second, the dependency scholars linked their understanding of the international context to an analysis of internal social and class structures of individual countries, pointing out that certain elites benefited by maintaining the dependent relationships, even as the majority of people were left behind in the economic growth that did occur.[16] In terms of the analysis of development issues, this perspective was clearly influenced by neo-Marxism and Lenin's writing on imperialism and international capitalism.

Although both modernization and dependency theorists emerged before the contemporary period of neoliberal globalization, both schools assumed an international context. Moreover, their approaches are part of the lineage of worldviews and policy recommendations that carried into the twenty-first century. To illustrate, in the case of modernization theory, the broad conceptualization of the characteristics of development, including urbanization, labor efficiency, and secular decision making, is with us today; and the core assumptions are still shared by many feminists, even though the failure of many modernization policies over time led to some rethinking of this conceptualization. Most of dependency theory also accepted the basic worldview of development, although it drew our attention to the international class and nation-state power structures. Contemporary debates over the role of the state in development and a clearer understanding of the unequal effects of development policies are one heritage of dependency approaches.

Anti-colonialism and Postcolonialism

Although it has had little impact on policy formulation or implementation, the postcolonial intellectual movement is important to the story of post–World War II decolonization and development. The genesis of postcolonialism lies primarily in countries that received their independence from colonial regimes in the 1940s, 1950s, and 1960s. Although influenced by some of the European post-structuralist theories, such as those of Michel Foucault, theorists in Asia (especially India), Africa, and Latin America were at the forefront of deconstructing the multiple meanings of colonialism and its implications for "subaltern" peoples. They draw our attention to what is *not* in the dominant narratives of history or international relations, emphasizing the structures of both our worldviews and our institutions. In this way, postcolonial perspectives—despite their enormous diversity—tend to be culturally situated as well as generalizing about the destructive power of colonialism and Western institutions.[17]

Critics frequently deride postcolonialism for its lack of policy recommendations or its use of convoluted language, but it has been broadly influential throughout academic communities, particularly the humanities and social sciences. However indirectly, it has contributed to greater awareness of the diversity of cultures and populations that both participate in development and are the "subjects" of development policy making. Feminists have been actively engaged in the postcolonial debates, and most share the characteristics of what we have identified in chapter 2 as deconstructionist feminists. The strains of the postcolonial movement have also influenced some diversity feminists, despite its inability to transform the dominant thinking about development.

Alternative Development

One of the most important premises of both modernization and dependency approaches was to define development in terms of national economic growth, and it was this linkage that by the 1970s initially provoked widespread criticism of both sets of theories. The criticisms followed several different lines of analysis, each reflecting a variety of intellectual traditions and ethical concerns. We characterize this group of critics as those calling for "alternative development" concepts and strategies.

Although these critics were (and are) exceedingly diverse in their thinking, they share a few characteristics. They pointed out that both the capitalist-inspired and the Marxist-inspired approaches rested on similar, European-derived, ideas of progress, including the faith in industrialization and technology; and they argued that development was much more complex than traditional economic growth.[18] They challenged the focus on nation-state and class structures to the exclusion of other forms of social organization and the role of human agency. Liberation Theology, for example, sought a return to the essential Christian message as a way of mobilizing the poor in Latin America to challenge the linkages between the Catholic Church hierarchy and traditional elites.

Many critics focused specifically on the environmental damage caused by development, whether born of liberal capitalist or Marxist communist precepts. The contemporary concept of "sustainable development"—embraced even when it is ill defined—reflects the preoccupation with damage to the natural environment and the pollution of air, water, and land resources.[19] Some environmental critics (including a number of ecofeminists) embraced alternative development strategies, although many of those sensitive to the environmental issues focused on strategies that maintained the dominant development trajectories while moderating policies to accommodate environmental concerns.

This cluster of critics also included practitioners who attacked "overtheorizing" and the lack of understanding about grassroots reality that seemed to permeate development debates. Many of these critics emphasized the importance of indigenous, local knowledge and "appropriate technology," and called for some form of "grass-roots development" or "participatory development."[20] The dissenters thus addressed both the way development had been conceptualized and the way development policies were implemented, echoing themes dating to the beginning of the twentieth century and Gandhi's criticisms of European-style development. These alternative approaches have become central to contemporary thinking about development, and we will return to them in succeeding chapters.

Overview

For the most part, neither modernization nor dependency theorists included a gender analysis or addressed the impact of their proposed policies on gender relations. It was left to WID and GAD advocates to rethink the shortcomings of the prevailing policies of development. The women in development advocates argued that women needed to be integrated into development policy planning and implementation, whereas the gender and development advocates focused more clearly on the context of gender relations and the reality of class and race differences (see chapter 2). Thus together, by the late twentieth century, liberal feminists (who primarily informed the WID perspective), diversity feminists (the GAD perspective), and deconstructionist (postcolonial) feminists were all part of the broad rethinking of development.

The importance of what we have called "alternative development" approaches to gender and development is more complex because the assumptions and focus of the different approaches are varied. To illustrate, Liberation Theology, grounded in Roman Catholic Christianity, was not hostile to gender concerns, but gender tended to be subsumed in the general focus on the poor. Thus Liberation Theology scholars and activists, largely men (partly because many were priests), did not emphasize the diversity among poor populations in Latin America.[21]

GLOBALIZATION

Many of the forces that undergird contemporary globalization are congruent with the European trajectory of development thought and practice. Science and technology, capitalism and industrialism, are all central to today's globalization. Put differently, direct historical links between the twenty-first-century characteristics of globalization and the changes in European society go back several centuries. For example, the sixteenth- and seventeenth-century European voyages of "discovery" laid the groundwork for international trade, then commercial systems, and subsequently colonial empires. These processes brought non-European societies into contact with European forms of economic production, technologies, social and cultural norms, and modes of political organization. All of these are part of modern international systems. We argue, however, that globalization, properly understood, is more complex and penetrates our daily lives in ways that are more profound than the reality of earlier eras.

To examine globalization and its implications for gender and development, we begin with the definition proposed by Anthony Giddens, a well-known British sociologist, more than two decades ago. Globalization, argued Giddens, can be defined "as the intensification of worldwide social relations which link distant localities in such a way that local happenings are shaped by events occurring many miles away and vice versa."[22] Giddens characterized globalization as a multifaceted process consisting of the universal expansion of the nation-state system, world capitalism, the diffusion of machine technologies, and the international division of labor. Giddens wrote in advance of some of the features of today's life that we take for granted, such as cell phone technology and the Internet, but these have only intensified the globalization process.

This multifaceted formulation of globalization carries a number of implications that are central to our discussion of gender relations. Three of these are worth explaining at this juncture. First, capitalism is inherently dynamic and international in scope, a fact that Marxists, including Lenin, recognized long ago; and booms and busts are a natural part of its processes. Capitalism survives through constant technological innovation. Capitalism and industrialism, with which it is historically linked, disconnect us from nature in ways that would be hard to imagine for people living in an agricultural world. Both capitalism and industrialism, because of their inevitable links with the expansion of new forms of communication and transportation, also drive the globalization of culture. One of our goals, therefore, is to look for ways in which capitalism—for example, through the division of labor—along with global cultural trends, impacts the daily lives of women and men.

The second point is that the nation-state for some time has been the dominant form of political organization. We are no longer a world organized along the lines of tribes, city-states, or colonial empires. This does not mean remnants or mixtures of these are no more; it means simply that nations—either in reality or in aspiration—want to be states, and states want national cohesion. Nation-states have long sought to use capitalist development as a way of strengthening state power, even though the dynamics of capitalism make it difficult to restrain economic growth within the territorial boundaries of a state. Similarly, the dynamics of the international market economy, combined with contemporary technology, have generated a wide array of transnational organizations that influence gender and development issues, often in tension with nation-state organizations.[23]

In addition to the economic dimensions of stateness, the ideological and coercive dimensions are significant from the perspective of gender relations. Insofar as governments seek to build national identity and loyalty, and define the boundaries of citizenship, they often create or reinforce certain notions of gender. They establish institutions that are grounded in particular assumptions of the appropriate roles of women and men and the relations between them. More will be said of this later, but a quick example would be laws on property rights and on marriage, where governments have often institutionalized the rights and obligations of women and men in different ways.

The third implication of our understanding of globalization is the role of coercion and violence in our lives. Coercion and violence have always been present in societies, of course, but the contemporary era has seen their intensification and extension as a consequence of industrialism. *Intensification* of coercion is found in the way that states, in their efforts to exert internal control over domestic populations and resources, control information and structure the lives of all citizens, using techniques that range from socialization and surveillance to outright violence. Intensification also refers to the kinds of weaponry now available—for example, nuclear, chemical, and biological weapons, which, along with sophisticated "conventional" weapons, sustain the lucrative international arms trade.

The *extension* of violence refers to the expansion of the geographical space in which it occurs, and the elimination of traditional warfare distinctions between military and civilian populations. Extended violence reflects both the kinds of weapons employed and the strategies and tactics used, such as terrorism and "ethnic cleansing," both of which deliberately target civilian populations. The gender implications here are obvious and include the calculated use of rape as a weapon of war.

The Political Economy of Globalization

The term *political economy* means that politics and policy agendas both determine and are conditioned by economics. Thus politics and economics have an interdependent, dynamic relationship, both within nation-states and transcending them. As noted above, capitalism and the attendant forms of industry and technology are central to globalization, but they do not exist independently of political decisions and organizations. To clarify this point, we turn to the way in which political leaders and governments have endeavored to structure the global economy since the end of World War II in 1945.

The international organizations or intergovernmental organizations (IGOs) that are central to the global political economy today are all rooted in decisions taken in the late 1940s. Thus they belong to the same era as the United Nations. In 1944, delegates from forty-four countries met at Bretton Woods, New Hampshire, to discuss the postwar reconstruction of Europe as well as the trade and monetary problems they saw as contributing to the global depression of the 1930s. Their goal was to create a stable international economic system in order to prevent the political and economic chaos that affected Europe in the 1920s and 1930s, after the end of World War I. The International Bank for Reconstruction and Development (IBRD, or World Bank) and the International Monetary Fund (IMF) were the two organizations created to implement the goals of the Bretton Woods Agreement. The World Bank and the IMF became key players in decisions that today affect not only international commercial and monetary transactions, but also national-level decision making.

In 1947, a number of the same governments that had negotiated the Bretton Woods Agreement negotiated the General Agreement on Tariffs and Trade (GATT), whose purpose was to reduce barriers to international trade. In the early 1990s, the provisions of GATT were updated and the World Trade Organization (WTO) created. The WTO, which began operations in 1995, has more than 150 member states, states that also belong to the World Bank and the IMF. In fact, with the demise of the Soviet Union and the Eastern bloc system in the early 1990s, and the commitment of countries such as China and Vietnam to market economies, very few countries remain outside this overarching structure. Thus the goals of coordinated management of a system of international capitalism, including free movement of goods, services, and money across national borders, were largely realized by the end of the twentieth century. This in no way means that it is a seamless system or that it always works smoothly; clearly, this is not the case. Debt crises, bank failures, and trade barriers still exist, and both the organizations and their policies are frequently contested. Nonetheless, very few countries are left untouched by the decisions these organizations make. The multiple ways in which the international systems of production, finance, and trade are linked became obvious during the collapse of major financial institutions that spiraled from the United States across the globe in 2008–2009.

The one area left largely unregulated is the international movement of labor: A truly global, integrated capitalist system would include not only the free movement of capital, goods, and services, but also labor. However, for reasons having to do largely with national security concerns, this has not been the case outside the European Union.[24] Subsequent chapters will illustrate the importance of the barriers to the free movement of labor for gender and development issues.

The United States has always been a central player in the World Bank, IMF, and WTO, both in the negotiations leading to their creation and in their subsequent management. The United States has been joined in its aspirations for a smooth functioning of a global trading and monetary system by countries sharing its economic worldview, if not always its national political priorities. One result of US preeminence throughout the second half of the twentieth century was that shifts in American priorities and decisions taken by the US government had much wider international impact than the priorities and decisions of other governments. A good example of this impact was the set of macroeconomic policies known as the "Washington Consensus."

Neoliberalism

The basic elements of the Washington Consensus, a term attributed to the American economist John Williamson in 1989, are fiscal discipline, tax reform, market-determined interest rates, competitive exchange rates, trade liberalization, openness to foreign direct investment (FDI), privatization of state enterprises, deregulation, and security for property rights. Taken together, these became known as structural adjustment policies (SAPs) when they became preconditions for loans from international institutions. In Williamson's own words: "The three big ideas here are macroeconomic discipline, a market economy, and openness to the world (at least in respect of trade and FDI)."[25]

Another dimension of what is now known as global neoliberalism has been the emphasis on political decentralization. In principle, decentralization offers the advantage of bringing decision making closer to the people whose lives are influenced by public policies. Decentralization may take different forms. For example, it may entail moving policy decisions from the national to the regional or local levels. It may be part of a broader strategy of privatizing activities that formerly were carried out by public (government) agencies. As a consequence, new groups—people formerly excluded from decision making—may be better positioned to make their voices heard and to exercise their priorities. At the same time, decentralization may shift burdens of time and money to people who are already stretched thin by caring for families and coping with the demands of their work. Chapter 5, which addresses gender and water, illustrates these contradictory aspects.

GENDER AND GLOBALIZATION

The "big ideas" of neoliberalism had become the driving force behind economic globalization by the late 1980s, during the same period that debates on the relationship between gender and development had also become global. Increasingly the World Bank, the IMF, and other multilateral agencies required implementation of SAPs as conditions for loans or debt relief for developing countries. The new macroeconomic orthodoxy was premised on the theory that the key to debt reduction and development lay in reducing the state's role in the economy while promoting exports and encouraging greater foreign investment. Even countries that had long opposed market economics, such as China and Vietnam, became enthusiastic adherents to strategies of economic competition, government downsizing, tax reform, and foreign investment. "Although it was a package designed for indebted countries, it became the policy framework for all countries wishing to 'modernize', even those without a debt crisis."[26] Countries were drawn into the global economy to a much greater degree than ever before.

Both scholars and activists were quick to see the implications of the new policies for women. Most of the criticism of globalization's impact during the past thirty years has focused on the effects of SAPs on the socially most vulnerable, those who are typically more dependent on publicly financed employment or programs than people with more private resources. Peggy Antrobus labeled the 1980s the "lost decade," referring to government cuts in allocations to key sectors such as education, health, welfare, and agriculture.[27]

Feminist scholars have argued that the devastating effect of these policies for many women was a result of the basic assumption that macroeconomic policy and SAPs were gender neutral, when they are not. Diane Elson, for example, has analyzed the way in which the internationalization of markets increases the risk of malfunctions or shocks from which people can no longer isolate themselves. Thus a financial crisis in the United States has a ripple effect that contributes to unemployment and government cutbacks in Europe and elsewhere, which happened beginning in 2008. Historically, economists have tended to see the household or domestic sector as the safety net that absorbs the negative effects of economic instability, without understanding the role of the household in maintaining and replenishing the resources necessary to ensure long-term economic and social stability. Privatization and cutbacks in public expenditure may seem more efficient in the short run, but by transferring costs to the domestic sector, where the gender division of labor is central to household functioning, these policies over time lead to a destruction of human energy and a deterioration in the quality of "labor services" necessary to maintain the overall system.[28] A simple example would be working mothers who commute farther to low-paying jobs, with less time for supporting and monitoring their children. The health of both mothers and children is at risk, but the public health infrastructure, which is critical to low-income parents, is crumbling or nonexistent. In addition, the decline of energy and time at the household level may undermine social stability in the long run.

In the past two decades, much gender and development research has substantiated the argument that neoliberal economics and structural adjustment policies have had particularly pernicious effects for women, children, and the elderly in much of the world. Despite these findings, however, both the impact of the policies and the responses to them have been uneven, with the result that we must be cautious about overgeneralizing. In her research on West Africa, for example, Lucy Creevey stressed the importance of looking at SAPs within the broader context of ethnicity, religion, geographical location, and family status. Niger and Senegal, both low-income countries, undertook structural adjustment in the mid-1990s. Government downsizing meant a loss of services and employment, and currency devaluation resulted in a sharp rise in the price of imports and even domestic commodities. Even though the groups of women that Creevey studied in both countries were Muslim, different religious customs, social linkages, and labor patterns resulted in structural adjustment having substantially different consequences for women in the two countries.[29] Some women were able to adjust and actually benefited from the changes, although on balance the effects for the majority of women tended to be negative. Creevey's findings are an example of the contributions of a diversity approach in feminist research.

How should feminists respond to the diverse implications of neoliberal globalization? As the twenty-first century opened, activists pursued both inclusionary and transformative approaches. Chapter 2 explained that the former requires engagement with established political and legal structures, whereas the latter confronts these structures in an effort to provoke a redistribution of power. The Millennium Development Goals and the global justice movement illustrate the contrasting approaches that feminists used to alter or challenge global structures.

The Millennium Development Goals

By the beginning of the twenty-first century, several trends in development think-ing converged. Although neither international institutions nor national governments abandoned neoliberal economic strategies, policy makers increasingly debated the costs and benefits of these strategies. Both national and IGO leaders expressed concerns about duplication of efforts and contradictions in development planning, and they proposed a common development approach defined by specific goals and targets. In assessing the impact of development within the context of neoliberal glo-balization, feminists increasingly argued that *in general* poor women had lost more than they had gained in the preceding decades.

Meeting at the United Nations in September 2000, world leaders committed their governments to a partnership to reduce extreme poverty. This public commit-ment acknowledged that, despite decades of bilateral and multilateral development assistance programs, the numbers and conditions of the "poorest of the poor" had scarcely improved. Billions of people around the world continued to be locked in wretched conditions. Although neoliberalism was not disavowed, the Millennium Development Goals (MDGs) did coincide with some reconsideration of the negative impacts of structural adjustment programs in areas that particularly affect the poor, such as health services. The MDGs were crafted and announced in 2001 without any input from civil society groups.[30]

In the MDGs, world leaders pledged to work toward the achievement of eight goals by 2015, including ending extreme poverty, achieving universal primary education, combating HIV/AIDS, and reaching environmental sustainability.[31] Many people applauded the MDGs, saying they reflected an international consensus with clear, achievable targets. Recognition was widespread that the accomplishment of develop-ment goals could not be separated from an understanding of gender relationships; and, in particular, the status of women was highlighted in the third MDG, gender equality, and also in the fifth goal, improving maternal health. Some viewed this as evidence that the feminist organizing of the previous three decades had finally borne fruit in this international consensus on a targeted strategy to help the poorest people.

From a feminist perspective, one could feel gratified that eliminating poverty was the primary rationale of the MDGs, and that gender equality was central to several of the goals. Feminists could also recognize that attempts to measure the MDG targets were one of the results of years of their demands for gender-sensitive data.

Despite the apparent consensus on the development–gender connections, how-ever, some feminists were quick to note that the MDGs fell short of what was needed for successful and inclusive development policies. In particular, feminist groups maintained that political and economic empowerment were not addressed in the gender equality goal (Goal 3), which was expressed solely in terms of education. Peggy Antrobus went so far as to label the MDGs "A Major Distraction Gimmick," criticizing "their inadequate targets and indicators; their restriction to indicators that are quantifiable, when much of what is most important—such as Women's Equality and Empowerment—is not easily quantifiable."[32] Clearly, the MDGs did not and could not overturn repressive structures that block women's empowerment.

The Global Justice Movement

Variously labeled the antiglobalization, alter-globalization, or global-justice movement (GJM), a broad coalition of groups has organized to confront the inequalities created or exacerbated by neoliberal globalization. Antiwar activists are also part of this movement, protesting the US-led wars in Iraq and Afghanistan. In 1999, the movement generated enormous publicity with its large-scale demonstrations against the World Trade Organization in Seattle.

The GJM is actually a network linking organizations with different priorities. Some target the World Bank and IMF with their criticisms. Longtime progressive organizations, such as the American Friends Service Committee, participate, as do identity or issue-based feminist, indigenous, labor, and environmental organizations. Some development NGOs located in the Global South are engaged, as well as radical social movements such as the Zapatistas in Chiapas, Mexico. The policies and strategies these groups advocate are as diverse as the groups themselves, ranging from substantive reform of international structures to de-linking from the global political economy. Despite this diversity, ideology coheres around shared values supporting transformative change: participatory democracy, restorative and redistributive justice, equal access to resources and opportunities, universal rights, global solidarity, and environmental sustainability.[33]

Since 2001, the global justice movement has held an annual conference called the World Social Forum (WSF), in which to share experiences and strategies. The Forum mimics the World Economic Forum, which is held annually in Davos, Switzerland, and represents the global capitalist elites. In 2013, 4,500 organizations from 120 countries met in Tunis, the first World Social Forum to be held in an Arab country.[34]

Although women have been active in the World Social Forum since its inception, feminism has had a problematic relationship with the coalition. In the early years, gender issues were largely absent from the debates and negotiations. However, beginning with the 2004 meeting in Mumbai (Bombay), a strategy of intersectional feminist organizing has generated more attention to gender issues. This strategy has contributed to the increased recognition that "gender is fundamental to the operation of global capitalism."[35]

At present, the WSF is important for feminists because of the vision that "another world is possible" and as a site for forging coalitions with groups that share their basic values. In this way, feminist participation recalls the "consciousness-raising" that defined the flourishing of women's movements and feminist activism sparked by the UN world conferences on women from the 1970s through the 1990s. The challenge for feminists is to maintain the focus on gender issues while participating in efforts that engage so many diverse groups and causes.

CONCLUSION

The story of the Millennium Development Goals illustrates the changes in development thinking and planning and also the importance of understanding the *political economy* of globalization. International elite policy makers crafted the MDGs without consultation among the myriad civil society groups that have long been stakeholders in "doing" development. The content of the MDGs reflects some rethinking about the goals and practices of development (and, by implication, the impact of neoliberal globalization), without, however, radically questioning the fundamental premises of what it means to be "modern" or "developed" in the twenty-first century. To a degree, they are sensitive to the differences between women and men in critical areas such as health and education, differences that can only be "measured" as a result of gender-disaggregated data. At the same time, the MDGs are silent on the critical discrepancies in structures of power—from the household to the global system.

Many of the groups participating in the World Social Forum stand out precisely because they *do* have an alternative vision of capitalism. The weakness of the WSF is one that confronts most movements calling for systemic transformation: Multiple voices with weak organization are up against an entrenched power structure that—despite the inequities associated with it—still generates wide support, including among many women who see neoliberalism as offering greater opportunities.

A comparison of the MDGs and the global justice movement suggests that for feminists, inclusionary approaches may enjoy more success than transformative approaches. For example, in the case of the MDGs, some feminists criticized the goals as insufficiently transformative even as they worked with the Millennium Project Task Force to incorporate a clearer gender perspective. Their lobbying efforts ultimately resulted in an expanded definition of MDG 5.[36] In its original formulation, "MDG 5 Improve Maternal Health" included no reference to reproductive health. After intensive NGO lobbying, the phrase "Achieve universal access to reproductive health" was added in 2005 as a target for MDG 5. All feminists recognized, however, that articulation of goals and targets would not alone guarantee progress.

The history of the past two centuries, and particularly the experience since World War II, leads us to a number of conclusions that set the framework for subsequent chapters. First, the commitment to economic growth and prosperity, national power, and global markets is essentially universal. Second, despite the widespread dominance of capitalist and neoliberal economic policies, critics of this process still exist. The international and intra-national inequalities that date back to early colonialism persist, and in many places, have been exacerbated—a reality that the dissenters are quick to point out. Third, politics and economics are inextricably linked in both the creation of the inequalities and in the proposed solutions.

This is the story of the expanding debates—often in the context of the UN system—of the past three decades. Research and theorizing about these inequalities and solutions has also expanded, and feminist scholars and policy makers have been central to this process.

NOTES

1. M. K. Gandhi, *Hind Swaraj and Other Writings*, ed. Anthony J. Parel (Cambridge: Cambridge University Press, 1997), 37. Mohandas K. Gandhi (1869–1948) is usually referred to as Mahatma Gandhi. Mahatma is an honorific title, typically translated as "Great Soul." Gandhi was best known as an important Indian nationalist leader who espoused a philosophy of nonviolence in the fight against British colonialism. "Hind Swaraj" means Indian home rule.

2. Since the 1980s, some social scientists have systematically deconstructed the history, values, and policies that constitute the development "discourse." Philosophers such as Michel Foucault and anticolonial intellectuals deeply influenced their thinking. For an example of deconstructionist scholarship, see Arturo Escobar's *Encountering Development: The Making and Unmaking of the Third World* (Princeton, NJ: Princeton University Press, 1995).

3. See note 1. Gandhi was aware of, and undoubtedly influenced by, earlier nineteenth-century writers who criticized prevailing modes of development, although they were not necessarily critical of European imperialism.

4. The case of Israel also exposes the tensions accompanying the growth of conservative or fundamentalist religious movements. As a Jewish homeland, how does the government reconcile the demands of ultraconservative Jews who demand special status for their policies and the desires of more liberal Jews, including many feminists, who feel diminished or excluded by those policies? In recent decades, Hindu fundamentalists have claimed that India is (must be) a *Hindu* nation—a position that is ominous for the approximately 15 percent of the population that is Muslim. Finally, Americans are familiar with the common argument that the United States is a *Christian* nation, and the position among fundamentalist Christians that government policy should reflect their opposition to gay marriage and abortion.

5. The debate about secularism, development, and politics has come to permeate academic discussions. Two notable examples are the 2011 publication of *Rethinking Secularism* (New York: Oxford University Press), whose editors (Craig Calhoun, Mark Juergensmeyer, and Jonathan VanAntwerpen) have close ties to an influential American research institution, the Social Science Research Council; and the 2011 establishment of a new section, "International Development and Religion," in the massive American Academy of Religion.

6. Okin's article was originally published in the journal *Boston Review*, and republished in book form with multiple critiques and responses. See Susan Moller Okin with Respondents, *Is Multiculturalism Bad for Women?*, ed. Joshua Cohen, Matthew Howard, and Martha C. Nussbaum (Princeton, NJ: Princeton University Press, 1999).

7. Sally Engle Merry, "Constructing a Global Law—Violence against Women and the Human Rights System," *Law and Social Inquiry* 28, no. 4 (2003): 966.

8. Nida Kirmani, "Claiming Their Space: Muslim Women-led Networks and the Women's Movement in India," *Journal of International Women's Studies* 11, no. 1 (November 2009): 72–85.

9. For example, see Karl Marx's articles on India and China, including "British Rule in India," "The Future Results of British Rule in India," and "Revolution in China and in Europe," written for the *New York Daily Tribune* in the 1850s, http://www.marxists.org.

10. First written in 1879, *Women and Socialism* has been translated into many languages and reissued in multiple editions, sometimes titled *Women Under Socialism*. August Bebel (1840–1913) was an early founder of the Social Democratic Workers' Party of Germany (today's Social Democratic Party). Bebel was also a critic of the racism in Germany's African colonies.

11. Among the most famous were John Hobson (1858–1940), who wrote *Imperialism* (1902); and Vladimir Ilyich Lenin (1870–1924), who wrote *Imperialism: The Highest Stage of Capitalism* (1917). Hobson was British; Lenin was Russian, although he lived many years in exile during the early part of the century.

12. Gustavo Esteva, "Development," in *The Development Dictionary: A Guide to Knowledge as Power*, ed. Wolfgang Sachs (Atlantic Highlands, NJ: Zed Books, 1992), 6.

13. Leonard Binder, "The Natural History of Development Theory," *Comparative Studies in Society and History* 28, no. 1 (January 1986): 3.

14. W. W. Rostow, *The Stages of Economic Growth: A Non-Communist Manifesto* (Cambridge: Cambridge University Press, 1960), 4.

15. See, for example, the works of Samuel Huntington, such as *Political Order in Changing Societies* (New Haven, CT: Yale University Press, 1968).

16. The most important scholars include André Gunder Frank (1929–2005; born in Germany; lived widely in Europe, Latin America, and North America); Theotonio dos Santos (b. 1936; Brazilian economist); Samuel Valenzuela and Arturo Valenzuela (Chilean-born American academics); Fernando Cardoso (b. 1931; Brazilian sociologist and president of Brazil 1995–2003); and Guillermo O'Donnell (b. 1933 in Argentina). These scholars received academic training and positions in the United States.

17. For examples of the generalizing power of a postcolonial critique, see Edward Said's influential book *Orientalism* (New York: Random House, 1978) or the work of Indian psychologist Ashis Nandy. Frantz Fanon's *The Wretched of the Earth*, first published in 1963, combined an attack on colonialism with an understanding of its effects on individuals (especially in Africa). Illustrations of the culturally and historically embedded subaltern studies may be found in the work of Indian intellectuals who began publishing in New Delhi in the early 1980s. See, for example, Ranajit Guha and Gayatri Chakravorty Spivak, eds., *Selected Subaltern Studies* (New York: Oxford University Press, 1988).

18. For a discussion of the similar assumptions of modernization and dependency theorists, see Kate Manzo, "Modernist Discourse and the Crisis of Development Theory," *Studies in Comparative International Development* 26, no. 2 (Summer 1991): 3–36. An early critic of "development as growth" was Peter L. Berger in *Pyramids of Sacrifice: Political Ethics and Social Change*, first published in 1974. See also works by Norwegian sociologist and peace activist Johann Galtung; and the classic, *Small Is Beautiful: Economics as if People Mattered*, first published in 1973 by the British economist E. F. Schumacher.

19. Sustainable development became part of mainstream thinking about development with the report of the Brundtland Commission, chaired by Gro Harlem Brundtland, the former prime minister of Norway. The Commission (formally known as the World Commission on Environment and Development) published its report, *Our Common Future*, in 1987. The Commission defined sustainable development generally as that development meeting the needs of current generations without compromising the ability of future generations to meet their needs.

20. Michael Edwards emphasized the practitioner's point of view in "The Irrelevance of Development Studies," *Third World Quarterly* 11, no. 1 (January 1989): 16–35.

21. Although essentially a Latin American protest movement, the definition of "liberation theology" has become more expansive over the years. See, for example, the website "Liberation Theologies" at http://liberationtheology.org. The website is based in San Francisco.

22. Anthony Giddens, *The Consequences of Modernity* (Stanford, CA: Stanford University Press, 1990), 64.

23. Transnational organizations are both intergovernmental and nongovernmental. Intergovernmental organizations (IGOs) are typically formal in the sense that treaties create them and primarily nation-state governments are the constituent members. These include the United Nations and its affiliated organizations (such as the World Health Organization), the European Union and other regional associations, and the World Bank. Nongovernmental organizations (NGOs) are both large and small and generally consist of member NGOs based in a few or many countries. Criminal and terrorist organizations are often also transnational.

24. The European Union originated during the same period as the IBRD, IMF, and GATT. The original proposals for European integration, designed primarily to prevent another war between Germany and France, date to the late 1940s. In 1950, the so-called Schuman Plan (after its French sponsor, Robert Schuman) led to the creation of the European Coal and Steel Community, with six European members. Subsequently, the same six states established the European Economic Community (EEC) and Euratom, the latter to coordinate the peaceful development of nuclear energy. These three organizations, later named the European Community, are today's European Union, which has twenty-seven members and three more negotiating to join. See the EU's website at www.europa.eu.

25. John Williamson, "Did the Washington Consensus Fail?" Speech given at the Center for Strategic and International Studies, Washington, DC, November 6, 2002. Williamson is a senior fellow with the Peterson Institute for International Economics. He has worked in various capacities with the World Bank, the IMF, and the US Treasury Department. See http://www.iie.com/publications/papers/paper.cfm?researchid=488, retrieved March 16, 2009.

26. Peggy Antrobus, *The Global Women's Movement: Origins, Issues and Strategies* (London: Zed Books, 2004), 68–69.

27. Antrobus, *The Global Women's Movement*, chap. 5.

28. Diane Elson, "Gender at the Macroeconomic Level," in *Towards a Gendered Political Economy*, ed. Joanne Cook, Jennifer Roberts, and Georgina Waylen (London: Macmillan, 2000), 77–97. See also Shirin M. Rai, *Gender and the Political Economy of Development* (Cambridge, UK: Polity Press; and Malden, MA: Blackwell Publishers, 2002), especially chap. 4.

29. Lucy Creevey, "Structural Adjustment and the Empowerment (or Disempowerment) of Women in Niger and Senegal," in *Women in Developing Countries: Assessing Strategies for Empowerment*, ed. Rekha Datta and Judith Kornberg (Boulder, CO: Lynne Rienner, 2002), 93–112.

30. Rosalind P. Petchesky, *Global Prescriptions: Gendering Health and Human Rights* (London: Zed Books, 2003), 68–69.

31. See the website of the Millennium Development Goals at http://www.un.org/millenniumgoals.

32. Antrobus, quoted in Patrick Bond, "Global Governance Campaigning and MDGs: From Top-down to Bottom-up Anti-poverty Work," *Third World Quarterly* 27, no. 2 (2006): 340.

33. Manfred B. Steger and Erin K. Wilson, "Anti-Globalization or Alter-Globalization? Mapping the Political Ideology of the Global Justice Movement," *International Studies Quarterly* 56, no. 3 (2012): 439–54.

34. Claire Provost, "World Social Forum Begins with March through Streets of Tunis," *The Guardian*, March 27, 2013, http://www.guardian.co.uk/global-development/poverty-matters/2013/mar/27/world-social-forum-march-tunis.

35. Lyndi Hewitt and Marina Karides, "More Than a Shadow of a Difference: Feminist Participation in the World Social Forum," in *Handbook on World Social Forum Activism*, ed. Jackie Smith et al. (Boulder, CO: Paradigm Publishers, 2012), 86.

36. K. S. Mohindra and Béatrice Nikiéma, "Women's Health in Developing Countries: Beyond an Investment," *International Journal of Health Services* 40, no. 3 (2010): 543–67.

4

Debates and Dilemmas:
Global Sex Trafficking

In the twenty-first century, *all* development occurs within the context of a global system. The institutions of globalization create new opportunities for some people and foreclose them for others. A good example of the way in which development in a globalized setting produces contradictory effects is sex trafficking, which has become headline news in recent years.

Sex trafficking is one form of human trafficking, which includes other forms of forced labor. In 2012, the International Labor Organization estimated that about twenty-one million people annually are victims of forced labor; of these 55 percent are women and girls. Ninety percent of forced laborers are exploited in the private economy, and of these, about 22 percent are victims of forced sexual exploitation.[1] Although sex trafficking is not numerically the most common form of human trafficking, it has received the most publicity, partly because the primary victims are women and girls.[2]

In choosing trafficking as our first case study, we see the significance of globalization processes as they condition both the idea of development and the context within which it occurs. Globalization facilitates international migration, and cross-border movement is closely associated with forced sexual exploitation, although sexual exploitation and trafficking frequently occur within countries as well.[3] Trafficking highlights the uneven impact of development and the multiple ways in which individuals cope with the changes around them. Trafficking also publicizes the inequality between women and men that persists in the twenty-first century, even when it does not involve forced sex.

Sex trafficking takes place within complex networks of individuals, communities, organizations, and governments—all of which vary widely across spaces and through time. These networks illustrate in concrete terms the necessity for a levels-of-analysis approach to conceptualizing the problems of trafficking.

Although human trafficking has patterns, no uniformity of opinion exists about why and how trafficking occurs. The multiple patterns of trafficking account for the debates among scholars and policy makers over the *nature* of transporting and exploiting humans. The variability in trafficking patterns, combined with our own *assumptions* about gender, sexuality, and crime, leads to conflicting opinions about the kinds of *policies* needed to address trafficking. Put differently, our policy recommendations reflect our assumptions about the nature of the problem.

The first section of this chapter describes two cases of women from different parts of the world trafficked for sexual exploitation. Maryam and Jharna, the women featured, have very different life experiences. Both, however, show us something about two central characteristics of the modern global order. First, the *structure* of contemporary globalization sets the economic and political context for trafficking. Second, despite powerful global forces at work in trafficking, national and local institutions—from governments to families—still influence the kinds of decisions we make as individuals. Human *agency* thus is bounded by webs of formal and informal relationships.

The debates about the nature of trafficking referred to above derive from different understandings of how and why the global order came to be as it is, and the costs and benefits we all experience as a result of the interaction of global, national, and local structures. But these costs and benefits are inescapably linked to the choices we make as individuals—that is, our ability to act as agents of our own lives. As the analysis following the stories of Maryam and Jharna will show, gender is central to both structure and agency.

An important reminder is in order when contrasting the importance of structure and agency: The dichotomy is not absolute. Both analysts and policy makers often fall into the trap of assuming that all development issues must be understood solely in terms of the global forces of international finance, trade, migration, and culture. Other analysts and policy makers assume that too much emphasis is put on these factors, ignoring the role of human choices and willpower. Sex trafficking, like the other case studies that follow in this book, is a mixture of both; and the mixture varies from place to place, individual to individual.

The second half of the chapter shows the way in which different understandings frame the debate about sex trafficking and condition the solutions that individuals, organizations, and governments advocate to address it. As a point of departure, we use the definition of the United States government in its *Trafficking in Persons Report*: "'Trafficking in persons' and 'human trafficking' have been used as umbrella terms for the act of recruiting, harboring, transporting, providing, or obtaining a person for compelled labor or commercial sex acts through the use of force, fraud, or coercion."[4]

Despite the apparent clarity in this definition of sex trafficking, we will see that it contains "gray areas" that are open to debate, and it doesn't address the broad economic and social context within which sex trafficking has blossomed. The stories of Maryam and Jharna illustrate these gray areas and the challenges of understanding and addressing the contextual factors that drive trafficking. These stories also set the stage for debate among feminists—who generally abhor trafficking—over the appropriate policy responses. We will see that general approaches to gender inequality that were examined in chapter 2 become central to understanding why those who care so much about the women who are trafficked have such great difficulty in reaching agreement over anti-trafficking strategies.

TWO CASES

Maryam (Russian Federation)

Maryam had just turned sixteen years old, and she was optimistic and excited about her future.[5] It had been more than twenty years since the old Soviet Union had broken up, but she didn't remember any of the turmoil of the 1990s, even though her mother and grandmother still talked about it a lot. Her grandmother, in fact, thought things used to be a lot better and blamed her son's constant drinking on all the changes that had taken place in the new Russia. Maryam, though, figured that in a year or two, she could make enough money to escape her town and her family's problems. She'd finished school, she knew a little English, and soon she would have enough money to go to Moscow or St. Petersburg.

A year later, Maryam's dreams were turning to desperation. She'd lost her part-time job during the global recession that began in 2008, her parents fought all the time, and she'd broken up with her boyfriend. So when she saw the ad on the Internet for waitresses and salesgirls in Moscow, she jumped at the chance. Her employer would pay her way, and she would have a year's contract. She'd heard the rumors that sometimes sex was part of these kinds of jobs, but if that's what it took to get ahead, it was worth it.

Six months later, Maryam had become part of the parade of "Natashas" lured into prostitution first in Moscow, then transported through Poland to the Netherlands.[6] She had been sold twice, the first time for nearly US$10,000, she heard. Her passport, which she had seen only once, was kept with other papers by the man she first saw in Moscow. All she really remembered was that he pushed her into the car at the airport and told her she was being trained for her new job. She was taken to an old house on the edge of the city and raped that first night. When she begged to be let go, they beat her and threatened to hurt her family back home. She saw only a little of the money she made for her captors; they told her that she owed them money for her transportation to the city, along with her lodging and food.

When Maryam was moved from Russia, she was sold a second time, but for much less money. She had been sick a lot and looked older. On the eve of her twentieth birthday, she was taken over the border at night from Russia to Ukraine, then Poland, and finally to the Netherlands, where she ended up in another seedy house on the outskirts of Amsterdam. A local feminist anti-trafficking group had been suspicious about this house for some time. Finally, under pressure from both feminist

NGOs and the city government, the police raided the brothel and freed the eight women held there.

Now Maryam was confronted with a dilemma. Technically, she was in the country illegally; moreover, although she did speak some English, she knew only a few words of Dutch, and her health was bad. All of these factors combined meant that she couldn't get a legal job, at least until she had a residency permit and some skills.

With the help of a small group, CoMensha/LaStrada International, Maryam was accommodated in a shelter and linked with local health and social services.[7] Meanwhile, she learned that her father had died and her grandmother was ill. Feeling that her options in the Netherlands were limited, she chose to be repatriated to Russia, despite the risk that the group that had originally kidnapped her might seek retribution.

Eventually, Maryam was sent back to Russia with new clothes, medicine, and a small amount of money. However, her future back in her hometown was uncertain, both because of her personal situation and also because both a local job center and the fledgling women's crisis center had suffered budget cutbacks. She wanted to publicize her story, but her mother found it shameful and begged her just to get a job. Discouraged, Maryam decided to concentrate on her health for the time being and maybe take some courses to improve her job prospects. She was convinced that the central government had made no significant efforts to prevent sex trafficking;[8] perhaps she would volunteer at the crisis center.

Jharna (Bangladesh)

In contrast to Maryam, Jharna lived in a village with her aunt and uncle, who had agreed to raise her after her parents died.[9] She had a good childhood, roaming around with her friends, climbing trees, and swimming in the river. However, this life was coming to an end because her guardians insisted that she marry a much older man whom they had chosen. Jharna rebelled: She had fallen in love with a village boy who had left to find a job in India, and anyway she was repulsed by the idea of marrying a man more than twice her age. An older woman in the village offered an alternative: If Jharna went with the woman, she would help Jharna find her boyfriend. Excited by the prospect, Jharna went with the woman, crossing the river into India where they stayed in a small town for a few days. But quickly the young woman became impatient again, wanting to find her boyfriend. At this point, Jharna was betrayed by the woman who led her to a brothel in Kolkata (Calcutta) and sold her as an indentured prostitute.

A few months later, the madam (called a *malkin*) took Jharna to Mumbai (Bombay) and sold her to another brothel. Ironically, the police raided the brothel the same evening that Jharna arrived, and she was taken with the other sex workers to a shelter for prostitutes. The people at the shelter were abusive, but Jharna, like the others, was told she could leave if she gave up sex work. This would qualify her for a government rehabilitation package. However, in order to leave the shelter, her guardians had to agree to take her into custody. But Jharna was in India illegally, and if she told people this, she would be further trapped: She would either have to bribe the police to release her, go through a lengthy court and bureaucratic battle—which she could scarcely afford—or somehow contact the guardians who had arranged the unwanted marriage that had caused her to run away in the first place. By now, she was more than a thousand miles from home, speaking only her native Bengali in a region where people spoke a different language.

At this point, the madam who had sold Jharna to the Mumbai brothel paid off the authorities and took her back to Kolkata and another brothel. Once again, Jharna fled, this time with a client she really liked. They went to live in her lover's home, but she eventually tired of putting up with his father's sexual harassment, gave up, and went back to become a sex worker. This time she was able to negotiate a position as an *adhiya*, a sex worker who splits her income with the *malkin*. Finally, she saved enough money to rent a room with a friend in Kolkata's red-light district and gradually became her own madam. In the end, Jharna stayed in the sex industry, but was able to work independently.

What Do These Cases Tell Us?

These two cases bear both similarities and differences. Although Russia and Bangladesh are very different in terms of their level of development, Maryam and Jharna were trafficked as a result of conditions that both push individuals out of their families and communities and pull them into situations where they are exploited.

Maryam and Jharna are economically and sexually exploited, but their exploitation is partly a consequence of their own aspirations and decisions. Maryam seeks opportunities, including more consumer choices, in a big city; she wants to escape family bickering, her father's drinking, and unemployment in her town. Ultimately, she takes the initiative to respond to an advertisement. Jharna's life circumstances are very different at the outset, but she is eager to leave her village to avoid marrying a man chosen by her relatives. Instead, she goes with her neighbor, hoping to find the love of her dreams. Both women are realistically constrained by the options available to them if they stay home; wanting a better life, they take risks that ultimately trap them. Modern forces shape their aspirations: a better job and consumer choices for Maryam, romantic love for Jharna. Both are moved illegally and surreptitiously across international borders, a situation that makes it difficult (if not impossible) to complain to local authorities. Finally, language is an issue at some point in the story for both women: Maryam knows a little English, but not Dutch; and Jharna doesn't speak Marathi or Hindi, the dominant languages in Mumbai.

The stories also have some notable differences. Maryam becomes part of a sophisticated network of traffickers operating throughout Eastern Europe. Much has been written about the networks operating in Europe in the wake of the collapse of the Soviet Union and the other communist countries, and the subsequent introduction of strategies of economic liberalization and development.[10] These networks are elaborate, interconnected, and vicious. Ultimately, Maryam is repatriated to Russia, but her options are limited: She is back in Russia, in poor health, with few job skills.

In contrast, Jharna's case involves a much more limited network: She is lured by an individual woman who has contacts in Kolkata and Mumbai, and ultimately is able to make choices that give her a few options as a prostitute. She becomes part of the system. As an *adhiya*, Jharna becomes an entrepreneur with a little freedom and perhaps even a sense of empowerment—at least in contrast to her prospects had she remained in the village.

Both women illustrate the role of structure and agency noted in the introduction. Constrained by economic, social, and cultural structures, they make choices that illustrate their personal agency. The next section contrasts the structures that confronted Maryam and Jharna in Russia and Bangladesh respectively and provides more insight into the options available to the young women who share their fate.

RUSSIA AND BANGLADESH: GLOBAL CHANGES AND LOCAL REALITIES

In economic, social, and cultural terms, it is hard to imagine two countries more different than Russia and Bangladesh. Spanning the Asian continent and much of Eastern Europe, Russia has the largest landmass of any country in the world, whereas Bangladesh is one of Asia's smaller countries. Russia is a sparsely populated and resource-rich country; Bangladesh is densely populated and resource poor. Russia boasts large industrial complexes, but Bangladesh is predominantly agricultural. Educational and income levels are vastly different in the two countries.

The cultural differences are also significant. For seventy years, Russia was the largest federation in the avowedly atheist political system of the Soviet Union (USSR). After the dissolution of the Soviet Union in 1991, large areas that had been dominated by Muslim populations broke away to form independent republics. Bangladesh continues to be overwhelmingly Muslim. Both countries have strong patriarchal traditions. During the Soviet period, both the Communist party and the government stressed gender equality. However, in the 2000s under President Vladimir Putin,[11] Russia underwent a "gender regime change"—symbolized by Putin's "rhetoric of masculinism."[12]

Although Bangladesh has a recent tradition of prominent female political leaders (and Russia does not), Bangladeshi girls and women play a secondary role in most households, following a cultural pattern that is common throughout South Asia. The practice of patrilocal exogamy means that a bride leaves her natal family at marriage, lives with her husband's family, and no longer contributes resources to her natal family. Consequently, a girl's family tends not to prioritize her education. These patterns are slowly changing, as more and more Bangladeshi women become income earners in the garment industry. Although women gain increased status from wage earning,

Table 4.1. Comparative Human Development Statistics: Russia and Bangladesh

Measure	Russian Federation		Bangladesh	
	Male	*Female*	*Male*	*Female*
Life Expectancy at Birth, 2009	63	75	66	68
Adult Literacy (percent population age 15 and older, 2009)	99	98	61	51
Technical Workers, 1999–2007	36	64	78	22
Legislators, Officials, Managers, 1999–2007	61	39	90	10

Source: Adapted from databases of the United Nations Development Programme (UNDP); the United Nations Educational, Scientific and Cultural Organization (UNESCO); and the World Bank. Data shown are for the most recent years compiled by the organizations; percentages are rounded.

the horrible safety record of the garment industry leads to many deaths from fires, building collapse, and industrial accidents.

Table 4.1 provides an overview of some of the gender differences between the two countries, and the numbers help explain some of the conditions that make life so difficult for people such as Maryam and Jharna. The data show, for example, that while the gap in life expectancy between Bangladeshi males and females is not large, in Russia the gap is surprisingly large. Men such as Maryam's father are far more likely to die at an early age due to the circumstances discussed below. Male-female literacy rates are equivalent in Russia, but not in Bangladesh. But the gaps are significant in the numbers of technical workers (line 3) and highly placed legislators, officials, and managers (line 4). In all these categories, men are far more likely than women to be employed in Bangladesh; in Russia, women predominate in the category of technical workers (which includes office workers), but not in the category of legislators and officials, the individuals who are best placed to make decisions that affect development priorities.

Russia

Maryam's story reflects the reality of thousands of women caught in an explosion of trafficking throughout Europe that began in the late twentieth century. Trafficking escalated dramatically when the communist states of east and central Europe began to fall apart after 1989 as centrally planned economies were replaced by liberalized market economies open to global trade and finance. Despite some movement in the direction of democracy, the regime changes failed to stimulate the women's movements that many Western feminists anticipated.[13] During this same period, civil wars in the Balkan Peninsula brought political and economic chaos and social dislocation, all of which led to intra-regional migrations of large numbers of people. Patterns of trafficking shift quickly, reflecting changing economic and legal conditions, but by 2005, the strongest flows occurred in Europe.[14] Maryam is Russian, but she could as easily be Ukrainian, Romanian, Turkish, or Albanian.

The combined phenomena of "marketisation, migration and militarization"[15] across western, central, and eastern Europe resulted in a shadow trafficking economy valued in excess of more than US$7 *billion* by the turn of the century—that is, within the first decade after political and economic liberalization took hold.[16]

To better understand why trafficking grew so rapidly, one needs to look more closely at the changes that occurred in the 1990s. The changes resulted from intentional policies, but because of the context in which they occurred they often produced unintended consequences. In order to liberalize the rigid Soviet economic and political system, the central government of the new Russian Federation removed state controls on the economy to encourage entrepreneurial activities. In downsizing the state role in the economy, the government also withdrew from many social service programs built up during the development of the Soviet Union. For example, the provision of maternity, health and child care, and old-age pensions took a sudden downturn. The consequences of liberalization spread unevenly across Russia. Urban men with education and connections (frequently due to Communist party ties under the old system) often flourished and even created the elaborate Mafia organizations that still play a central role in human trafficking in Russia. In contrast, old people, as well as younger people with less education and few skills or heavy family responsibilities, suffered, especially in those regions that had always been poorer.[17]

Put differently, both winners and losers appeared under liberalization. Those with connections or with entrepreneurial skills and ambitions contributed to the growth of the middle class. In contrast, Maryam and her family were among those hit hardest by the economic changes of the 1990s. Unemployment rose quickly, while real wages fell. Life expectancy in Russia fell as a result of the sudden decline in the provision of health services and the rise in illnesses, murder, alcoholism, and road traffic accidents. In 2000 alone, two million abortions were registered in Russia; this represented 80 percent more than the number of births.[18] Maryam's father was especially at risk. As table 4.1 shows, his life expectancy at birth in 2009, nearly twenty years after the liberalization began, was sixty-three years of age, a dozen years less than the life expectancy of Russian women. In the first decade of the new economic policies, infectious diseases, including tuberculosis, increased by one-third, and respiratory diseases increased by 23 percent; the rate of alcohol poisoning rose by more than 44 percent.[19] Russia was hit hard by the 2008–2009 recession; and although the economic situation had shown some improvement by 2010–2011, it was slow and uneven.[20]

Maryam is from the Irkutsk region of the Russian Federation, in the far southwest of the Siberian plateau. The main industries of the region are in the metals, energy (such as oil), logging, and hydroelectric sectors, areas of the economy where women are underemployed, but growth has been slowing in recent years and income inequality growing. Male life expectancy in this region is lower than the national norm, and the HIV infection rate in the region was the highest in Russia in 2006. Women, in particular, have few economic opportunities and play few political roles.[21] Although more women than men are found in higher education, a great deal of gender segregation exists in the subject areas of study. In fields such as geology, the energy sector, and metallurgy important in the area where Maryam comes from, the proportion of men training ranges from 79 to 94 percent.[22] The global recession of 2008–2009 hit families such as Maryam's the hardest: Already close to the poverty line, the jump in unemployment left the family with no steady income.[23]

To summarize, a "paradoxical situation has arisen: in a country where the number of women exceeds the number of men by almost 11 million, where women account for almost half of all professional employees (49.6%), and where their level of education is higher than that of men, decision-making remains a largely male preserve."[24] Thus the two main gender problems in Russia, low life expectancy for men and low political representation for women, are very characteristic of Maryam's geographic region.

Bangladesh

In the much poorer setting of Bangladesh, some of the same dynamics occur for women. Bangladesh is a densely populated rural nation where, in 2010, 35 percent of the rural population lived below the poverty line.[25] The choices of rural Bangladeshi women, such as Jharna, are limited by a patriarchal family system and a conservative Muslim society. Sons are preferred, as they support their parents in old age whereas daughters will be working in their husbands' households. Although more Bangladeshi girls are going to primary school today, and the gender literacy gap has been narrowing in recent years (see table 4.1), many families do not let girls continue to secondary school.[26] Consequently, the lack of education beyond the primary level means fewer life choices for girls, including Jharna, who had no secondary education.

The shift from a subsistence economy to a market economy has been accompanied by a rise in the practice of dowry, which further devalues women.[27] Jharna's guardians probably chose an older man for her husband because they lacked the financial resources to pay dowry, but she was horrified by the prospect of marrying an old man. Jharna may have been aware of the prevalence of domestic violence in marriage. For example, one study found that 61.7 percent of Bangladeshi rural women had experienced physical or sexual violence from their partners.[28] Jharna probably also had romantic notions about love from pop songs on the radio, leading her to be swayed by her neighbor's suggestion that finding her "true love" was possible.

The oppression grounded in both class and gender is situated in a nation mired in poverty, inequality, and political instability. Bangladesh's neoliberal development strategy has created a monetized economy pushing both men and women to migrate away from work as unpaid family laborers in rural areas to seek wage labor jobs in the cities. Some women find employment in the ready-made garment industry, which supplies the world market. However, a horrific fire in 2012 and a building collapse in 2013 focused international attention on the safety violations that are widespread in the garment industry, where the minimum wage is the lowest in the world.[29]

Men also frequently migrate, although they are more likely to leave the country, finding work in India and the Middle East, with the result that remittances have been a critical component of Bangladesh's GDP.[30] Bangladesh's long border with India makes undocumented movement from one country to the other relatively easy. Jharna's neighbor belonged to a small network of traffickers who have been able to take advantage of a young woman's dissatisfactions with rural life.

Bangladesh, like Russia, was hit hard by the 2008–2009 recession: The garment industry laid off workers, and remittances dropped as many of the men who had migrated also lost their jobs. As a consequence, the structural factors that made girls such as Jharna vulnerable to trafficking guaranteed that others would likely follow her. Nevertheless, Bangladesh has made more strides in female literacy and health indicators than many other low-income countries because of the extraordinary role of nongovernmental organizations (NGOs) in promoting poverty-centered development strategies and women's empowerment in Bangladesh.[31] Sadly, none of these organizations operated in Jharna's village.

FRAMING THE DEBATE, SEEKING SOLUTIONS

Policy makers and NGOs, including feminists, human rights advocates, and social conservatives, all condemn trafficking, but they frame the issue in different ways. These frames, or conceptualizations of the issues, both complement and contradict each other. Individuals and groups disagree about the origin and nature of human trafficking: Is it a criminal justice and national security problem, a global economic inequality problem, a women's human rights problem, or a multilayered phenomenon encompassing all three of these dimensions? Disagreement continues over the causes of and solutions to these problems. In this section we explain these different conceptualizations of trafficking, discuss the ways they inform policy, assess the impact of policies on human trafficking, and identify some promising approaches developed by feminist organizations.

Human trafficking reemerged on national and international policy agendas in the 1990s as the dramatic increase in the trade of poor women taken to rich countries focused attention on the global sex industry. Policy makers in the West have understood human trafficking primarily as a problem involving organized crime and illegal migration that threaten national security and public safety.[32] The role of global economic inequality in the illegal migration of trafficked women is obscured in the national security debates on trafficking.

The question of human rights of the trafficked women is of secondary importance to many policy makers, but of primary importance to feminists. But how to promote the human rights of trafficked women is mired in controversy. To understand this controversy, we look at the two different positions feminists have put forth on trafficking, one called the "sexual domination" perspective and the other the "sex work" perspective. Although these perspectives circumscribe the debate about international trafficking, their origins lie in different positions about prostitution in cases where no trafficking is involved. They also reflect the contrasting assumptions seen in the analysis of feminist positions laid out in chapter 2: equality, difference, and diversity.

Sexual Domination or Sex Work?

The two approaches to trafficking represented by the terms *sexual domination* and *sex work* reflect different assumptions about the underlying causes of both prostitution and sex trafficking.[33] These differing assumptions lead to different organizing strategies and policy recommendations put forth by two rival global networks of feminist anti-trafficking organizations. The Coalition Against Trafficking in Women (CATW) emphasizes the sexual domination perspective in its approach to trafficking, whereas the Global Alliance Against Trafficking in Women (GAATW) favors a sex work perspective. Neither of these feminist networks has been powerful enough to set the anti-trafficking policy agenda at the global or national levels, but each has tried to influence the policy process directly through lobbying and indirectly by defining the discourse on trafficking. The sexual domination perspective, represented by CATW, has been more influential because its analysis resonates with the dominant position that condemns prostitution—and, by extension, trafficking—on moral grounds. This position characterizes conventional wisdom and has been vigorously advanced by conservative social groups in many countries.

According to the *sexual domination* perspective, the underlying cause of trafficking is male sexuality. Although male sexuality is understood to be socially constructed, it is also seen as the coercive foundation of domination over women. Trafficking and all forms of prostitution are instances of sexual violence that are violations of women's human rights. According to this perspective, women cannot give meaningful consent to trafficking or prostitution because of the underlying condition of male domination. Based on these assumptions, the sexual domination perspective argues that the feminist goal should be the abolition of both prostitution and trafficking by punishing business owners *and* male clients, as well as traffickers. Trafficked women, like prostitutes, are seen as victims to be rescued and rehabilitated. Feminist organizations that follow the sexual domination philosophy have created shelters for trafficked women and have initiated a number of prevention campaigns in source countries to educate women about the dangers of trafficking. CATW has also worked with conservative lobbies in the United States seeking the abolition of prostitution by making it illegal or preventing its legalization.

In contrast, the *sex work* perspective views trafficking primarily as a migration issue, with the underlying cause being global inequality that forces people to migrate in search of work. Instead of viewing prostitution as inherently damaging to women, the sex work perspective frames it as an economic survival strategy, not much different from any other type of work in which poor migrants are engaged. Based on these assumptions, the feminist goal should be to ensure that both the conditions of migration and subsequent economic activities are safe and not characterized by coercion. The sex worker perspective argues that feminists should attempt to improve the working conditions of prostitutes, whether trafficked or not, through legalization or decriminalization and political organization.

Sex workers first articulated this perspective internationally in opposition to the sexual domination perspective advanced by some Western feminists. It underlies the philosophy of Durbar, a feminist sex-worker organization in Kolkata that is committed to establishing prostitution as a legitimate occupation freed from the exploitation of traffickers. Jharna's story is drawn from Durbar's files. Durbar criticizes anti-trafficking interventions for assuming "that those who are trafficked remain in a situation of everlasting powerlessness."[34] This assumption, according to Durbar, creates anti-trafficking efforts that paradoxically harm women and expand trafficking. For example, in 1982, in response to news stories about Bangladeshi maids being mistreated in the Middle East, the Bangladesh government prohibited the migration of women to the Middle East, which had the effect of diverting female migration into illegal trafficking.[35]

The strengths and weaknesses of both of the sexual domination and sex work perspectives mirror each other. Both sexual coercion and global inequalities contribute to sex trafficking, but each of the perspectives highlights one of these and neglects the other. *Sexual domination* illustrates the assumptions of difference feminism, which emphasizes the fundamental differences between men and women and the universal domination by men of our social, economic, political, and cultural structures and norms. The primary weaknesses of this approach are its failure to address the impact of globalization, economic inequality, and rural/urban differences on young women in poor countries, and its denial of agency to trafficked women. The sexual domination approach depicts trafficked women as "modern-day slaves," who are lured into sexual slavery by evil men. The denial of the agency of trafficked women sets up the situation in which anti-trafficking feminists and their allies must rescue them. Obscured in this analysis is the fact that many women "rescued" from brothels return, because, in their assessment, prostitution is their least bad option for making a living.[36]

In contrast, the sex work perspective, which is rooted in diversity feminism, expresses the viewpoint of those sex workers who challenged their portrayal as victims. This perspective does not recognize sufficiently the sexual objectification of women's bodies or the role organized crime plays in many instances of trafficking. The contribution of deconstruction feminism in this debate is that it enables us to recognize that trafficking is exceedingly complex; viewing a trafficked woman in binary terms as either victim or free agent is simplistic. Both the claim that all prostitution and trafficking occur under duress and the assertion that it is easy to distinguish forced from voluntary prostitution neglect the complexities of structure and agency that are present in the cases of Maryam and Jharna, for example.

Given the weaknesses in the fundamental assumptions governing each perspective, it is not surprising that the solutions each advocates also present problems. In the current global context, states are unlikely to agree with those who view prostitution as sex *work* and who therefore recommend the creation of safe conditions of migration for undocumented migrants.[37] Even when states make prostitution illegal, which is the central policy demand of those adhering to the sexual domination perspective, this does little to curb its occurrence. The debate on whether prostitution should be legal or illegal is largely irrelevant to women trafficked across national borders—as happened to both Maryam and Jharna—because any benefits that come to prostitutes from legalization (such as health care and better pay) are unlikely to be extended to them as illegal migrants. Trafficked women experience sexual violence, which is assumed in the sexual domination position, but they also experience other aspects of gender inequality in the family, society, and economy in both source and destination countries. Sex trafficking shares these characteristics with other forms of human trafficking.

THE GLOBAL POLITICS OF TRAFFICKING: STATES AND INTERNATIONAL ORGANIZATIONS

The reemergence of human trafficking on the policy agendas of states in the 1990s occurred within a context of a dominant global discourse of neoliberalism, uniformly restrictive immigration policies, and varying state stances toward prostitution. Prostitution was legal and regulated in some European states. Sweden represents a unique case; a 1999 law made the purchase of sexual services illegal and the selling of sexual services legal. In other European states and in the United States (except in Nevada), prostitution was illegal.[38] United States policies during the administration of President George W. Bush (2001–2008) reflected a sexual domination perspective and urged states to prohibit prostitution. The issue of trafficking has also arisen in the various UN peacekeeping missions that have been established since the end of the Cold War.[39]

The standards, laws, policies, and programs developed since the 1990s to curtail human trafficking, including sex trafficking, involve transnational cooperation and networking among states, international organizations, and NGOs. The United Nations provided guidelines to address human trafficking with the adoption of the Palermo Protocol in 2000. This protocol, a supplement to the UN Convention Against Transnational Organized Crime, is embedded within a criminal justice framework. The drafting of the protocol was characterized by intense lobbying by states and NGOs representing both sexual domination and sex work positions on prostitution.[40] The definition of human trafficking used in the protocol represents a compromise between the two positions, implying both that consent is irrelevant (see "b" below) and that coercion is necessary (see "a" below) for trafficking to occur:

(a) "Trafficking in persons" shall mean the recruitment, transportation, transfer, harbouring or receipt of persons, by means of the threat or use of force or other forms of coercion, of abduction, of fraud, of deception, of the abuse of power or of a position of vulnerability or of the giving or receiving of payments or benefits to achieve the consent of a person having control over another person, for the purpose of exploitation. Exploitation shall include, at a minimum, the exploitation of the prostitution of others or other forms of sexual exploitation, forced labour or services, slavery or practices similar to slavery, servitude or the removal of organs; (b) The consent of a victim of trafficking in persons to the intended exploitation set forth in subparagraph (a) . . . shall be irrelevant where any of the means set forth in subparagraph (a) have been used.[41]

Since 2000 several international agreements, shown in table 4.2, have set out common legal standards for criminalizing trafficking. The most significant of these have been the Palermo Protocol and the directives issued by the European Union (EU). The first European instrument on sex trafficking, the 2002 European Union Council Framework Decision, identified the victimization of trafficked women by organized criminal networks as the problem and the criminal prosecution of traffickers as the solution.[42] In 2011, the EU Council and Parliament adopted more ambitious legislation, expressing frustration over "insufficient or erratic implementation in Member States," as evidenced by few prosecutions.[43] Although victims' rights are mentioned, support for victims is delegated to NGOs; and curbing "irregular" migration, although not mentioned, is seen by scholars as the underlying rationale of EU policy.[44] The EU migration management approach is a state consultative process, called the Berne Initiative, which shares biometrical tools for detecting and tracking the hidden bodies engaged in irregular migration while attempting to encourage legal migration.[45]

The United States has also been a major influence in shaping national anti-trafficking policies. The US Trafficking Victims Protection Act (TVPA), initially enacted in 2000, attempted to strengthen efforts to prosecute traffickers and assist victims domestically as well as to prevent trafficking activities in other countries.[46]

Table 4.2.   Selected International Anti-Trafficking Conventions

Date	Title	Issuing Organization
2000	Protocol to Prevent, Suppress and Punish Trafficking in Persons, Especially Women and Children, of the United Nations Convention against Transnational Organized Crime (Palermo Protocol)	United Nations
2002	Framework Decision on Combating Trafficking in Human Beings	European Union—Council
2002	Convention on Preventing and Combating Trafficking in Women and Children for Prostitution	South Asian Association for Regional Cooperation
2005	Convention on Action against Trafficking in Human Beings	Council of Europe*
2011	Directive on Preventing and Combating Trafficking in Human Beings, and Protecting Victims (repealing 2002 Framework Decision)	European Union—Council

*Not to be confused with the Council of the European Union.

Both the US TVPA and the 2002 and 2011 EU policies on Combating Trafficking in Human Beings established systems of monitoring the adequacy of anti-trafficking efforts by source country governments and threatening to withhold foreign aid from countries judged to be lagging in this area. However, the TVPA categorization of certain countries as "Tier 3," and thus ineligible for foreign aid, appears more related to US foreign policy objectives than those countries' anti-trafficking policies. For example, in 2005, Bolivia and Venezuela were classified as "Tier 3," whereas India and Thailand were not. This judgment possibly reflects the presumption at that time that as Asian countries, India and Thailand were strategically more important to the United States than the Latin American cases. Thus criticism of government policies in India and Thailand—where trafficking is widespread—was muted. In the United States, as elsewhere, policy initiatives are imbedded in larger political considerations.

In keeping with these international legal standards and US and EU pressure, states have enacted laws and put increased resources into law enforcement and prosecution to criminalize sex trafficking. Although policy makers have described their policy goals in terms of the "three P's"—prevention, protection of victims, and prosecution of traffickers—the policies are primarily criminal justice initiatives against traffickers and illegal migration, and most of the available funding has been for law enforcement and criminal justice.[47] Typically, victims are only offered residence permits in the destination country if they cooperate with the police in the prosecution of traffickers; otherwise they are repatriated.

Nation-states, including the United States, and international institutions, such as the EU and UN, have funded a number of NGOs, especially those groups willing to work with the police, to carry out victim-protection programs and prevention programs in countries from which trafficked women come. This kind of effort has assisted the European coalition and its Dutch branch that helped Maryam find a safe house and ultimately repatriate.

Groups affiliated with the two rival anti-trafficking networks have tried to raise women's human rights issues during the processes of trafficking policy formulation and implementation, and they have crafted some prevention and protection programs funded by governments, but their impact has been reduced by their opposing positions on prostitution, which has led them to attack each other as much as to address the problem of trafficking. In the United States, only groups with a strong antiprostitution stance were able to get funding during the administration of President George W. Bush; more than $300 million was distributed to feminist groups associated with CATW and also to socially conservative faith-based groups.[48] In Europe and Asia, the range of organizations funded has been much broader, but the conflict between the rival feminist networks has also been apparent.[49]

How effective have been the criminal justice-oriented anti-trafficking regimes in Europe, the United States, and Asia in stopping trafficking? Several assessments of the anti-trafficking regimes in the United States and Europe find their effectiveness limited.[50] Estimates of the number of people convicted for trafficking (sex trafficking and forced labor) globally and in the United States in 2011 were 4,239 and

141, respectively.[51] Many European states have stiffened penalties for trafficking, but prosecution of traffickers appears to have had the effect primarily of pushing the criminal networks further underground. Victim protection is inadequate, leading most trafficked individuals to refuse to be prosecution witnesses. Reintegration programs are deficient, as they do not provide the repatriated women with economic opportunities or assist them in coping with community censure. Prevention efforts are extremely narrow, consisting primarily of education and awareness programs in source countries. Few programs provide economic development assistance in the source countries to former or potential trafficked women. States have not considered rethinking their migration policies to grant work permits to potential or actual victims of trafficking. Finally, few programs are designed to reduce the demand for sexual services.

What have been the effects of these counter-trafficking regimes on trafficked women and/or those women vulnerable to be trafficked? The ineffectiveness of the criminal justice approach in stopping trafficking and the lack of emphasis on programs promoting economic development and women's empowerment in the countries of origin result in a situation in which women continue to resort to illegal migration to improve their lives by escaping untenable situations at home, and trafficking networks continue to take advantage of them. In the absence of a comprehensive policy approach going after traffickers through criminal justice mechanisms; addressing the economic inequalities that have been exacerbated by globalization and financial crises; and targeting gender discrimination in the family, society, and the economy, ending human trafficking is unlikely.

SEEKING A FEMINIST APPROACH

In spite of the conflict between the sexual domination and sex work feminist perspectives, both perspectives share a gender analysis of the structural causes of sex trafficking, drawing attention to the subordination of women in the family and society, insufficient economic opportunities, and women's disempowerment. Although the counter-trafficking regimes of both nation-states and international organizations have been ineffective, feminist organizations have developed a number of promising approaches to address sex trafficking. In different combinations these approaches reflect the assumptions of the equality, difference, and diversity strands in feminism.

At the national and international levels, feminist organizations from both camps seek to expand the counter-trafficking policy agenda by emphasizing women's human rights. In addition to testifying at legislative hearings, they have offered workshops; developed materials to educate legislators, judges, police, and teachers; and published articles and books about women's human rights in trafficking. These rights-based approaches, which emphasize education, development, and freedom from violence, point out the gender inequalities underlying women's vulnerability to trafficking.

Although feminist organizations of different persuasions may work together, the tensions between the difference and diversity strands in feminist theory are still seen in the different versions of women's human rights emphasized in the sexual domination and sex work perspectives. Yet these contending perspectives can also be seen in some ways as complementary, each drawing attention to important components of women's human rights. Reducing the male demand for sexual services and increasing women's economic opportunities are both important in advancing women's human rights. The efforts of both groups expose policy makers to a gendered counter-trafficking agenda that addresses underlying structural forces. For example, CATW publicizes its school-based programs for boys that examine male sexual attitudes in an attempt to prevent sexual exploitation.[52] Feminists associated with the sex work perspective call for greater coordination between anti-trafficking and economic development programs in source countries, so that vulnerable women have additional economic options.[53]

Although the two feminist approaches are in some instances complementary, the demand for the legal prohibition of prostitution by those in the sexual domination camp has been harmful in several ways. The most persuasive criticism of the sexual domination perspective is that it hasn't ended prostitution, and arguably it has only made conditions worse for sex workers. Many feminists in this camp, particularly Americans, have furthered the work of conservative Christian evangelical groups, which reinforces the idea that heterosexual marriage is the only appropriate option for women, and they have exacerbated racial and gender stereotypes. Some feminist scholars have labeled this approach as "carceral feminism," arguing that strengthening the coercive power of the state harms marginalized individuals.[54] That said, the sexual domination perspective *does* call attention to the harmful process of sexual objectification inherent in the demand for sexual services, and the pattern of violence that often accompanies this demand.

At the local level, feminists in many nations have created grassroots anti-trafficking initiatives that incorporate participatory strategies to foster local leadership development and women's empowerment. These initiatives are able to address specific cultural contexts and give voice to women of the community, principles espoused by diversity feminism. Community-based anti-trafficking interventions include monitoring of trafficking activity and enlisting former trafficking victims to identify traffickers and victims at local border crossings. For example, Durbar promotes a model of a community-based anti-trafficking intervention in Kolkata.[55] Local Self-Regulatory Boards (SRBs), composed of sex workers and other members of the community, have been set up to monitor the working conditions of prostitutes. These SRBs assist trafficked individuals to get out of situations of coercion.

Other community-based initiatives focus on the empowerment of women and girls through education, vocational training, or micro-finance programs. Encouraging girls to stay in school increases their economic options, and a number of innovative programs have this focus. One successful activity in several Indian states has been teaching karate to girls, which has increased their self-confidence and their likelihood of staying in school.[56]

In a number of countries, these kinds of local initiatives have been weakened by the political and economic dynamics of the global system, as well as national policies. Innovative initiatives often depend on support from national and international donors, making them vulnerable to shortfalls in donor funds, shifts in donor interests, or legal restrictions on their activities. In Russia, for example, opportunities for feminist activism have been circumscribed by the conservative ideologies propagated by the Putin presidencies, and the 2006 law regulating nongovernmental organizations has hampered international support for Russian NGOs, including those focusing on gender issues.[57] This makes planning for sustainability a crucial element in the long-term survival of local initiatives. In Russia, the establishment of crisis centers was part of the global pattern of feminist activism in the 1990s, but competition for funding and government efforts to establish publicly funded and controlled centers undermined the momentum of the NGOs, both their numbers and their self-identification as feminist.[58]

CONCLUSION

In this chapter we have examined how global, national, and local structures create conditions that result in trafficking. These structures—globalization, national government policies, families and local communities—all reflect gender inequalities, making women economically and sexually vulnerable. We have also looked at the role of human agency: women attempting to escape untenable situations. Their choices are constrained and may lead to outcomes worse than their initial situations. Nevertheless, it is clear that these women are not just passive victims of oppressive structures.

International institutions and nation-states have undertaken innumerable counter-trafficking initiatives that emphasize national security and criminal justice. These policies and programs reflect a particular gender ideology—that women are victims requiring protection (even though the policies fail to protect them). The gendered economic and familial inequalities that push women to consider trafficking are typically obscured by this approach. Meanwhile, the often-acrimonious debate among feminists detracts from their efforts to address women's human rights—both rights to livelihood and to freedom from violence—in discussions of anti-trafficking policies.

Nonetheless, the issue of sex trafficking has energized many organizations reflecting diverse perspectives. Some of these are clearly feminist, others less so. But together, they have developed a broad array of arguments, strategies, and services drawing on the strengths of equality, difference, and diversity feminisms. They illustrate the vibrancy of contemporary feminist activism on sex trafficking, and they offer many opportunities for individuals to become engaged on this issue.[59] These initiatives, considered as a whole, offer some promise.

As we have seen, sex trafficking is facilitated by globalization, but individual cases can be imbedded in complex economic, cultural, and political structures from the local to the global level. Thus a levels-of-analysis approach is necessary to understanding trafficking patterns. Except in the most egregious cases of trafficking (e.g., children), individual agency is also a factor in both the circumstances and outcomes. A comparison of our two cases from Russia and Bangladesh illustrates different trafficking contexts and mixtures of structure and agency.

In view of these complexities, no one set of policies is sufficient to curb or eliminate trafficking. For example, we can assume that if Maryam's hometown had better job opportunities, as well as a more vibrant cultural life, she would be less apt to respond to the lure of an ad to come to Moscow. Her family life would likely be more stable if her father and mother had predictable jobs and incomes and if her father had not fallen prey to the alcoholism and communicable diseases that became so prominent in the wake of Russia's commitment to a neoliberal economic strategy in the 1990s. But none of these is a guarantee, given the force of other structural conditions, including the role of the Mafia, the ease of transportation and communication, and the pervasiveness of a consumerist ideology.

Similarly, if Jharna's aunt and uncle belonged to a less conservative culture, were not committed to an arranged marriage, and not preoccupied with paying Jharna's dowry, and if Jharna herself had training and economic opportunities, she would also be less vulnerable. But nothing guarantees that a young woman will not succumb to the images of romantic love and the potential for a better life.

So what are the realistic alternatives? First, we all need to be more conscious of the lenses we bring to the issue. A dominant preoccupation with "rescuing victims" reflects a humanitarian impulse, but it may also be patronizing and neglect the mixture of structure and agency that operates in most cases. Second, and logically connected, we need to rethink the terms and conditions of globalization. Who are the winners and losers in the neoliberal global strategies that have swept the world in the past quarter century? What is the trade-off between more cheap T-shirts in our closets, job opportunities in offshore garment factories, and conditions that approximate indentured servitude? The global consumer economy that improves our material lives in so many ways also imprisons us in cultural norms of sexuality and unfilled aspirations. Liberal trading regimes have contributed to the growth of drugs, arms, and sex as the most valuable international commodities. But a free global labor market has not accompanied free trade. In reassessing our own lenses and the conditions of globalization, we will better understand the commonalities and differences in trafficking patterns and therefore be able to craft more viable policies to deal with trafficking.

NOTES

1. International Labor Organization, "2012 Global Estimate of Forced Labor: Executive Summary," http://www.ilo.org/wcmsp5/groups/public/---ed_norm/---declaration/documents/

publication/wcms_181953.pdf. The full report is also at the ILO website; it details the methodology used to calculate the numbers of people trafficked into forced labor, but notes that there are multiple difficulties in determining the exact numbers.

2. See the *Trafficking in Persons Report*, issued annually by the US Department of State at http://www.state.gov (hereafter abbreviated as *TIP Report*).

3. International Labor Organization, "2012 Global Estimate."

4. US Department of State, *TIP Report* 2012, 33.

5. Maryam's case is compiled from research and testimonies of women from Russia, Ukraine, Moldova, Albania, and other central and east European countries. For example, see "Marina's Story: A Survivor's Fight against Human Trafficking," posted on the IREX website, April 7, 2011; accessed April 18, 2013.

6. Victor Malarek's book, *The Natashas: Inside the Global Sex Trade* (New York: Arcade Publishing, 2003), gave currency to the name "Natasha" for women trafficked into prostitution from Russia and Ukraine.

7. CoMensha (the Coordinational Centre Human Trafficking) is the Dutch affiliate of La Strada International, the European Network Against the Trafficking in Human Beings. See http://lastradainternational.org. La Strada branches provide data on trafficking, as well as networking with a variety of support groups for victims of trafficking.

8. This is the conclusion of the State Department's *TIP Report* 2012, 295–96. "Russia is a source, transit, and destination country for men, women, and children who are subjected to forced labor and sex trafficking," 295.

9. The story of Jharna (not her real name) is adapted from the story told by Nandinee Bandyopadhyay with Swapna Gayen et al., "Streetwalkers Show the Way: Reframing the Debate on Trafficking from Sex Workers' Perspective," in *Feminisms in Development: Contradictions, Contestations and Challenges*, ed. Andrea Cornwall, Elizabeth Harrison, and Ann Whitehead (London: Zed Books, 2007), 88–89.

10. On the pattern of trafficking represented in Maryam's story, see Chris Corrin, "Transitional Road for Traffic: Analysing Trafficking in Women From and Through Central and Eastern Europe," *Europe-Asia Studies* 57, no. 4 (June 2005): 543–60; Liz Kelly, "'You Can Find Anything You Want': A Critical Reflection on Research on Trafficking in Persons within and into Europe," *International Migration* 43, no. 1/2 (2005): 235–65; and Alexandra V. Orlova, "From Social Dislocation to Human Trafficking: The Russian Case," *Problems of Post-Communism* 51, no. 6 (November/December 2004): 14–22.

11. Putin was elected for two terms as president (2000–2004 and 2004–2008), and was prime minister from 2008 to 2012, when he was again elected president. Most observers see Putin as reinforcing the authoritarian trends in Russian politics.

12. Janet Elise Johnson and Aino Saarinen, "Twenty-First-Century Feminisms under Repression: Gender Regime Change and the Women's Crisis Center Movement in Russia," *Signs* 38, no. 3 (Spring 2013): 543–67.

13. Johnson and Saarinen argue that this is characteristic of countries without "thick democracy"; the resurgence of neo-authoritarianism under Putin has made it harder for NGOs to organize. Johnson and Saarinen, "Twenty-First-Century Feminisms," 543–44.

14. Kelly, "'You Can Find Anything You Want,'" 204.

15. Corrin, "Transitional Road for Trafficking," 544.

16. Corrin, "Transitional Road for Trafficking," 547.

17. These trends are confirmed in the 2011 UNDP-sponsored study, *National Human Development Report for the Russian Federation: Modernization and Human Development*, ed.

Alexander A. Auzan and Sergei N. Bobylev (Moscow, 2011). The report emphasizes the ongoing problems of excessive smoking and alcohol consumption as health factors, 88–95.

18. United Nations Development Programme, *Human Development Report for the Russian Federation 2001: General Aspects of Human Development*, 53.

19. United Nations Development Programme, *Human Development Report for the Russian Federation 2001: General Aspects of Human Development*, 53.

20. United Nations Development Programme, *National Human Development Report for the Russian Federation 2011: Modernization and Human Development*, chap. 1.

21. United Nations Development Programme, *Russia's Regions: Goals, Challenges, Achievements* (National Human Development Report 2006/2007), "Human Development Index in the Regions of Russia" (2003), http://hdr.undp.org/en/reports/nationalreports/europethecis/russia/RUSSIAN_FEDERATION_2007_en.pdf, 120; maps for "Officially Registered Cases of HIV Infection in Russian Regions" (1987–2006); and "Gender Composition of Regional Parliaments in the Russian Federation" (2006), 128–29, retrieved March 26, 2009.

22. United Nations Development Programme, *Millennium Development Goals in Russia: Looking into the Future*, 2010, 51.

23. World Bank, "Russian Economic Report No. 18," March 2009, particularly chap. 3. Retrieved April 2, 2009, from http://siteresources.worldbank.org/INTRUSSIAN FEDERATION/Resources/rer18eng.pdf.

24. United Nations Development Programme, *Millennium Development Goals in Russia*, 2010, 51.

25. International Monetary Fund, "Bangladesh: Poverty Reduction Strategy Paper," IMF Country Report (March 2013), 13, at http://www.imf.org/external/pubs/ft/scr/2013/cr1363.pdf.

26. International Monetary Fund, "Bangladesh," 295.

27. Elora Halim Chowdhury, "Feminist Negotiations: Contesting Narratives of the Campaign against Acid Violence in Bangladesh," *Meridians: Feminism, Race, Transnationalism* 6, no. 1 (2005): 67.

28. Claudia Garcia-Moreno et al., "Prevalence of Intimate Partner Violence: Findings from the WHO Multi-Country Study on Women's Health and Domestic Violence," *Lancet* 368, no. 9543 (October 7–13, 2006): 264.

29. It was about US$37 per month in 2013. Neither the fire nor the building collapse was the first in an industry focused on minimizing costs while providing clothing for European and American manufacturers and consumers. In these two cases alone, more than twelve hundred people, mostly garment workers, were killed. Violations of building codes and other safety provisions are widespread, with Western companies, factory owners, and government inspectors sharing in the responsibility for the tragedies.

30. Remittances rose to $14 billion in 2012. "Bangladesh Remittances Jump 16.5 Pct in 2012," Reuters, http://in.reuters.com/article/2013/01/05/bangladesh-remittance-idINL 4N0AA0ED20130105. See also Zahid Hussaine, "How Remittances Grease the Wheels of Bangladesh Economy," *World Bank Blog: End Poverty in South Asia*, February 7, 2013, http://blogs.worldbank.org/endpovertyinsouthasia/node/803, retrieved April 20, 2013.

31. "The Path Through the Fields," *Economist*, November 3, 2012, online version; International Monetary Fund, "Bangladesh."

32. Heli Askola, "Violence against Women, Trafficking, and Migration in the European Union," *European Law Journal* 13, no. 2 (2007): 204–17.

33. Joyce Outshoorn, "The Political Debates on Prostitution and Trafficking of Women," *Social Politics* 12, no. 1 (2005): 141–55.

34. Bandyopadhyay, "Streetwalkers Show the Way," 33.

35. Bimal Kanti Paul and Syed Abu Hasnath, "Trafficking in Bangladesh Women and Girls," *Geographical Review* 90, no. 2 (2000): 270.

36. Julia O'Connell Davidson, "New Slavery, Old Binaries: Human Trafficking and the Borders of Freedom," *Global Networks* 10, no. 2 (2010): 244–61.

37. GAATV does work with migrant-worker groups trying to improve working conditions for undocumented workers. In the long term, it might be possible to make migration safe and create good working conditions for migrant workers through cross-border worker organizations that would enforce worker rights, a scenario sketched out by Jennifer Gordon in "Transnational Labor Citizenship," *Southern California Law Review* 80 (2007): 5038–87. This would provide alternatives to being trafficked for both men and women workers.

38. In the fall of 2008, voters in San Francisco were asked to approve Proposition K, "Changing the Laws Related to Prostitution and Sex Workers." Proposition K sought to decriminalize prostitution and represented clearly the sex work perspective. It did not pass. http://www.smartvoter.org/2008/11/04/ca/sf/prop/K, retrieved November 15, 2008.

39. Sandra Whitworth, *Men, Militarism, and UN Peacekeeping: A Gendered Analysis* (Boulder, CO: Lynne Rienner, 2004).

40. Janie A. Chuang, "Rescuing Trafficking from Ideological Capture: Prostitution Reform and Anti-Trafficking Law and Policy," *University of Pennsylvania Law Review* 158, no. 6 (2010): 1655–1728.

41. The Palermo Protocol can be found at http://www.uncjin.org/Documents/Conventions/dcatoc/final_documents_2/convention_%20traff_eng.pdf.

42. Sarah H. Krieg, "Trafficking in Human Beings: The EU Approach between Border Control, Law Enforcement and Human Rights," *European Law Journal* 15, no. 6 (November 2009): 783.

43. EU, Directive 2011/36/EU of the European Parliament and of the Council, April 5, 2011. *Official Journal of the European Union*, L101/1, April 15, 2011, http://eurlex.europa.eu/LexUriServ/LexUriServ.do?uri=OJ:L:2011:101:0001:0011:EN:PDF.

44. Krieg, "Trafficking in Human Beings," 790.

45. IOM, The Berne Initiative, http://www.iom.int/cms/en/sites/iom/home/what-we-do/migration-policy-and-research/migration-policy-1/berne-initiative.html; Jacqueline Berman, "Biopolitical Management, Economic Calculation and 'Trafficked Women,'" *International Migration* 48, no. 4 (2010): 84–113.

46. The US TVPA was reauthorized in 2003, 2005, and 2008. It expired in 2011, but in February 2013, Congress reauthorized it. President Obama signed the bill into law on March 7, 2013. See http://www.endslaveryandtrafficking.org/trafficking-victims-protection-reauthorization-act.

47. In addition to these "three P's," the US State Department now emphasizes a fourth: partnership between governments, civil society, and the private sector. *TIP Report* 2012, 9.

48. Ronald Weitzer, "The Social Construction of Sex Trafficking: Ideology and Institutionalization of a Moral Crusade," *Politics and Society* 35, no. 3 (2007): 460.

49. Vidyamali Samarasinghe and Barbara Burton, "Strategising Prevention: A Critical Review of Local Initiatives to Prevent Female Sex Trafficking," *Development in Practice* 17, no. 1 (2007): 51–64.

50. H. Richard Friman and Simon Reich, eds., *Human Trafficking, Human Security, and the Balkans* (Pittsburgh: University of Pittsburgh Press, 2007); Askola, "Violence against

Women"; Cornelius Friesendorf, "Pathologies of Security Governance: Efforts against Human Trafficking in Europe," *Security Dialogues* 38, no. 3 (2007): 379–402.

51. Department of State, *TIP Report* 2012, 44, 361.

52. CATW at http://www.catwinternational.org/campaigns.php#curb.

53. Gail Kligman and Stephanie Limoncelli, "Trafficking Women after Socialism: To, Through, and From Eastern Europe," *Social Politics* 12, no. 1 (Spring 2005): 118–40.

54. Elizabeth Bernstein, "Militarized Humanitarianism Meets Carceral Feminism: The Politics of Sex, Rights, and Freedom in Contemporary Antitrafficking Campaigns," *Signs* 36, no. 1 (Autumn 2010): 45–71.

55. Bandyopadhyay, "Streetwalkers Show the Way."

56. Samarasinghe and Burton, "Strategising Prevention,"58.

57. Johnson and Saarinen, "Twenty-First-Century Feminisms under Repression."

58. Johnson and Saarinen distinguish between feminism ("activism to challenge and change women's subordination"—a definition we share) and women's movements, which are defined by their constituencies. "Twenty-First-Century Feminisms under Repression," 551. They found that more than half of the crisis centers run by NGOs consulted on sex trafficking, whereas none of the governmental agencies addressed trafficking.

59. For example, the Laboratory to Combat Human Trafficking, http://www.combat humantrafficking.org.

5

Debates and Dilemmas: Water

Humans use water for drinking, cooking, and bathing. They use it for growing, and often processing, food crops. Animals also drink and bathe in water. Manufacturing and waste disposal rely heavily on water. From northern Europe to the Himalayas to Canada, countries depend on water flows to generate hydroelectric power. Water sustains all life, and the need for it is universal, leading one woman from the Kyrgyz Republic in central Asia to comment, "We need water as badly as we need air."[1]

Although people disagree over the extent of global water shortages, the consensus is growing that—given current patterns of use—the amount of water drawn from the natural ecosystem threatens agriculture, numerous wildlife forms, commerce, and human well-being. A number of major rivers, including the Indus, Colorado, Rio Grande, and Yellow, no longer reach the sea. Around the world, freshwater fish populations have declined dramatically. Every dimension of development is affected by water.

Three broad trends account for the decline in both the quantity and quality of water: population increases, changes in diet and other consumption patterns, and climate change. The world's population has doubled in the past half century and will continue to grow at least until the middle of the twenty-first century. More people leads to a greater demand for water. Perhaps of greater significance, however, is the change in patterns of human consumption. To cite one example, with development and improved standards of living, people consume more meat. Growing a kilogram of wheat requires approximately 1,400 liters (about 370 gallons) of water, but producing a kilo of beef takes 16,000 liters (4,227 gallons) of water.[2] Thus one of the unintended consequences of development is to reduce the quantity and quality of the water that enables economic growth.

Climate change also affects water quality and quantity, although the impact varies by geographic locale. To illustrate, in the first decade of the twenty-first century, a prolonged drought in southwest Australia led to widespread fires, the depletion of the Murray-Darling River, and shifts in agricultural patterns. Elsewhere, floods destroy lives and homes, as well as cropland. The impact is felt at all levels of the global system, from the individual farmer who watches her children and animals suffer, to communities that fight over scarce resources, to governments and international agencies that wrestle with water supply and delivery problems. People in countries as diverse as Bulgaria, Egypt, and Ecuador increasingly complain about water pollution and its impact on the health of humans and animals alike.[3]

This chapter focuses on the role of water in gender and development. In both urban and rural settings, women are primarily responsible for the domestic tasks for which water is central, such as food preparation and washing. In rural areas, women typically are also responsible for procuring water. In rural Rajasthan, India, women carry the water long distances on their heads and shoulders. In a small Ghanaian town, the source is closer—a municipal water tank—but the average woman makes six to seven trips daily to supply her household with water (see photos 5.1 and 5.2). In addition, women often spend long days on a variety of agricultural activities that require water, including farming, processing crops, and animal husbandry.

Gender analysis of water access and use emerged during the early phase of women-in-development studies, but only more recently has it played a visible role in studies and policy discussions in the most important organizations dealing with water management.[4] One important aspect of gender analysis has pointed to the traditional distinction between household use and irrigation. This distinction reflects assumptions about the dichotomy of the "private" or "domestic" sphere, historically viewed as female, and the "public" (male) sphere. This distinction is often institutionalized in the establishment of different agencies or departments for household and irrigation water in government and private bureaucracies. Such a division "renders invisible the different priorities that men and women assign to water in each sphere . . . [and] is overly simplistic as it obscures the many interconnections between the varied uses and users of water."[5]

The different priorities of women and men, and the interconnections between the various uses and users of water, are particularly visible in rural and peri-urban areas where farming occurs. In these settings, women and men share responsibility for agricultural production, although their roles differ. In all rural and urban settings, the availability and quality of water raise important issues for women and men, and the cost of water affects users everywhere.

This chapter examines the complexity of these issues in the context of globalization. Globalization generally increases pressures on water quality and quantity, although in some instances international transactions may improve water supplies. Neoliberalism, a dominant feature of globalization, has become central to water management in much of the world for two reasons. First, neoliberal policies have generated pressures to privatize water delivery services; and second, these policies have prompted decentralization of water management from central and regional governments to local governments and associations. Although the extent of privatization

Photo 5.1.   Carrying Water, Rajasthan, India. Photo courtesy of James W. Boyd

Photo 5.2.   Municipal Water Tank, Bonwire, Ghana. Photo by Sue Ellen M. Charlton

and decentralization varies considerably from place to place, both have important gender implications.

Much of the recent feminist debate about development and globalization focuses on neoliberal policies and decentralized management, and the impact of both on women's access to water. In this debate, we see the links to the early approaches to women in development (WID) and gender and development (GAD), as well as the tensions in feminist theories explored in chapter 2.

TWO CASES

Jennifer (South Africa)

Jennifer lives with her five children, disabled sister, three unemployed brothers, and her mother in Phiri Township, Soweto, which is part of the city of Johannesburg, South Africa.[6] The family subsists on the grandmother's pension of 115 Rand per month (less than US$15). With a 65 percent unemployment rate in Soweto, Jennifer and her brothers have been unable to find work. In 2003, Johannesburg Water launched a "Save Water" campaign that included the introduction of prepaid water meters as part of a project to replace the dilapidated water supply infrastructure, offer residents a basic supply of free water, and realize cost recovery for infrastructure and maintenance by charging for additional water.

Jennifer's household receives six thousand liters of free water a month, after which their water is shut off until they pay at the municipal office for additional water. The Save Water campaign sent Jennifer a pamphlet showing how to budget her family's water consumption: "20 litres of water for cleaning, 6 body washes per day, 6 flushes of the toilet per day, 2 kettles of water per day, 1 sink full of dishes per day, 1 clothes wash every second day, 12 liters of drinking water a day."[7] The new water limitations caused hardship for Jennifer's family. With eleven people in the house, only six toilet flushes a day meant that their small house smelled, they didn't have enough plates and cups to limit dishwashing to once a day, and every member of the family had to share bath water. They used up the six-thousand-liter limit halfway through the month and lacked the money to buy more water.

Out of frustration, Jennifer joined a "water for all" protest campaign in the township. The residents organized a civil disobedience campaign that included marches and the destruction of some of the water meters. Jennifer also joined the Coalition Against Water Privatization, which sued the city of Johannesburg in 2006, arguing that the prepaid meters were unconstitutional. In 2008, the High Court sided with the plaintiffs, finding that the prepaid water meters violated equal rights, because they existed only in traditionally black townships and not in affluent white communities and because the free water allotment was inadequate to fulfill the constitutional guarantee of a right to water. The court held that individuals should receive fifty liters of water per day to fulfill the constitutional guarantee and to address the needs of people with HIV/AIDS.

The prepaid meter system continued, however, because the mayor of Johannesburg appealed the court ruling. In February 2009, Jennifer and more than sixty other women marched through downtown Johannesburg to the mayor's office wearing unwashed and bloody underwear over their clothes to demonstrate that water is a human right. The women chanted, "We demand free water now, especially for women." "Water is a basic need, so it should be free for all." A spokeswoman for the Coalition Against Water Privatization that organized the protest stated, "When the ANC were lobbying for the elections they said 'free water, free this and free that'—it is time that they started to practice what they are preaching."[8]

Unfortunately for Jennifer and the other township residents, in March 2009 the Constitutional Court handed down a judgment in the Phiri water case that had mixed implications. The court held that prepaid water meters were unconstitutional because they were not authorized by Johannesburg bylaws, and it ruled that Phiri residents were entitled to forty-two free liters of water a day. However, the court suspended implementation of its ruling for two years to give the Johannesburg municipality time to change its laws and stated that access to the increased water would be available only to residents who were registered as indigents. Now, in order to qualify for the forty-two liters of free water, Jennifer had to go to the municipal office to begin the process of being classified as indigent.

Maria (Peru)

Maria lives in the arid southern highlands of Peru, where she works at thirteen thousand feet (nearly four thousand meters).[9] The average annual rainfall of about one hundred millimeters, less than four inches, means that Maria relies on irrigation water for her crops of maize, potatoes, and vegetables, as did her ancestors.

The region where Maria lives is characterized by widespread poverty, in large part due to degradation in the quality of natural resources, particularly water and land. The government of Peru, with the collaboration of the International Fund for Agricultural Development (IFAD), has worked to increase the productivity of the region's natural resources as part of the larger strategy of combating poverty. Project training undertaken as part of the Management of Natural Resources in the Southern Highlands Project, called MARENASS, emphasizes community involvement, including that of women, and Maria participated in one of the training sessions. The training, along with her participation in women's organizations, gave her the confidence to confront her husband and the community in order to better provide for her children.

Maria has been separated from her husband for nearly ten years and alone has been responsible for the care of their four children. Her husband has had a long-standing drinking problem and disapproved of Maria's assertiveness; he mistreated her, especially when he was drunk. He wouldn't take care of their farm, so she became the only source of income for the family. As a consequence, and increasingly with the help of her children, Maria has been responsible not only for the household tasks, but also running their small farm and participating in the communal meetings and other activities of the water users' association to which she and her husband belonged. Many of the villagers criticized her public activities, saying that it was the husbands who should go to the meetings and carry out the other obligations such as canal cleaning. But Maria persisted, and even held two different offices in the water users' association.

Maria complained to the communal association about her husband's physical abuse, but the members of the association weren't sympathetic; they said the abuse was the result of her not playing her proper role in the home. Nonetheless, after years of putting up with the abuse, she decided to separate from her husband. She didn't pursue a formal divorce, however, because she was afraid she would lose the two assets that made it possible for her to support her children: land and water. To guarantee her control of both, she had to begin by becoming an official member of the community, which manages the communal lands. This entailed that her name, rather than her husband's, be registered. It took her a long time to get the board's acceptance, and Maria had to show that she was responsible for all of the farm and household activities, and had also assumed the public responsibilities of a community farmer. Finally, one of her relatives, a member of the communal board, supported her request for membership, and her petition was successful.

After this battle, Maria then had to become an official member of the *Comisión de Regantes*, the committee responsible for managing irrigation water. This required proof that she is a landholder and head of household, the approval of a government irrigation agency, an official declaration from a local judge stating that she had separated from her husband, and testimonies from the water users' association about her husband's alcohol abuse and irresponsibility. After several years of effort, Maria finally succeeded in gaining official control of the water and land necessary to support her family.

What Do These Cases Tell Us?

Both Jennifer and Maria have assumed the primary responsibility for the well-being of their families, although for different reasons and under different circumstances. Except for the small pension from Jennifer's grandmother, neither woman has a steady, predictable income. Although she occasionally finds some part-time, temporary work, Jennifer has been unable to find a regular job. Maria is a small farmer who earns whatever she can by selling her surplus crops in a local market. Both struggle on a daily basis to provide for their children.

Maria chose to separate from her husband due to his continual abuse, and he provides no financial or moral support for his family. In fact, he has tried to stop Maria from acquiring the resources needed to farm. Jennifer never married, so like Maria she is the de facto head of her household. Both women are part of the growing percentage of female-headed households around the world—domestic units headed by women who are never married, widowed, divorced, or separated. In South Africa, 42 percent of all households are headed by women; in Peru, more than 22 percent. These percentages may be higher in certain regions of each country.[10] The universal pattern is that female-headed households are poorer than those with two parents or one male parent.

Both Jennifer and Maria also experience indirect gender discrimination. They receive some help from their older children in daily reproductive and household maintenance activities, and Jennifer's mother tries to do what she can—but Jennifer's disabled sister adds to the family's difficulties, and her brothers aren't very helpful. Both mothers thus struggle with the "double burden" common to women, especially poor women, around the world.

Jennifer and Maria are further disadvantaged by race or ethnicity. Like the overwhelming majority of South Africans, Jennifer is black. But majority status has not brought economic equality, despite the formal termination of the apartheid regime in the 1990s. By one estimate, 45 percent of female-headed households are below the South African poverty line.[11]

Maria, like approximately one-third of all Peruvians, belongs to an indigenous group and speaks a Quechua dialect.[12] In many ways, her situation is characteristic of indigenous peoples throughout Latin America. Although indigenous peoples constitute only 10 percent of the region's population, they always represent a much higher proportion of the poor. In surveying the status of indigenous peoples throughout Latin America, the World Bank found that despite the declaration by the United Nations of the Indigenous Peoples Decade (1994–2004), the poverty gap with non-indigenous peoples persists, even though education and health care have seen some improvements. Indigenous people recover more slowly from economic crises, and women and children are especially vulnerable. In Peru, indigenous people receive lower wages (if they are employed), have access to fewer services, and are more likely to be poor. Maria's household is one of those without access to drinking water or sewage facilities.

In addition to the structural constraints that are economic and social, Jennifer and Maria confront environmental constraints that make access to water more difficult. Maria's high Andean region is arid; and for centuries, farmers have relied on some type of irrigation. For example, much of the land in the Peruvian highlands is terraced to facilitate plowing and water retention; and Maria has learned to use *composturas*, a long-forgotten system of zigzag irrigation. Jennifer is entirely dependent on the urban infrastructure for water, and South Africa's urban water supply relies on the multi-dam Lesotho Highlands Water Project. The combination of an expanding economy, a growing population, and increased evaporation caused by climate change means that "South Africa is chronically water-stressed."[13]

Maria confronts traditional gender norms that condition her access to water and land. Water laws do not formally discriminate on the basis of gender, but customary norms and practices do. Men are assumed to be the formal decision makers in water users' associations, so women must confront these norms in order to gain access to irrigation rights. Maria was successful, although it took her years of surmounting various hurdles; and in one instance, she needed support from a male relative on the communal board. Still, the people of her village criticize her for breaking with tradition. They call her a *machista*, a woman whose behavior has trespassed "symbolic and normative gender boundaries."[14] Maria's story makes it clear that although important structural constraints affect a woman's access to irrigation rights, agency may overcome many of these—but at a personal cost.

Although the South African constitution guarantees gender equality, and South Africa has a vibrant array of women's rights organizations, traditional norms continue to assign less status to women—for example, in matters of sexual autonomy. It is interesting to note, however, the way in which Jennifer and the other women protesting the water meters manipulated traditional gender expectations by publicly flaunting their dirty underwear in their 2009 march to the mayor's office. Like Maria, Jennifer found a way to exercise agency both by challenging and by circumventing traditional norms.

SOUTH AFRICA AND PERU:
GLOBAL CHANGES AND LOCAL REALITIES

The struggles of Jennifer and Maria mirror many of the struggles of the people around the world who, already confronting multiple burdens, are now facing problems of availability and cost of a fundamental necessity—water. Water scarcity is not a new problem, any more than floods; both have affected societies for millennia. What is new in our era is the way in which water issues have become global-ized. International, government, and local agencies, along with nongovernmental organizations, play a role in the experiences of Jennifer and Maria, and confirm the importance of understanding connections between different levels of organization.

Two dimensions of contemporary neoliberal globalization are notably relevant to our cases. First is the commitment of national governments, typically in response to international pressure, to adopt development policies that reduce national govern-ment expenditures and open domestic markets to international trade and invest-ment. A second dimension of the new global order is the greater emphasis on de-centralization in policy formation and implementation from the national to regional and local levels. As noted in earlier chapters, neoliberal development strategies vary widely from one country to another, with some people benefiting but others left worse off. Those disadvantaged by the changes are less and less suffering silently, as recent grassroots protests in both South Africa and Peru illustrate.

The institutions of globalization have affected local realities in both countries, but in different ways due to varying government policies at the national level. For example, although the World Bank encouraged national strategies to improve greater efficiency and cost recovery in the provision of water and sanitation services in both Peru and South Africa, the former was slower than the latter in implementing legal changes to encourage private investment. Peru has experienced several changes in na-tional governments since the mid-1990s that resulted in shifts in development poli-cies. The frequent changes in Peruvian laws and government structures have resulted in shifting policies at the regional and local levels, few of which have substantially improved access to water for poor farmers. In South Africa, on the other hand, the African National Congress (ANC) has consistently governed; despite turnover in ANC leadership, the overall approach to development has been similar in the past two decades.

United Nations agencies have provided development assistance to both countries over the past two decades, and in some instances these UN affiliates have had a direct impact on local conditions. An example is the role of the International Fund for Ag-ricultural Development in Peru. Finally, multinational corporations are increasingly global players in water distribution projects, as the cases of both South Africa and Peru demonstrate.

South Africa

From the early twentieth century until the early 1990s, South Africa was orga-nized under a system of racial segregation and white domination, which, in the 1940s, became known as apartheid. During this period, the central government pro-vided subsidized services and infrastructure, primarily to whites, but blacks in some townships also received subsidized water and electricity services.[15] In the transition to democratic rule, the ANC initially promised a central role for poverty alleviation and community participation in its 1994 Reconstruction and Development Programme.

The postapartheid constitution of 1996 subsequently guaranteed a right to water to every citizen,[16] a fact that later provided the legal basis for the case that the Johannesburg Coalition against Water Privatization argued in the South African courts.

After it took over the government of South Africa in 1994, the ANC faced increasing political pressure from international organizations such as the World Bank, as well as from domestic sources, to confront the problem of declining state revenues. In response, the government adopted a new market-based development strategy called Growth, Employment and Redistribution (GEAR), which emphasized privatization and international investment. The central government drastically cut intergovernmental transfers to local governments and instituted policies of "cost recovery" for services. The City of Johannesburg entered into public-private partnerships with Johannesburg Water (JW), an affiliate of the global water company Suez, to operate and manage its water system.[17] In 2003, JW began installing prepaid water meters in Phiri Township, Soweto.

Urban blacks in South Africa have a long history of political activism stemming from their resistance activities during the apartheid era. In the current era, many black residents such as Jennifer have joined resistance activities to protest unemployment, crumbling or nonexistent infrastructure, and the increasing commodification of public services such as water. The protests number in the thousands; according to one report, as early as 2005 protests took place in 90 percent of the poorest municipalities in South Africa.[18]

Peru

In the past four decades, Peru has gone through cycles of centralization and decentralization in the provision of water services. In 1990, the administration of then president Alberto Fujimori adopted policies designed to commercialize and privatize the provision of water and sanitation services; and in 1991, the Private Investment Promotion Law (for water and sanitation) was enacted. Over the next two decades, subsequent administrations created, changed, and abolished water administration agencies. For a variety of reasons, it was not until 2005 that the government began to award water and sanitation concessions to private companies. The move toward privatization was supported by the World Bank, as well as by some bilateral government donors.

Over recent decades, a number of UN agencies have provided development assistance to Peru. As noted earlier, the International Fund for Agricultural Development (IFAD), in cooperation with the Peruvian government, has been important for its role in helping to design and craft the MARENASS Project, which was designed to enhance natural resources, food production, and community development in the region where Maria lives. One of the project's findings has been that local farmers do not distinguish between household and farming activities when they think of water and other natural resources. Rather, their vision "begins with their own dwelling and extends outward from there to encompass the garden, animal corrals, farmland, irrigation, organic production and pastures. . . . They have a logical conception of an undivided whole that is the space within which their lives and their productive activities take place."[19] Put differently, the traditional conception of space and activity is holistic. Hence it is logical that no clear distinction is made between water for household and for agricultural use.

Maria took advantage of the community training opportunities provided by MARENASS. However, the project's strategy had a built-in contradiction. It emphasized the recognition and enhancement of traditional community norms at the same time as it provided training in gender awareness. But the community norms privileged men in water and land-use decisions, as did government bureaucrats not engaged in the project. It was only with considerable effort that Maria was able to overcome the structural hurdles, although one may conclude that in the end, she was much better off having participated in the project than if she had not.

Despite Maria's relative success, the scenario for the future does not look promising. "Peru is South America's most water-stressed country," and researchers have identified Peru "as the world's third most vulnerable country to the impacts of climate change."[20] Andean glaciers have shrunk at an alarming rate over the past thirty years, and the stresses in Peru's water supply have been exacerbated by two trends that are grounded in Peruvian engagement in the global economy: the agricultural export economy and mining activities (also designed for export production). Export cropping, which is water-intensive, is centered in Peru's coastal lowlands, but many mining concessions, which are under concession to multinational companies, are located in headwater areas of the Andes and thus threaten the water quality of rivers and aquifers downstream. Many local communities, particularly among the indigenous peoples, are suspicious of both corporations and the central government, and conflicts and protests have risen over the past decade. The protests have yet to reach Maria's village, but it is not implausible to suppose that Maria, like Jennifer, could join an antigovernment protest in the future.

Table 5.1 summarizes several factors that describe the structures within which Jennifer and Maria live. Three indexes illustrate the levels of development and inequality that prevail in South African and Peru: the Human Development Index (HDI), the Gini Index, and the Gender Inequality Index (GII). The HDI and the GII have been developed by the United Nations to determine the progress countries have made in raising the level of human development and "the loss in human development due to inequality between female and male achievements in reproductive health, empowerment and the labour market."[21] The Gini Index is a long-standing measure of the degree of inequality within a country. Life expectancy statistics are included because they show a different dimension of development—the low life expectancy in South Africa and especially the disadvantaged situation of men. Finally, the information on water demonstrates differences between the two countries, as well as between urban and rural areas.

The next section provides more background on the complicated international context of globalization and water that has grown over the past half century. This is

Table 5.1.　Comparative Development Indicators: Peru and South Africa

Development Indicators	Peru	South Africa
Human Development Index Rank (2013)	77	121
Gender Inequality Index Rank (2013)	73	90
Gini Index (2000–2010)	48.1	63.1
Female Life Expectancy at Birth (years, 2005–2010)	75.9	52.1
Male Life Expectancy at Birth (years, 2005–2010)	70.6	50.1
Proportion (%) of urban population with improved drinking water (2010)	91	99
Proportion (%) of rural population with improved drinking water (2010)	65	79

Sources: United Nations Development Programme, 2013 *Human Development Report,* http://hdr.undp.org; UNICEF, *Progress on Drinking Water and Sanitation 2012 Update,* http://www.unicef.org; UN, *World Population Prospects 2010 Revision,* http://esa.un.org/wpp. All data are best estimates for the years indicated.

followed by the feminist responses and the efforts to craft a feminist approach to the global issues of water access and quality.

THE GLOBAL POLITICS OF WATER

A half century ago, international thinking about water reflected the post–World War II optimism about the course of development in Asia, Africa, and Latin America. National governments and international institutions, including the United Nations and the World Bank, adopted a technical approach toward water issues, confident that modern technology and engineering would solve the water problems facing developing countries. For example, the World Bank emphasized large dams and water infrastructure projects when granting loans to the new nations of the South. The UN launched the International Hydrological Decade (1965–1974), which brought together water scientists and managers to promote global research and education on water. The first UN Conference on Water took place in 1977, and the UN designated the 1980s as the International Drinking Water Supply and Sanitation Decade. However, the technical and state-centered approaches proved unsuccessful, failing to meet the goals of universal access to safe drinking water and basic sanitation services by 1990.

By the 1980s, challenges to the prevailing notions of technical solutions to water issues (and development more broadly) were growing. The emergence of a transnational anti-dam movement in the mid-1980s symbolized the new voices in what was quickly becoming an international debate: Political activists, intellectuals, and some policy makers challenged the environmental effects and human displacement caused by large-scale dam and irrigation projects, most of which were funded by international financial institutions. The globalization processes of the past two decades have added questions of sustainability, accountability, and management to the contentious political debate about water. The remainder of this section describes the global water scenario, the primary "players" in the debates and policy making on water, and the role of gender in these debates.

The global politics of water in the twenty-first century raises questions of how water resources should be governed, who should decide, and who should be involved in the implementation of water policies. Gender issues have become visible, but they have been overshadowed by tension between two competing, fundamental perspectives: water as an *economic good* versus water as a *human right*. The dominant orthodox position derives from neoliberal assumptions and views water as an economic good, a natural resource that must be managed efficiently. Those who share this position critique the failure of the state in water management, claiming it has often been inefficient, failing to maintain and upgrade infrastructures and, at the same time, failing to recover the costs of operation. As a result, they advocate market-based solutions ranging from full-cost pricing to privatization of water utilities. The opposing position disputes neoliberal principles and emphasizes water as a human right, opposing water privatization. Those who view water as a human right maintain that water is a common good and that control over water systems must be held by public entities, in the public interest. However, this position is not without its own contradictions because it often falls short of offering practical policies for building and repairing costly infrastructures and may not provide guarantees that—even though public—such entities actually operate in a broad public interest.

People on both sides of this debate generally support decentralization of decision making on matters pertaining to water. Both support, in principle, greater local control, stakeholder participation, and community involvement. Despite these similar positions, the logic and worldview that undergird them differ between the two sides. In the neoliberal perspective, decentralization and local participation improve overall governance and decrease the administrative and financial obligations of central governments. Critics argue that neoliberal approaches to participation depoliticize citizen input and fail to address conflicts of interest between rich and poor, resulting in decisions that benefit the rich and hurt the poor. They also point out that privatized water supply and delivery systems advocated by neoliberals have the effect of diminishing local control in the interests of corporations—often multinational—that are by their nature concerned primarily with profit. The human-right-to-water advocates believe that democratic decision making will lead to pro-poor water policies.

The "Players"

Joining states and international institutions in addressing these questions are organizations of water professionals, transnational corporations in the water business, and transnational networks of activists opposed to water privatization. One of the most influential organizations articulating the interests of water experts at the global level is the International Water Resources Association (IWRA), established in 1972. Two corporations, Veolia and Suez, which dominate the global water industry, formed a trade association, Aquafed, in 2005.[22] Anti-privatization activists form a loosely organized "water justice movement" made up of social movements, NGOs, and trade unions.[23]

One strand of global water politics consists of the creation of and debate over norms, standards, and best practices for the management of water resources. These norms, generally embodying neoliberal values, come out of the reports, conferences, events, and organizations established by international institutions and by multi-stakeholder groups of water professionals from development agencies, private firms, international institutions, and international professional associations.

The UN system has been central to the globalization of water since 1965, when it launched the International Hydrological Decade. One of its initiatives has been to improve coordination between the water-related programs in its various affiliated organizations, including the World Health Organization (WHO), the UN Development Programme (UNDP), and the UN Environmental Program (UNEP), by creating an interagency task force, UN Water, in 2003.

One of the best-known UN initiatives was the International Conference on Water and the Environment in Dublin, Ireland, in 1992. Conference delegates agreed on four guiding principles for water management that have since become integral to international discussions of water issues:

1. Fresh water is a finite and vulnerable resource, essential to sustain life, development, and the environment.
2. Water development and management should be based on a participatory approach, involving users, planners, and policy makers at all levels.
3. Women play a central part in the provision, management, and safeguarding of water.
4. Water has an economic value in all its competing uses and should be recognized as an economic good.[24]

Shortly thereafter, Agenda 21, the report of the 1992 United Nations Conference on Environment and Development (UNCED), reinforced these principles of sustainability, participation, the central role of women, and water as an economic good, bringing them together in the concept developed by water professionals of "integrated water resources management" (IWRM), a holistic, multi-sectoral approach to water policy.[25] It is notable that both the Dublin Conference and UNCED, although emphasizing the importance of sustainability, stakeholder participation, and the role of women—positions with which almost all players in water politics concur—simultaneously emphasized the economic value of water. This last principle is at the core of the differences between the neoliberal and human rights perspectives described earlier.

Other influential sources of neoliberal principles in the water sector are the World Bank and the World Water Forum. The World Bank, in a 1993 report, announced its new approach to water based on the "treatment of water as an economic good, combined with decentralized management and delivery structures, greater reliance on pricing, and fuller participation by stakeholders."[26] The triennial, multi-stakeholder World Water Forum (WWF) has roots in the International Water Resources Association. In 1996 the IWRA created the World Water Council, a think tank composed of water elites from international and national development agencies, the private sector, and professional associations. The WWC, in turn, set up the WWF, a triennial conference of water professionals, along with a parallel conference of government water ministers. At the second WWF in 2000, a report was released calling for expanding investment in water-supply infrastructure primarily through "privatization and full-cost pricing of water."[27]

Reinforcing the neoliberal tenor of international water organizations, both private and public, is what Ken Conca calls the "visible fist" of water marketization, "the process of creating the economic and policy infrastructure for treating water as a marketed commodity."[28] Two factors have been central to the push for treating water as a commodity: the World Bank and IMF requirement that developing countries accept water privatization as a condition for receiving loans; and the 1994 General Agreement on Trade and Services (GATS), which created opportunities for transnational corporations to enter into national markets to provide water services. In this way, World Bank, IMF, and international trade policies together reinforce neoliberal norms, which, without this pressure, might otherwise have little effect on loan recipients. Other factors promoting water marketization have been the efforts of transnational water corporations to expand investment and the necessity for governments to attract capital investment when public financing for infrastructure projects is unavailable. Thus it is not surprising that both South Africa and Peru have been responsive to privatization agendas as part of their broader development strategies.

Although treating water as a market commodity remains the dominant agenda in global water politics, a vigorous opposition has emerged that recalls the earlier anti-dam movement. Beginning with local protests against privatization in the 1990s, national and transnational activist networks have expanded. They meet annually at the World Social Forum, orchestrate demonstrations at World Water Forums, mount campaigns focused on GATS negotiations on liberalization of services, and use the Internet as a central tool for communication and network building. It is this anti-privatization movement that has framed water as a human right, articulating "a positive, people-centered vision of globalization."[29] Upon occasion women have played a noteworthy role in the anti-privatization movement. Their activities have been particularly significant since 1999 in Latin American and African protests that have led to the cancellation of state contracts with global water companies.[30]

In recent years, the UN and a number of states have endorsed the idea of water as a human right. In 2002, the UN Committee on Economic, Social and Cultural Rights issued an interpretation of the International Covenant of Economic, Social and Cultural Rights that there is "a human right to water," and that "Water should be treated as a social and cultural good, and not primarily as an economic good."[31] By 2009, thirty national governments had enacted constitutional or legal provisions establishing a human right to water.[32] On July 28, 2010, the UN General Assembly officially recognized access to clean water and sanitation as a human right.[33]

Private-sector water proponents have responded to the growing strength of the anti-privatization movement in several ways. The World Bank has softened (but not abandoned) its commitment to privatization, and in its 2003 water sector guidelines emphasized public-private partnerships.[34] A 2006 World Bank study acknowledged the increased recognition by international institutions and national governments of the human right to water.[35] Meanwhile, the large private water corporations have found that providing water to the poor majority in cities of the South is not cost-effective, and they ask for government subsidies in order to extend water service to all.[36] Aquafed, the International Federation of Private Water Operators, asserts that it supports the right to water, declaring that its members are the appropriate means for governments to implement this right.[37]

An examination of the events surrounding the Fifth World Water Forum in Istanbul, March 16–22, 2009, offers some insight into the contemporary state of global water politics and how women have been only partially successful in efforts to engender the process. According to the Forum organizers, more than thirty-three thousand participants from 192 countries attended.[38] Presenters at the official sessions included UN agencies, the World Bank and regional financial institutions, national government agencies, research institutes, Aquafed, and professional associations. The themes addressed included governance and management, finance, human development, capacity development, and the implications of the global economic crisis for water.

Envisioned as a meeting place for professionals, the Fifth WWF (like earlier forums) instead became an arena where the conflicting agendas in global water politics played out.[39] On the first day the police turned water cannons on three hundred Turkish activists protesting at the forum entrance. Water justice activists characterized the WWF as a trade show for the water industry. They organized several alternative meetings, including a Water Tribunal, a Peoples Water Forum, a Water Justice Conference, and an Alternative Water Forum to denounce water privatization and demand that water be considered a human right. The official conference culminated in a ministerial declaration that made no mention of water as a human right, instead calling access to safe drinking water and sanitation a basic human need. Twenty-five governments from the Global South signed a counter-declaration recognizing a human right to water, and sixteen governments called for the UN "to develop a global water forum within the framework of the United Nations, based on the principles of democracy, full participation, equity, transparency and social inclusion," two demands of the water justice activists.[40]

SEEKING A FEMINIST APPROACH

Feminist scholars, activists, and practitioners engaged with gender and water issues have used three distinct arguments.[41] First, women have been left out of development and must be integrated into development planning. This argument grows out of a WID perspective, which, in turn, reflects a liberal feminist theoretic framework. Second, it is argued that women are closer to nature than men, which makes them better stewards of natural resources. This argument reflects an ecofeminist perspective that is grounded in difference feminism. Third, the achievement of gender equality requires addressing the power relations of gender as well as race and class in particular contexts; it is insufficient to follow a single strategy for integrating women into development projects. This argument is based on a gender and development (GAD) perspective inspired by diversity feminism.

The WID perspective on water was dominant in the 1970s when feminist scholars and practitioners documented the drudgery involved in the work of women and girls in water procurement. In the 1980s ecofeminist and WID arguments were put forth in advocacy of women's participation in water management projects, while GAD arguments tended to target broader reforms, such as granting women land and water rights.

In 1990s the growth of international women's movements led to a focus on women's rights in development that was consistent with all of these approaches. The high point for global feminism was the 1995 Beijing Women's Conference. The Beijing *Platform for Action* advocated "gender mainstreaming," an approach intended "to make the state an agent of transformative change for women" by embedding gender equality into the entire developmental planning process.[42] However, gender mainstreaming has been a disappointment for feminists, as it has often come to mean counting the number of women in decision-making positions rather than measuring the extent of gender analysis in policy formulation. Multilateral and bilateral foreign assistance programs in water have emphasized the inclusion of women in water projects, but they have not addressed the broader structural issues disempowering women. For example, the February 2005 "Women and Water" issue of a UN publication, self-described as "published to promote the goals of the Beijing Declaration and the Platform for Action," highlighted the need to include women in water-project design and implementation in order to improve project effectiveness.[43] Although the "Women and Water" issue used GAD language, it did not raise the question of whether the commodification of water might be a major obstacle to women's rights to water.

Since the 1970s, the UN has taken a leading role in bringing gender issues into the global discussion of water management norms and practices. As early as the First World Conference on Women in 1975, one of the resolutions in the *World Plan of Action* addressed water: "Improved easily accessible, safe water supplies (including wells, dams, catchments, piping, etc.), sewage disposal and other sanitation measures should be provided both to improve health conditions of families and to reduce the burden of carrying water which falls mainly on women and children."[44]

The Dublin Principles mentioned women's central role in water management, and the report of the 1992 UNCED Conference, Agenda 21, recommended "enhancement of the role of women in water resources planning and management" through women's participation in these processes.[45] A global network of feminist activists was able to get an entire chapter on women's roles in sustainable development written from an ecofeminist perspective added to Agenda 21, creating increased visibility for gender issues in environmental management.[46] In the twenty-first century, female water professionals increasingly have played a role in engendering the global discussion on water issues through their own associations and in women's caucuses at the World Water Forum. Two important global women's networks of water professionals committed to gender mainstreaming are the Gender and Water Alliance (GWA), formed at the 2000 World Water Forum; and the Women for Water Partnership (WfWP), formed at the 2002 UN Conference on Sustainable Development in Johannesburg.[47]

In spite of gender-inclusive principles in international conference documents and donor commitments to women's full involvement in water management, feminist scholars writing in the mid-1990s found a large gap between policy principles and policy implementation, noting the lack of gender analysis or women's participation in most water projects and arguing that privatization weakened women's roles in water management.[48] Nevertheless, recent reforms in water policies have incorporated women into local decision making in some cases. For example, India has adopted rural water governance policies featuring neoliberal principles of decentralization and user fees. A study of programs in two Indian states found that a 50 percent mandate for women's representation in *pani samitis* (water committees) responsible for domestic water use led to the active participation of women, especially where NGOs were active in mobilizing women.[49] In contrast, lower levels of women's representation in the water users' associations responsible for irrigation were associated with a lack of participation by women. The study criticized the narrow scope for decision making of the *pani samitis* in a context "where policies of privatization, pricing and centralized, technocratic delivery systems (large dams, pipelines and the Indian state's river linking project) dominate the political discourse on water management."[50] In short, the degree and effectiveness of women's participation in water decision making varies by context.

Today, two camps generally divide feminist scholars, practitioners, and activists who emphasize gender equality in the area of water. In the first school of thought, the main objective is to amplify the voice of women in water management at all levels in order to empower women. Even here, some division exists between those who see women's participation in local water management associations as always positive and those who are more circumspect, asking questions such as whether participation increases women's workload, improves women's lives, and/or empowers women in particular contexts. Feminists adopting WID and ecofeminist positions tend to be more positive, whereas those espousing a GAD position tend to be more circumspect. The second school of thought sees the main objective as fighting water privatization and advancing the idea of water as a human right. These divisions played out in the 2009 World Water Forum described above.

Gender advocates participated in both the official and alternative conferences but had some difficulty creating visibility for gender issues at both venues. At the official conference, the Gender and Water Alliance and Women for Water Partnership focused attention on gender issues and women's participation by creating a Women and Gender Coalition, organizing a women's preparatory conference in Istanbul in March 2009, and holding daily Women's Caucus meetings during the conference.[51] Their organization of the seventeen gender-related panel sessions showed that GWA and WfWP had gained a foothold in the Forum structure. There was also an awareness of women's marginalization within WWF leadership. Speaking to a reporter, Joke Muylwijk, executive director of GWA, pointed out that "the opening ceremony of the 5th World Water Forum was conducted by men only and out of 19 members on the forum steering committee there are no women."[52] Nevertheless, gender advocates took advantage of the WWF platform to make recommendations for better gender monitoring of water projects, gender mainstreaming, land rights for women, and increased participation of women at all levels of decision making on water. Gender advocates at the official conference also supported the human right to water. At the close of the Forum, Sara Ahmed, chair of GWA on behalf of the Women and Gender Coalition and "Women Major Group," criticized the ministerial declaration, stating that it "seems to forget earlier commitments made by governments to insure the right to water and sanitation."[53]

At the alternative conferences, some panels focused on gender and water issues. Sara Ahmed spoke on gender-water justice struggles at the March 18 Water Justice Conference; and a panel of women from India, South Africa, Germany, and Turkey talked about water and women at the Alternative Water Forum.[54] But the focus of the water justice movement is not on gender issues per se, but on the human right to water and democratic control of water policy. Within that framework, water justice advocates acknowledge gender (and ethnic and class) discrimination in existing water policies and call for equitable access to water for all marginalized groups, including women, and the participation in water decision making by women and other groups in civil society. "The Peoples Water Forum Declaration 2009" makes no references to women but does reaffirm the principles of the 2006 "Joint Declaration of Movements in Defense of Water," which committed "[t]o value the contribution of women, indigenous and aboriginal peoples, youth and all people incorporating the defense of their rights in the development of models that show that another form of water management is possible."[55]

CONCLUSION

The events surrounding the 2009 WWF illustrate two contrasting feminist strategies. Women leaders and gender issues were visible at both the mainstream WWF (an "inclusionary" strategy) and the alternative forums organized by the water justice movement (a "transformation" strategy). However, the 2009 events also demonstrate that gender issues tend to remain marginal, albeit in different ways, in both strategies. Women's organizations were in charge of sessions examining gender issues at the

WWF, but these were placed in a separate section of the conference program, most likely attended only by those already interested in gender issues. The water justice movement claims that women and gender issues are important, but they have been subsumed in the broader coalition fighting for the human right to water. Inclusion and transformation have been undertaken in an "either/or" instead of a "both/and" manner, which has compromised efforts to ensure that social justice includes women's voices and that gender perspectives are sensitive to issues of class and race—that is, that they reflect a diversity perspective.

Even if the human right to water is assured, issues remain about how water is supplied and paid for, at what levels (national, local) these decisions are made, and by whom. A recent study found that poor women were excluded from decision making in both state-led and public-private partnership water-governance systems in Dhaka and Manila.[56] These and other findings suggest that despite the many examples articulating the cause of women in the global politics of water, the effect at the local level is uneven. A more successful strategy might be to emphasize gender-sensitive democratic accountability, universal access to clean water at affordable prices, and ecological sustainability as solutions to water politics.[57] Thus gender advocates should focus on creating strategies that transcend the inclusion–transformation dichotomy and that promote environmental stewardship.

A few cases exemplify successful strategies that have both bridged this dualism and encourage conservation. The case of the Self-Employed Women's Association (SEWA) in India is one such example of rural water management (see the description of SEWA in chapter 6). SEWA has a long history of working with poor women in the western Indian state of Gujarat. Although the organization began its work in cities, it has branched out to rural areas. In the arid countryside of Gujarat, SEWA initiated a campaign to augment existing water supplies through practices such as harvesting rainwater, improving the water supply infrastructure by maintaining and repairing pipes and hand pumps, and increasing women's awareness of water issues. By 2004, SEWA had trained 2,500 female "barefoot technicians" and facilitated the creation of village-level water committees that were at least 50 percent female.[58] The significance of this project is twofold. It demonstrates that decentralized decision making can be both practical (from the standpoint of financing and maintaining water infrastructures) and gender sensitive and contributing to the empowerment of women. In this way, it also bridges the gap between those who maintain that women need to be full participants in developing resources and those who argue that a strategy of grassroots participation by poor people puts into practice the philosophy of water as a human right.

An example of urban water management that appears to be democratic, transparent, and sustainable is the municipal water system of Porto Alegre, a city of four million in Brazil. This system is operated by an autonomous city agency, DMAE.[59] Internationally recognized for excellent water quality, DMAE provides 99 percent of city residents with access to water and sewerage services. The citizens of Porto Alegre engage in a participatory budgeting process; and the Deliberative Council, made up of representatives from thirteen civil society groups, representing constituencies such as medicine, business, neighborhoods, and municipal workers, must approve water policies on an ongoing basis. Porto Alegre demonstrates that public management can work well, with democratic decentralized decision making a key to success. Although women participate in this process, the civil society groups that send representatives to the Deliberative Council do not include women's organizations. Likewise, no long-term effects of women's involvement are evident. The enhancement of women's voices would engender the democratic process in urban water governance in Porto Alegre and might provide a model that would benefit poor women elsewhere, such as Jennifer in Johannesburg.

Existing strategies of decision making for irrigation are more problematic. Women's access to water for crop irrigation continues to be limited throughout the world. Water users' associations, the bodies that make decisions about access to irrigation water, are typically male-dominated. The example of Maria in Peru illustrates how important participation in a water users' association can be. Many women lack land rights—an obstacle to participation in irrigation decision making, which usually is reserved for property owners. Ideally, irrigation systems should be designed to address the needs of all farmers—men and women—and water user associations should include all those with either property or use rights. The gender division of labor means that women bring different experiences to decision making about water. With responsibility for both household and agricultural water use, women tend to see water needs in an integrated manner. For example, women might favor a continuous flow of irrigation water, so they can wash clothes and water crops, whereas men, without the household responsibilities, might favor rotational irrigation.[60] Researchers have found that even when women are included in meetings of water users' associations, they are reluctant to speak. Thus gender-sensitive changes need to go beyond the inclusion of women in these associations to foster transformations capable of "structurally addressing gender inequities."[61]

NOTES

1. Quoted in Deepa Narayan, Robert Chambers, Meera K. Shah, and Patti Petesch, *Voices of the Poor: Crying Out for Change* (New York: Oxford University Press, for the World Bank, 2000), 72.

2. For water consumption information, see the Water Footprint Network website at http://www.waterfootprint.org.

3. Narayan et al., *Voices of the Poor*, 73–75.

4. Isha Ray, "Women, Water, and Development," *Annual Review of Environment and Resources* 32 (2007): 421–49.

5. Margreet Zwarteveen and Vivienne Bennett, "The Connection between Gender and Water Management," in *Opposing Currents: The Politics of Water and Gender in Latin America,*

ed. Vivienne Bennett, Sonia Dávila-Poblete, and María Nieves Rico (Pittsburgh: University of Pittsburgh Press, 2005), 14.

    6. This case study is drawn from Antina von Schnitzler, "Citizenship Prepaid: Water, Calculability, and Techno-Politics in South Africa," *Journal of South African Studies* 34, no. 4 (2008): 899–917; David McKinley, "The Struggle against Water Privatisation in South Africa," *Water Justice*, September 17, 2004, http://www.waterjustice.org/?mi=1&res_id=77; Patrick Bond, "The Battle over Water in South Africa," *Africa Files* (February 2004), http://67.199.57.196/article.asp?ID=4564; and "Freedom Flows in South Africa," *Multinational Monitor* 30, no. 1 (July/August 2008): 8–9, http://www.multinationalmonitor.org/mm2008/072008/front.html.

    7. Von Schnitzler, "Citizenship Prepaid," 914. An empirical study of actual water usage in a South African township found that the average person used at least four times the limit set for free water: J. A. Smith, "How Much Water Is Enough? Domestic Metered Water Consumption and Free Basic Water Volumes: The Case of Eastwood, Pietermaritzburg," *Water SA* 36, no. 5 (October 2010): 600.

    8. Louise McAuliffe, "Bloody Underwear Protest in Johannesburg—To Demand Free Water," *Sowetan*, February 12, 2009, available from Abahlali baseMjondolo, http://www.abahlali.org/node/4796.

    9. This case study is adapted primarily from Juana Vera Delgado and Margreet Zwarteveen, "The Public and Private Domain of the Everyday Politics of Water," *International Feminist Journal of Politics* 9, no. 4 (December 2007): 503–11; and descriptions of the region from the International Fund for Agricultural Development (see note 19).

    10. General statistics are from the United Nations database, GENDERSTATS.

    11. Paula Armstrong, Bongisa Lekezwa, and Krige Siebrits, "Poverty in South Africa: A Profile Based on Recent Household Surveys," Stellenbosch Economic Working Papers, April 4, 2008, 13.

    12. "Indigenous" in Peru is defined by the language spoken by household head and/or spouse. Where the head uses an indigenous language, such as Quechua, more frequently than Spanish, the percentage is about 25 percent. But as many as 48 percent are considered indigenous when including the households in which either the household head and/or the head's spouse has parents or grandfathers who spoke an indigenous mother tongue. Gillette Hall and Harry Patrinos, "Peru Highlights," in *Indigenous Peoples, Poverty and Human Development in Latin America, 1994–2004* (World Bank, 2004), http://web.worldbank.org/WBSITE/EXTERNAL/COUNTRIES/LACEXT/0,,contentMDK:20505839~pagePK:146736~piPK:146830~theSitePK:258554,00.html.

    13. UN Office for the Coordination of Humanitarian Affairs, *IRIN News*, "South Africa: Clock Ticks towards Water Scarcity," May 22, 2009, retrieved October 15, 2009, http://www.irinnews.org/Report/84517/SOUTH-AFRICA-Clock-ticks-towards-water-scarcity.

    14. Delgado and Zwarteveen, "Public and Private Domain," 507.

    15. David A. McDonald, "No Money, No Service," *Alternatives Journal* 28, no. 2 (Spring 2002): 16–20.

    16. Sean Flynn and Danwod Mzikenge Chirwa, "The Constitutional Implications of Commercializing Water in South Africa," in *The Age of Commodity: Water Privatization in Southern Africa*, ed. David A. McDonald and Greg Ruiters (London: Earthscan, 2005), 59–76. Article 27 of the Constitution states that everyone has the right to sufficient water; and the state must ensure, through reasonable legislation, the realization of this right.

17. The French-based multinational company has gone through a number of organizational changes in the past twenty years. In 2008, the publicly traded company known as Suez Environnement was established to invest and manage water and wastewater treatment. See http://www.suez-environnement.com.

18. Patrick Heller, "Democratic Deepening in India and South Africa," *Journal of Asian and African Studies* 44, no. 1 (2009): 123–49. Heller notes that almost six thousand protests were held during the 2004/2005 year.

19. "Republic of Peru: Management of Natural Resources in the Southern Highlands Project (MARENASS)," http://www.ifad.org/evaluation/public_html/eksyst/doc/agreement/pl/pe386.htm; and IFAD, "Gender and Water," paper prepared by Robina Wahaj, http://www.ifad.org/gender/thematic/water/gender_water.pdf.

20. Anthony Bebbington and Mark Williams, "Water and Mining Conflicts in Peru," *Mountain Research and Development* 28, no. 3/4 (August–November 2008): 190–95, http://www.bioone.org/toc/mred/28/3%2F4.

21. UNDP, Human Development Reports, Gender Inequality Index (GII), http://hdr.undp.org/en/statistics/gii.

22. Ann Christin Sjolander Holland, *The Global Water Business: Corporations Versus People* (New York: Zed Books, 2005); see also the Aquafed website, http://www.aquafed.org.

23. Philipp Terhorst, "'Reclaiming Public Water': Changing Sector Policy through Globalization from Below," *Progress in Development Studies* 8, no. 1 (2008): 103–15; and Paul Nelson and Ellen Dorsey, "New Rights Advocacy in a Global Public Domain," *European Journal of International Relations* 13, no. 2 (2007): 187–216. Organizations in this movement include the Blue Planet Project, http://www.blueplanetproject.net; the Public Citizen's Water for All Campaign, http://www.citizen.org; the Inter-American Network for the Defense of the Right to Water; La Red Vida, http://www.laredvida.org/noticias.php?tipo_noticia=Noticia; and Public Services International, http://www.world-psi.org.

24. The Dublin Statement on Water and Sustainable Development, http://www.un-documents.net/h2o-dub.htm.

25. UNCED, Agenda 21, http://sustainabledevelopment.un.org/content/documents/Agenda21.pdf. The World Bank, UNDP, and the Swedish International Development Agency created the Global Water Partnership in 1996 to implement IWRM principles in water management. Ken Conca, *Governing Water: Contentious Transnational Politics and Global Institution-Building* (Cambridge, MA: MIT Press, 2006), 150.

26. World Bank, *Water Resources Management* (Washington, DC, 1993), 10.

27. Conca, *Governing Water*, 1. The report, *World Water Security, A Framework for Action*, was prepared by the Global Water Partnership.

28. Conca, *Governing Water*, 215.

29. Conca, *Governing Water*, 248.

30. Nina Laurie, "Gender Water Networks: Femininity and Masculinity in Water Politics in Bolivia," *International Journal of Urban and Regional Research* 35, no. 1 (2011): 172–88; and Michael Goldman, "How 'Water for All!' Policy Became Hegemonic: The Power of the World Bank and Its Transnational Policy Networks," *Geoforum* 38, no. 5 (2007): 786–800.

31. UN Economic and Social Council, General Comment No. 15, November 29, 2002, 2, 5, http://www2.ohchr.org/english/issues/water/docs/CESCR_GC_15.pdf.

32. Yigal Schleifer, "Is Access to Clean Water a Basic Human Right?," *Christian Science Monitor*, March 19, 2009, http://www.csmonitor.com/2009/0319/p06s01-woeu.html.

33. "General Assembly Declares Access to Clean Water and Sanitation Is a Human Right," UN News Centre, July 28, 2010, http://www.un.org/apps/news/story.asp?NewsID=35456& Cr=sanitation&Cr1.

34. Conca, *Governing Water*, 233.

35. M. A. Salman and Daniel D. Bradlow, *Regulatory Frameworks for Water Resource Management: A Comparative Study* (Washington, DC: World Bank, 2006), 158–60.

36. Goldman, "How 'Water for All!' Policy Became Hegemonic," 796.

37. Aquafed, "Key Messages for the Istanbul Water Forum," March 17, 2009, http://www .aquafed.org/pdf/KeyMessagesforWWF5_Press%20Release_Final_Pd_ENG_2009-03-17 .pdf.

38. Fifth World Water Forum, "Bridging Divides for Water," http://www.worldwater forum5.org/index.php?id=1870&L=0%2522%2520onfo.

39. This section is based on coverage of the Fifth WWF by activist organizations: Hilmi Toros, "Development: Troubled Waters Hard to Bridge," *IPS (Inter Press Service)*, March 22, 2009, http://ipsnews.net/news.asp?idnews=46227; and Jeff Conant, "Fifth World Water Forum Marked by Violence and Repression," *Alternet*, March 17, 2009, http://www.alternet.org/water/132066/fifth_world_water_forum_marked_by_violence_and_repression.

40. Briefing on the World Water Forum, *Wiser Earth*, March 23, 2009. Retrieved June 5, 2009, from http://www.wiserearth.org/article/dcc22209c42d53bdafc5ea19b9891c95.

41. For a discussion of WID, ecofeminist, and GAD perspectives on environmental issues, see "Part 1," *The Women, Gender and Development Reader*, ed. Nalini Visvanathan et al. (Atlantic Highlands, NJ: Zed Books, 1997), 17–32, 54–74.

42. Ramya Subrahmanian, "Making Sense of Gender in Shifting Institutional Contexts: Some Reflections on Gender Mainstreaming," in *Feminisms in Development Contradictions, Contestations and Challenges*, ed. Andrea Cornwall, Elizabeth Harrison, and Ann Whitehead (New York: Zed Books, 2007), 112.

43. Division for the Advancement of Women, United Nations, "Women and Water," February 2005, at http://www.un.org/womenwatch/daw/public/Feb05.pdf.

44. In Irene Tinker and Michele Bo Bramsen, eds., *Women and World Development* (Overseas Development Council, 1976), 208.

45. UNCED Agenda 21, chap. 18, 12, n.

46. Mary Haney, "Women's NGOs at UN Conferences: The 1992 Rio Conference on the Environment as a Watershed Event," *Journal of Women, Politics and Policy* 27, no. 1/2 (2005): 181–87; and UNCED, Agenda 21, chap. 24.

47. Information on these organizations can be found on their websites, http://womenfor water.org/openbaar/index.php and www.genderandwater.org.

48. Frances Cleaver and Katja Jobes, "Donor Policies and Gender in the Water and Sanitation Sector," *Natural Resources Forum* 20, no. 2 (1996): 111–16; and Christine van Wijk, Ester de Lange, and David Saunders, "Gender Aspects in the Management of Water," *Natural Resources Forum* 20, no. 2 (1996): 91–110.

49. Seema Kulkarni, "Women and Decentralised Water Governance: Issues, Challenges and the Way Forward," *Economic and Political Weekly* 66, no. 18 (2011): 64–72.

50. Kulkarni, "Women and Decentralised Water Governance," 72.

51. Women's summary report, http://www.worldwaterforum5.org/fileadmin/WWF5/ Preparatory_Process/Major_Groups/Major_Groups_Women_Summary.pdf.

52. Tasha Eichenseher, "Critical Role of Women in World Water Issues Is Missing, Advocates Say," *Natgeo Newswatch*, March 20, 2009. Retrieved June 5, 2009, from http://blogs .nationalgeographic.com/blogs/news/chiefeditor/2009/03/women-and-water-issues.html.

53. European Water Partnership, "Women Major Group Call in Istanbul: 'Stop the Word Game, Implement the Right to Water & Sanitation,'" March 25, 2009, http://www.ewp .eu/571/women-major-group-call-in-istanbul-stop-the-word-game-implement-the-right-to -water-sanitation.

54. Water Justice, conference-seminar, part of the "No to Commercialisation of Water" program taking place during the Fifth World Water Forum, Istanbul, March 16–22, 2009, http://www.concertacion.info/documentos/19.pdf.

55. For the 2009 Declaration, see http://worldwaterforum.blogspot.com/2009/03/ peoples-water-forum-declaration-2009.html; for the 2006 Declaration, see http://www.blue planetproject.net/documents/Joint_Declaration_Water_Mexico_2006.pdf.

56. Sayeed Iftekhar Ahmed, *Water for Poor Women: Quest for an Alternative Paradigm* (Lanham, MD: Lexington Books, 2013).

57. See, for example, Karen Bakker, *Privatizing Water: Governance Failure and the World's Urban Water Crisis* (Ithaca, NY: Cornell University Press, 2010).

58. Smita Mishra Panda, "Women's Collective Action and Sustainable Water Management: Case of SEWA's Water Campaign in Gujarat, India," CAPRi Working Paper, no. 61 (October 2006), http://www.genderandwater.org/content/download/8896/58996/file/capriwp61.pdf.

59. David Hall et al., "Water in Porto Alegre, Brazil: Accountable, Effective, Sustainable, Democratic," (2002), Public Services International Research Unit (University of Greenwich), http://www.psiru.org/reports/2002-08-W-dmae.pdf.

60. Vivienne Bennett et al., "Water and Gender: The Unexpected Connection That Really Matters," *Journal of International Affairs* 61, no. 2 (Spring/Summer 2008): 113.

61. Rhodante Ahlers, "From Increasing Participation to Establishing Rights: Evading the Gender Question in Water Resources Management," EMPOWERS Regional Symposium: End-Users Ownership and Involvement in IWRM, November 13–17, 2005, Cairo, Egypt.

6

Debates and Dilemmas: Work

Working is an inseparable part of human life. All of us work, have worked, or will work during our lives. Work, however, has different meanings for each of us; it varies by age and physical capacity, by gender, place, and class. Work may be paid or unpaid, and usually it is a combination of the two. For example, many people who work for an income also perform many household or farm duties that are essential to survival, but for which they receive no money.

STRUCTURE

Throughout most of the world, the way in which people work has changed dramatically in the past two centuries. The processes of development that first emerged in Europe and later spread across the globe have transformed both the purposes and the conditions of labor. In earlier chapters we pointed out that development, as we have come to know it, was defined by structures that both enabled and circumscribed the reality of modern work. Capitalism and liberalism led to the private ownership of property by individuals and corporations. For some people, this meant that for the first time in history, they could farm land that they owned and controlled. Others could only sell their labor, often in degrading conditions. Over time, improvements in material consumption spread, and these improvements justified for many the negative consequences of the new systems of production—consequences that included human exploitation and environmental destruction. By the mid-twentieth century in industrial capitalist economies, most individuals working in corporations, factories, and government had secure wage contracts and some level of social protection (health, unemployment, and retirement benefits); and their workplaces were subject to government regulation of wages and working conditions. These jobs constituted what was characterized as the formal economy, which was seen as a defining characteristic of the modern world.

The nature of work continues to evolve in the twenty-first century due to changes in the structure of international production. Technology and globalization are driving the changes, as they have in the past. We noted in introducing the topic of globalization that this is not a new phenomenon. Today's global systems were preceded by European voyages of exploration, trade, colonialism, and production processes.

Globalization in the twenty-first century is defined by four characteristics that are central to our study of work. The first trend is the internationalization of production, which has been under way for decades, but which has accelerated and fragmented. Transnational corporations are increasingly large and complex. Investment decisions, marketing, procurement, production, and assembling may occur in different places around the globe, making it more difficult to address quality control or working conditions. For example, a study of the Apple iPhone4 discovered that the phone was designed in the United States and manufactured in China, but the parts came from at least six other countries.[1]

An associated trend is what is commonly known as "outsourcing." Facilitated by sophisticated computer and information technologies, outsourcing leads to the rapid loss of jobs in some parts of the world and the creation of new jobs in other places. Jobs may shift suddenly, with the result that outsourcing is generally accompanied by job insecurity, even for those who initially benefit by the movement to new regions or countries.

The third noticeable trend is the significance of international migration. As in the cases of international capitalism and technological change, migration is not new. Large-scale migration, particularly during the past two centuries, was central to the development of industrialization and plantation agriculture. It made possible much of the economic growth in the United States, for example. However, international migration today is different in both quality and quantity. There are more migrants, moving in multiple directions, taking on new responsibilities. International migrants are almost evenly divided by gender, but men and women do different work. To illustrate, one characteristic of today's globalization and migration is the creation of the international "care chain," in which women have assumed positions around the globe as nannies, nurses, and teachers.

The fourth characteristic of contemporary globalization is the entry of new "players" into positions of power. Asian countries such as China, for example, increasingly drive globalization not just as producers, but also as consumers, bankers, and decision makers. In certain economic sectors, other new players, such as Russia or Brazil, are important in ways that undermine the long dominance of Western Europe and North America. Our study of the intersection of globalization, development, and gender must be sensitive to this new political economy.

AGENCY

In this chapter, our discussion of work in the twenty-first century distinguishes between four sectors: factory work, agriculture, professional and technical, and the growing category of informal labor. Informal labor may resemble family work and may be done in the home (for example, piecework sewing). But often it is carried out in small workshops, the street (as with petty vendors), or in the homes of others. In each instance, we are attentive to the interplay between structure and agency as they affect workers' lives. Workers exercise agency when they are able to choose between alternative employments: They may upgrade their skills, quit one job and take another, move to a new place, or protest working conditions. In all instances, their decisions are framed by the structures within which they live, as well as their own capabilities. In our discussion of work, we are guided by a number of questions regarding the interplay between agency and structure, particularly as it affects the quality of lives that workers are able to lead.

GENDER IN THE WORKPLACE

The dominant question is the nature of gender-specific issues in the workplace. In some instances, women's work, in particular, verges on invisibility. Earlier generations, for example, typically referred to the farmer as "he," overlooking the reality of women's work in farming throughout the world and its dominant role in sub-Saharan subsistence agriculture. Feminist scholarship, the "WID-GAD debate" examined in chapter 2, the depletion of female labor by AIDS and other diseases, and the demand for enhanced food production have all contributed to raising awareness of women's vital role in agriculture. Nonetheless, in other sectors of work, such as the global care chain, women's roles are poorly understood or largely invisible.

An additional gender-specific issue is the so-called double day that women typically confront in reconciling work and family roles. Although this issue has received a great deal of attention in the United States, where public support for child care is minimal, it is familiar throughout the world. As more women have entered the paid labor force and must leave home in order to work, child and elder care may suffer. Feminists around the world have long argued that men should assume a larger share of reproductive labor, including procuring and preparing food, cleaning, or caring for other family members. However, established gender patterns of labor are slow to change, and the dilemma of reconciling unpaid work in the family with paid work persists.

Harassment of workers is also a long-standing issue. Supervisors may harass workers for a variety of reasons, including lifestyle choices or political activity (especially union organizing). Women, in particular, are particularly vulnerable to sexual harassment, which may be blatant (sex in exchange for job security) or subtle (such as unequal access to information). In most of Europe and North America, laws and policies have been crafted in the past several decades to combat sexual harassment in public and private institutions; and female workers themselves are increasingly aware of their rights and willing to exercise agency in challenging harassment. However, in much of the world and in quasi-invisible work settings in the Global North (e.g., domestic labor), both blatant and subtle harassment continues.

The Race to the Bottom?

For most people, work is not a choice but a necessity, even when they are able to exercise some agency in the type of work they do. In those instances where some choice is involved, we ask whether—and to what extent—paid work is empowering. The answer to this question is complex and clearly depends on both structural and personal factors. Paid work makes it possible to buy things that people need and want, thus enhancing their capabilities to do other things. For many, work is simply a survival strategy. For others, it is not essential to survival, but it leads to improvements in material consumption or personal esteem despite possible trade-offs in terms of a sense of guilt ("abandoning" one's children), family disharmony, or health problems.

Linked to the question of trade-offs in paid work is a second issue. Does globalization generate improved work opportunities, particularly for women, or does it accelerate the "race to the bottom"? If one looks at the structures of production, global wage competition is unrelenting: There is always cheaper labor somewhere. At the same time, a job in an outsourced industry—to take one example—may be an opportunity to escape an unwanted marriage or a worse job in farming or cleaning. In one study of girls and young women who work in the coastal factories of southeast China, for example, the author found that the workers tolerated long hours, loneliness, and arduous working conditions in dreary factories and dormitories in exchange for a vibrant consumer lifestyle and escape from boring villages.[2]

LEVELS OF ANALYSIS

Throughout the world, workers experience conflicts of various kinds and devise strategies to cope with them. At the most intimate local levels, people negotiate conflicts in various ways. Amartya Sen refers to "social technology" in analyzing the organization of the household that makes possible its productive activities (see chapter 1). Gender and age patterns of work within the household are part of a larger social context that is defined by both cooperative and conflictual behavior. Some research shows that conflicts may ensue between men and women in instances where women's stature and autonomy are enhanced through their own paid work. In a compelling example of the strategies used under such circumstances, a midwife in the north-central African country of Mali copes with a shiftless, greedy husband while her father-in-law collects her salary, giving the midwife a small amount to live on and run her clinic. A combination of cultural, economic, and social structures limits her agency. Despite these constraints, she finds solace in her work and occasional visits to a neighboring town, as well as the respect of villagers for her work.[3]

At the regional, national, and international levels, structural constraints differ, as do opportunities for changing or navigating those constraints. Structures may contribute to gender conflicts, as suggested above in the case of the Malian midwife. But they also create opportunities. The midwife's job and pay are the result of a national government program, and the Chinese factory girls see freedom and choice in the options made available by outsourced industries and government development policies. Of particular interest in the sections that follow are the opportunities for collective action. Under what circumstances can workers come together to change structures, if only marginally, in order to enhance their opportunities?

The following sections first summarize the main sectors of work, emphasizing the impact of globalization and its significance for the gender division of labor. The discussion of global politics includes the role of organizations, both intergovernmental (such as the International Labor Organization, ILO) and transnational, ranging from formal trade unions to nonprofit networking groups. This section also includes an introduction to the controversy over micro-finance.

The final section of the chapter, "Seeking a Feminist Approach," examines work-based organizing as a strategy to increase the power and material welfare of women workers through collective action. Case studies of work-based organizing in Brazil and India illustrate two different types of trade unions responsive to the concerns of women workers. Usually trade unions are the organizational form that represents the interests of workers. However, trade unions generally have been male-dominated and not receptive to women's leadership or even organizing women workers in many cases. This situation is slowly changing through pressure from women workers, women's organizations, global justice NGOs, and the structural opportunities and dangers brought about by globalization. In this section we look at the STR Rural Workers Union in Brazil and the Self-Employed Women's Association (SEWA), an independent trade union in India, in the broader context of women workers organizing in the Global South.

THE WORLD OF WORK

Factories

Factories, as we think of them today, emerged in western Europe in the late eighteenth century, and have long been associated with the process of industrialization. The earliest factories in most countries are devoted to manufacturing that requires relatively simple technology. Textile manufacturing is a typical example, and it is not surprising that the mechanized fabrication of cloth and garments moved from the first countries to industrialize in the eighteenth and nineteenth centuries to countries that began to industrialize in the twentieth century, including China and India. Textiles are also a good example of the "race to the bottom": As Chinese wages rise, production shifts to countries where workers are paid less, such as Bangladesh. More complex fabrication processes, such as those required for automobiles, are slower to move, but by the second half of the twentieth century, the manufacture of vehicles had spread beyond western Europe and North America to East Asia. In this way, factory production serves as a primary example of globalization.

Factories range in size from very small to gigantic, but almost all are defined by the specialization of manufacturing tasks and by tight controls on workers in order to maximize efficiency and minimize costs. It is a hallmark of globalization that countries compete for factories by offering cheap land and labor in order to attract businesses that might otherwise be reluctant to move from one country to another. As more and more governments have promoted export-oriented manufacturing as a development strategy and a way of engaging in the global trading system, they have often set up "offshore" export-processing zones (EPZs) by offering favorable taxation and labor policies. Governments and manufacturers may also minimize health and safety measures designed to protect workers, with the result that today—as two centuries ago—factory accidents are common.

Women have become a large segment of the labor force in export-oriented industrialization (EOI) and predominate in labor-intensive industries such as garments and food production. Nancy Caraway argues that the feminization of factory production is a result of several factors. The initial stages of EOI generate such high demand for workers that both men and women workers are needed. Once women are hired in a particular industry, "stickiness" (continuation of gender-based hiring patterns), "spillover" (later industrializers copying the gendered hiring decisions of early industrializers), and "snowballing" (rapid expansion in feminized sectors) occur. The gender ideologies of owners, managers, and state agents characterize women as having "nimble fingers," but across regions and industries, employers and governments encourage or recruit different categories of women—young, middle-aged, rural, indigenous—as the appropriate labor force.[4]

Is the feminization of factory work a good or bad thing for women in developing countries? Scholars and activists debate the costs and benefits for women of working in EOI.[5] Critics, such as Oxfam, present a picture of a vulnerable female workforce, working long hours at low pay, on short-term contracts, with unreasonable production targets, and risking their jobs if they try to organize. Proponents, such as Jagdish Bhagwati, argue that women's jobs in EOI are much better than the alternatives and have liberating effects. Problems mark both of these positions—Bhagwati emphasizes agency without examining the structural constraints; Oxfam does the reverse. Recently scholars have provided a more nuanced and complex picture of the lives of women workers in global market factories, noting that they "experience contradictions, such as an increase of status in the family or greater autonomy from husbands and fathers, alongside continued subordination at home and work."[6] The workers themselves respond to factory conditions in a variety of ways, exhibiting resilience and, in some cases, resistance.

Agriculture

In contrast to factory-based employment, work in agriculture is more diverse, and the number of workers is harder to count. We use the term agriculture to include a variety of activities, including growing, weeding, and harvesting crops; raising livestock; forestry, fishing, horticulture, and aquaculture. All of these activities engage both male and female workers, but in different roles and with different time commitments. For example, land preparation, including clearing and plowing fields, is traditionally men's work, while hand weeding is women's work. One characteristic of the increasing mechanization of many agricultural tasks is that those areas in which men dominate, from field preparation to transporting crops to market, are mechanized before those areas with predominantly women workers. Hand weeding, which is both physically difficult and exceedingly time consuming, is one such example. Photo 6.1 shows an Indian worker engaged in hand weeding. Many agricultural activities overlap, particularly for small farmers. The farmer may be responsible for weeding crops, while she and her children also plant and tend a small vegetable garden and watch poultry or livestock.

Historically, a declining agricultural workforce accompanies the process of industrialization. For example, in western Europe and North America, the percentage of the workforce engaged in agriculture falls between 2 and 6 percent, whereas in countries as diverse as Ethiopia in East Africa, Bangladesh in South Asia, and Kyrgyzstan in

Photo 6.1.   Hand Weeding in India. Photo courtesy of Robert L. Zimdahl

Central Asia, more than 50 percent of the workforce is found in agriculture.[7] Although the decline in agricultural workers includes both men and women, the rate of decline is not necessarily the same; and, in some cases, the overall decline has been accompanied by a relative feminization of the workforce. For example, in 1950, 60 percent of all women workers in Japan were in agriculture, but fifty years later it was 6 percent. However, in the decade from the 1980s to the 1990s, the female share of all agricultural labor increased from 25 to 33 percent.[8] Elsewhere, feminization has occurred as a result of deaths from HIV and AIDS and, in these cases—as in Japan— the workers are older.

Globalization and development have changed agriculture as they have other work sectors. The creation of international markets has stimulated agribusiness, which in a general sense simply refers to for-profit agriculture. However, agribusiness is often very big business, engaging multinational corporations in structures of vertical integration, including seed selection and breeding, landholding, labor contracts, fertilizer and pesticides, marketing, and transportation. "These changes may create opportunities for greater market participation for both women and men; however, for women in particular, to date, equal access to these markets is still limited."[9] Long before the debates over the impact of agribusiness, women-in-development specialists drew attention to women's unequal access to education and technical assistance, secure property rights, and sources of capital. The smaller and poorer the farms, the more disadvantages women face in competing in the new markets. Cultural and social barriers often further handicap market access, particularly where women must rely on men for transportation, financing, and marketing.

Professional, Technical, and Managerial Jobs

Over the past few decades, the proportion of women in management and the professions has been increasing. These developments reflect the increase of women in higher education. Today more women than men students are studying in tertiary-level educational institutions globally, although inequalities persist: Women are clustered at lower degree levels and are less likely to be in natural science and technical disciplines.[10] Despite these inequalities, women constitute slightly more than half the professional workforce in the United States, Canada, many European countries, Australia, Argentina, Costa Rica, and Sri Lanka. Women are also just over half of the technical workforce in those countries, with the exception of Costa Rica and Sri Lanka.[11] Globally, 29 percent of scientific researchers are women.[12] By the early 2000s, women occupied 20 to 40 percent of the managerial positions in Europe, Canada, Australia, and Latin America and 46 percent in the United States. The highest proportion of women managers was in the Philippines (58 percent), but women continue to represent only a small proportion of managers in other Asian countries, such as Korea, Japan, and Pakistan, where they are 10 percent or less.[13] Across countries at all levels of development, the proportion of women managers is higher in the public sector than the private sector.[14]

Even though women have made strides in the professional, technical, and managerial workforce, a large gender pay gap remains in these occupations. The pay gap is due in part to horizontal and vertical occupational segregation by gender. Women are concentrated into lower-paying professions, such as teaching and nursing (horizontal segregation). For example, women are the majority of primary-school teachers in all but the least developed regions of the world: In North America, western Europe, Latin America and the Caribbean, East Asia and the Pacific, well over half of primary-school teachers are women, with percentages ranging from 60 to 85, and in Africa nearly half of primary teachers are women.[15] Even in female-dominated occupations such as teaching, men more often hold the top supervisory positions (vertical segregation). The gender pay gap is also due to male/female pay differentials within professional occupations. The lowest pay differentials are in female-dominated occupations, such as teaching and nursing. The largest pay differentials are in some male-dominated occupations requiring high skill levels: For example, the average pay of female accountants in the Republic of Korea is 33 percent less than that of male accountants.[16]

Improving the opportunities for women in managerial, professional, and technical fields requires a multipronged approach. The first step involves increasing the number of women pursuing higher education in scientific, business, and legal fields, which has gradually occurred. At the workplace, training, networking, and mentoring enable female professionals to become more successful. Balancing professional and family responsibilities continues to be a central issue for many women. Consequently, developing strategies to make the professional workplace more family friendly (for both women and men) is an important dimension of achieving gender equality in professional, managerial, and technical fields. Government policies and programs aimed at promoting gender equality in the workplace can make an important contribution as well. Professional women's associations in science, engineering, medicine, law, and business at both national and global levels are another mechanism for promoting gender equality and upward mobility for women in the professions.

Despite the persistent issues of access, pay inequity, and double-day burdens, women who do the kind of work described here enjoy substantial advantages in contrast to workers in factories and fields. Their physical workplace is less hazardous. By virtue of their formal education and workplace skills, they are assumed to have more personal agency. Although many workers in these fields are laid off during economic recessions and neoliberal restructuring programs, overall they enjoy more employment security and predictable incomes. This stands in stark contrast to the vast majority of informal economy workers.

Informal Economy Labor

More than 50 percent of the nonagricultural workforce in developing countries is found in what is known as the informal economy, where workers lack secure wage contracts or social protection (health, unemployment, or retirement benefits) and do jobs that are not regulated by the government.[17] The informal economy is extremely heterogeneous, encompassing self-employed and independent casual wageworkers as well as dependent workers in a chain of subcontractors in industrial production. In general, informal employment is divided into two types: self-employment in informal enterprises (as owners, own-account workers, or unpaid family members) and wage employment in informal jobs, which includes casual day laborers, domestic workers, and industrial outworkers. Informal economy workers are found in vastly different settings, including private homes, small workshops, and public places such as streets.

Early studies assumed that informal employment would fade away with modernization, but it has grown over time; informality now characterizes many jobs in high-income countries as well as low-income countries. Increasingly people work at temporary, short-term jobs, earning money on a day-to-day or week-to-week basis. Neoliberal globalization and economic recession have accelerated the contraction in formal employment, a trend made possible by technological changes. Both men and women have been forced into the informal economy. Public sectors have been downsized, and unionized factory jobs in high-income countries have been replaced by outsourced informal jobs in low-wage countries, typically without social protection and often without government regulation. Rural poverty and rural-to-urban migration in many countries guarantee a steady stream of people working as casual laborers or vendors.

Women are overrepresented in the informal economy; generally, they do more precarious jobs and are paid less than men. Some of the main occupational groups of women informal workers are domestic workers, street vendors, outworkers or unpaid family members in manufacturing, construction workers, and waste pickers. Although informal work offers women some benefits, such as flexibility and convenience, that enable them to combine their responsibilities as mothers, wives, and income earners, they come with costs: notably, low incomes, irregular or seasonal work, safety hazards, vulnerability in cases of health problems, and "lack of legal status, organization and voice."[18] Three occupations characteristic of female workers in the informal economy are described here.

Domestic Workers

Although boys and men may do domestic work within the home, women comprise the vast majority of domestic workers largely because the jobs they do have historically been part of their unpaid reproductive tasks. Household work by nonfamily members has a long history throughout the world, and the structures of feudalism, slavery, and colonialism depended as much on domestic labor as agriculture did. Globalization has accelerated the flow of migrant domestic labor from poorer to richer countries, so although some domestic workers come from the same villages or cities as their employers, they often come from distant places or foreign countries. Working in private homes doing cleaning, cooking, laundry, child care, and related household tasks, domestic workers are often invisible, and their work may be undervalued, unregulated, and unprotected. They may live in their employer's household or live outside. Live-in workers are often on call twenty-four hours a day and face the most abuse, especially if they are migrants.

The International Labor Organization estimates that domestic work comprises a significant proportion of the workforce: In developing countries, it accounts for 4 to 10 percent of total employment (both male and female), compared to industrialized countries, where the percentage is less than 3.[19] Over the past thirty years, the numbers of migrants from the Global South who work in more affluent countries as domestic workers have increased dramatically. In the North, the high labor-force participation rate of women coupled with inadequate child-care alternatives has led to a massive demand for nannies and maids, and the lack of opportunities for paid employment in the South produces the supply. The feminization of labor migration is especially high in the Philippines, Indonesia, and Sri Lanka, where women comprise 60 to 75 percent of the legal migrants, primarily serving as domestic workers in the Middle East, Singapore, Malaysia, and Hong Kong.[20] Governments generally encourage this type of migration because worker remittances provide needed economic resources for their economies. By the early twenty-first century, worker remittances exceeded 10 percent of GDP in twenty-two countries.[21]

Home-based Producers

Home-based production, like nonfamily domestic work, has a long history. In Europe, for example, women did carding, spinning, and weaving before the establishment of textile factories. Today, home-based producers in the informal economy may work for themselves or their families in independent microenterprises making simple products for daily use, such as brooms, incense sticks, or pots. They may be industrial outworkers dependent on subcontractors for work orders and raw materials. Frequently, multinational corporations create global supply chains that rely on subcontractors for production work, and these subcontractors in turn subcontract out labor-intensive assembly work, often to home-based producers. By "putting out" the work, subcontractors cut down on costs (wages, electricity, machinery, renting space) and transfer risks to the home-based workers who are paid by piece rate. Outworkers are especially common in the footwear and garment industries. The livelihoods of both the independent and dependent producers are precarious. The former generally face high levels of competition from other poor households trying to eke out a living. The latter suffer during economic downturns and when the global production system shifts supply chains to other countries.

Street Vendors

Both men and women work as street vendors in developing countries, usually sitting on the pavement or carrying wares on their heads or in pushcarts. This occupation, with low costs of entry, attracts many women. Women are the majority of street vendors in Africa, Southeast Asia, and Latin America, and are present in large numbers in other regions of the world, except in areas where social norms discourage women going outside their homes. Street vendors sell cooked food, vegetables, fruit, and inexpensive everyday items such as combs, mirrors, and plastic toys to both the urban poor and middle class. Researchers have reported a growing number of street vendors as a result of structural adjustment programs and economic crises.[22] Women vendors tend to have lower incomes because they have less capital to invest and must spend time on domestic responsibilities. Street vendors experience a number of problems related to their lack of legal status and voice: harassment by the authorities, lack of services, and infrastructure and health issues, such as respiratory problems from vehicle exhaust. Photo 6.2 shows a Ghanaian water vendor working a crowded highway under construction near Accra.

THE GLOBAL POLITICS OF WORK

The United Nations and the International Labor Organization have developed international norms to encourage states to enact policies that enhance the rights of women workers and workers more generally. Over the past two decades, gender advocates in the UN have set out a comprehensive policy agenda to promote gender equality and women's empowerment at work.[23] This policy agenda includes a host of policy recommendations designed to

1. reform macroeconomic policy to promote gender equality;
2. provide women full and equal access to productive resources (land, credit, technology), education, productive employment, social protection, and financial services;
3. ensure equal remuneration for work of equal value; and
4. assist in the reconciliation of work and family responsibilities.

The ILO has constructed a set of international labor standards through conventions, declarations, and recommendations. Most basic are five core labor standards "that all labor markets should strive to meet: freedom of association, the right to collective bargaining, abolition of forced or compulsory labor, elimination of child labor, and freedom from discrimination."[24] Recent ILO reports also call for decent work for women. "Decent work," as conceptualized by the ILO, is "work that takes place under conditions of freedom, equity, security, and dignity, in which rights are protected and adequate remuneration and social protection is provided."[25]

At present, this policy agenda is largely unrealized, and the work environments of the majority of the world's workers fall far short of the criteria set out for decent work. National governments argue that the global production system and free-trade agreements weaken their ability to ensure worker rights. Structural adjustment programs

Photo 6.2. Girl Selling Water Packets near Accra, Ghana. Photo courtesy of Gale Sherman

have resulted in governments eliminating many social programs and drastically cutting budgets in areas crucial to a gender empowerment agenda. Work in the informal economy by definition falls largely outside the reach of government regulation.

Chapter 3 explained the central premises of neoliberal globalization as the reduction of the state role in the economy and the promotion of international trade and foreign direct investment (FDI). Within this context, market-based approaches have become more popular than extending government laws and policies to address issues facing workers, and women in particular. Two approaches adopted over the past three decades illustrate this preference for market-based strategies: voluntary codes of labor conduct and micro-finance.

Voluntary Codes of Conduct

Chapters 4 and 5 on sex trafficking and water described the multiple new organizations that have emerged to address women's issues. Similarly, new actors have emerged in the global politics of women and work over the past few decades. Nongovernmental organizations and global labor unions have pressured corporations to establish voluntary codes of labor practice that define minimum labor standards required of their suppliers in global production systems. The primary strategy used by these NGOs is to increase consumer awareness and concern over exploitative working conditions. Egregious violations of labor standards can lead to consumer boycotts and harm brand reputations. Multi-stakeholder initiatives, such the Ethical Trading Initiative (UK) and Social Accountability International (US), involve coalitions of corporations, NGOs, and trade unions that develop, implement, and monitor codes of labor practice.

Assessments of the effectiveness of voluntary codes of conduct in improving working conditions and enhancing worker rights are mixed. It is clear that for any type of compliance to occur, NGOs need to monitor and expose conditions. Even then, victories have often been short-lived. For example, the Anti-Sweatshop Movement, a coalition of student NGOs and unions, initially achieved limited progress in its campaigns during the 1990s. Unions might be recognized, but corporations subsequently closed down the factories. However, three victories by the Anti-Sweatshop Movement suggest that improved cooperation between student organizations and labor unions and the transformation of the AFL-CIO Solidarity Center into a genuine advocate for worker rights may lead to progress. In 2010, Russell Athletic agreed to rehire Honduran workers; Nike agreed to pay severance owed by subcontractors in Honduras; and Knights Apparel, the largest supplier of college-logo clothing, agreed to raise wages substantially and recognize the union in a factory in Alta Garcia, the Dominican Republic.[26]

Micro-finance

The rapid growth of micro-finance has led proponents to call it "one of the great success stories of US foreign aid."[27] Micro-finance is a development strategy primarily targeted at women that has experienced exponential growth since its beginnings in the 1970s. By the early 2000s, estimates put the number of poor women globally with micro-finance loans at almost eighty-nine million, representing 82 percent of the poorest micro-credit clients.[28]

Micro-finance programs, which offer credit and savings services to the poor, originated in the 1970s when the Self-Employed Women's Association (SEWA), the Working Women's Forum in India, and the Grameen Bank and the Bangladesh Rural Advancement Committee (BRAC) in Bangladesh began to offer small loans mainly to women in the informal economy.[29] The self-employed poor in the Global South had been excluded from formal banking services designed for individuals and enterprises in the formal economy. Banks did not welcome illiterate clients who could not fill out forms, were badly dressed, female, and lacked collateral. The higher transaction cost of small loans was another obstacle preventing banks from serving those in the informal economy.

The early micro-finance programs developed a number of banking innovations. They issued identification cards with photos and thumbprints of their members. Generally, they used a group-lending model (in which the group of borrowers was responsible for the repayment of its members) instead of the conventional model that required collateral. The groups held regular meetings to do their banking and discuss both business and family problems. These early programs had explicit gender-empowerment goals and used micro-finance as an entry point for organizing women. As micro-finance grew in importance in the development community, the targeting of women was justified because of high repayment rates and because women spent any additional income on household necessities.

Micro-finance became very popular in the 1990s; as a market-based development strategy, it fit well with the ascendant neoliberal ideology. The emphasis was on the self-reliance of the poor instead of on an expanding developmental state. Increasingly, however, the expansion of micro-finance came with a new emphasis on financial sustainability that challenged the poverty alleviation and women's empowerment goals of the early micro-finance programs. The earlier programs frequently relied on some level of subsidies from donors to cover the high transaction costs. By the early twenty-first century, advocates of financial sustainability argued that setting interest rates high enough to cover costs would enable micro-finance to reach a much larger number of poor people than would be possible through donor-subsidized micro-finance programs. In contrast, advocates of the earlier poverty alleviation and women's empowerment goals of micro-finance worried that too much emphasis on financial sustainability would eliminate program elements that benefited the poor and promoted gender equality.

The financial sustainability approach has become dominant among donor organizations, such as the US Agency for International Development (USAID) and the Consultative Group to Assist the Poor (CGAP), a donor forum based at the World Bank. Commercial banks have also entered the micro-finance arena, and CGAP envisions the integration of financial markets and a global micro-finance industry designed to bring the poor into the global capitalist market.[30] Private capital has begun to invest in micro-finance with large initial public offerings (IPOs), generating headlines and questions about the purposes of micro-finance.[31]

Today, micro-finance service delivery has two main models: the original NGO-philanthropic model and the newer financial services/commercial-banking model. By 2010, commercial banks accounted for 60 percent of micro-finance borrowers; NGOs, 35 percent; and credit unions and rural banks, 5 percent.[32] With the growing presence of commercial lenders prioritizing financial sustainability and investor confidence, high interest rates and fees have become a point of contention in micro-finance. Interest rates as high as 125 percent have been reported, with average rates of 70 percent in Mexico and 74 percent in Nigeria compared to a global average of 37 percent.[33]

Scholars and development practitioners debate the efficacy of micro-finance in poverty alleviation and gender empowerment; research findings are ambiguous.[34] Critics appear on both the political left and the right. Conservatives, such as Thomas Dichter, argue that subsidies cannot be justified for "microfinance has no sustained effect on poverty reduction," and its gender empowerment effects "are less impressive than hoped."[35] Some feminists on the left, including Hester Eisenstein and Srilatha Batliwala, argue that subsistence strategies in the informal economy based on micro-finance are a poor substitute for formal sector jobs that constitute real economic development, and that micro-finance does little to transform hierarchical familial and social structures while increasing women's workloads and indebtedness.[36]

Other feminist advocates of micro-finance, such as Linda Mayoux, agree that existing micro-finance programs often fall short of their claims, but the solution lies in "improvement and innovation" rather than cynicism and dismissal.[37] Mayoux argues that empowerment concerns need to be mainstreamed into all program aspects, and a central component must be women's participation in program decision making. Assets purchased with loans must be registered in women's names. Borrower groups should be seen not merely as repayment vehicles, but as a means for building social capital through information exchange and problem solving. Micro-finance programs must link up with other women's networks to advocate property law reform and to provide women's rights training. She points to SEWA and other NGOs in India as embodying these progressive approaches.

An important trend in the global politics of work is the formation of multilevel networks and the expanding efforts to strengthen organizations and policies that generally advocate for workers, particularly low-wage, predominantly female workers. In the past, the global trade union movement showed little interest in organizing women and viewed the informal economy as a threat to union jobs and unionized workers. Economic globalization has threatened the viability of traditional union approaches by making it easier to move industries to lower wage "offshore" locations. But the technological and political changes of globalization have also facilitated the creation of transnational networks that link trade unions, grassroots activists, and nongovernmental development organizations.

Transnational Labor-Advocacy and Multilevel Networks

A crucial aspect of the new networks is that they are multilevel, linking local, national, regional, or global levels. These alliances seek actions by international organizations and national and local governments to promote and protect worker rights and to establish communication channels between local organizations in their occupations. Some early networks tended to be more organizations *for* women workers than *of* women workers, as illustrated by the Anti-Sweatshop Movement that framed women garment workers as victims and US activists as saviors.[38] However, transnational advocacy networks, such as the Coalition for Justice in the Maquiladoras (CJM) and the Anti-Sweatshop Movement, found that success depended on the empowerment of women workers and the formation of worker unions.[39] These transnational networks face tremendous challenges: power and resource inequalities among the constituent members, divisions among workers, and opposition by governments and corporations. Some networks have disintegrated; others have had to regroup and reorganize, but they are also expanding.

In the mid-1990s, two international networks of informal economic workers popped up. HomeNet, an alliance of home-based workers, was formed in 1994; and StreetNet, an alliance of street vendors, was formed in 1996. HomeNet was able to lobby successfully for the 1996 ILO Convention on Homework. In the lobbying process, HomeNet enlisted the assistance of Harvard University in compiling statistics and UNIFEM in working with Asian governments. This experience of joint action by research institutions, informal economic groups, and international organizations led to the creation of Women in Informal Employment: Globalizing and Organizing (WIEGO) in 1997. WIEGO is a global network intended to promote research, programs, and policies for women in the informal economy and support their organizing efforts.[40]

HomeNet survives as HomeNet South Asia, and a more recent international federation of homeworkers is based in the UK.[41] StreetNet, based in Durban, South Africa, was reorganized as Streetnet International in 2002, and has held regional workshops in Asia, Africa, and Latin America.[42] WIEGO has grown to encompass additional occupational groups in the informal economy: domestic workers, garment workers, and waste collectors. The past few years have witnessed the process of creating an international network of domestic worker organizations, spearheaded by the global labor federation, the International Union of Food Workers (IUF), and WIEGO.[43] In 2006, IUF organized an international conference of domestic workers, Respect and Rights: Protection for Domestic Workers!, which in turn led to the creation of the International Domestic Workers' Network. The Network lobbied the ILO for an international convention on domestic work, which was adopted in June 2011.[44]

What have these global networks accomplished so far? The ILO Conventions noted at the beginning of the section represent international norms around which campaigns for national legislation can be based. National networks have also achieved some success. To illustrate, a coalition of a domestic worker union, a feminist NGO, and the national trade union federation in South Africa influenced the government to include coverage for domestic workers in unemployment insurance.[45] International conferences and cross-national activist exchanges have led to strengthening local organizations by enabling activists to meet their counterparts, learn from each other, and challenge local power brokers.[46] For example, Streetnet International set up exchange visits between organizers of local street vendor associations in Maputo, Mozambique, and Durban, South Africa. The Maputo vendors gained confidence and innovative ideas from their international experience in crafting proposals to their local city government.

All of the efforts to influence the global politics of work show the influence of feminist thinking. The following section looks more closely at local and regional efforts to organize workers in a way that improves their opportunities to earn a living.

SEEKING A FEMINIST APPROACH

What does a feminist approach to women's labor rights look like? It might involve the formation of social movements of women workers able to develop their visions of gender and economic justice. The participation of women workers in democratic work-related organizations is an important first step. In this section, we sketch out several different types of organizing efforts and provide two case studies for a more in-depth look at work-based organizing. Collective organizing offers women opportunities for developing leadership skills and for articulating issues growing out of their experiences in productive and reproductive work. The exercise of collective agency by women through organizing "is both an end in itself—as women achieve a sense of empowerment and are able to support each other—and a means to leveraging wider impact on the local, national and international stage."[47]

At the level of both theory and practice, organizing female workers is a coalitional undertaking. Women workers are both workers and women, so both labor movements and women's movements are involved in the creation of a labor movement that serves women's interests. This process challenges the conventional assumptions of the labor and women's movements: "The first challenge is to the class-based solidarity of the labor movement, by acknowledging the differences of gender, race, sexuality and ethnicity within class. The second challenge is to the gender-based solidarity of the women's movement, by recognizing the class and ethnic differences among women."[48] The issues that emerge are ones the labor movement has championed historically—wages, working conditions, and social protection—along with new issues raised specifically by female workers: child care, sexual harassment, and dignity.

Elements of difference, diversity, and deconstruction feminism all can be seen in the work-based organizing of women workers. Difference feminism is found in the new issues women bring to the table, such as child care. Diversity feminism embodies the inclusive approaches and coalitional politics entailed in organizing women workers. Deconstruction feminism helps us see that the existing labor movement has been a movement mainly representing the interests, perspectives, and leadership of men working in formal employment. The changing nature of work under neoliberal globalization and declining trade union membership have led some trade unions to modify their stance and begin to see the organization of women, rural, and informal economy workers as central to the revival of the trade union movement.

Globalization has created formidable obstacles to women's collective action around work, but it has also opened up new possibilities. Labor market segmentation, the dispersed nature of the workforce in the informal economy, domestic responsibilities, discrimination, and familial resistance all act as barriers to women organizing. However, two cases, one from Brazil and the other from India, illustrate the types of collective action approaches available to workers to improve their working conditions and, as a result, their lives. The organizations in both cases are trade unions, although they differ considerably in their origins, structures, and activities.

Brazil: Sindicato dos Trabalhadores Rurais (STR/Rural Workers' Union)

In the past two decades, one of the most notable characteristics of neoliberal globalization has been the expansion of global value chains. These are chains of factories and farms across the world that produce high-quality goods for export to the countries whose consumers can afford to buy them. As a result of integrated production, transportation, and marketing processes, consumers are able to buy flowers, fruits, and vegetables out of season. These value chains rely on the availability of a flexible pool of labor in the producing countries in order to minimize labor costs. In many of the horticultural and produce chains, women predominate in certain positions, notably those that pay less or enjoy less job security.[49]

Brazil is one of the countries that has joined in the creation and maintenance of global supply chains, especially in the northeastern part of the country.[50] After two decades of military rule, Brazil returned to civilian government in the 1980s. The new government pursued a development strategy that included promotion of high-value export crops. In northeast Brazil, the most important of these crops is grapes, and the largest grape grower in the region is the Brazilian company Labrunier (itself a subsidiary of a larger corporate group). In 2008, Labrunier joined the Oppenheimer Group in order to sell high-quality grapes in the Northern Hemisphere, thus creating a global value chain for this fruit.[51]

In the São Francisco Valley of northeast Brazil, the country's most important grape-growing region, women comprise an estimated 65 percent of the field workers in the vineyards.[52] Increasingly, the vineyard workers have been unionized by the Sindicato dos Trabalhadores Rurais (STR). Formed initially in 1963 to represent small-scale farmers in the São Francisco Valley, the focus of the union's organizing activities shifted to the wage-labor force beginning in the 1980s. By the mid-1990s, when the grape sector was still relatively new, the STR recognized that production of high-quality fruit depended on meeting the complex requirements for pruning the vines, fertilizing, and picking the grapes. Delays would reduce fruit quality or even result in the loss of a crop. As a result, union workers have been able to use strikes to force employers to negotiate improvements in pay and working conditions.

In the early phase of organizing rural wageworkers, the STR largely ignored women. Within a few years, however, the union recognized the potential and necessity of organizing women. This, in turn, meant addressing their specific needs, as well as the general requirements for improved working conditions.

The vineyard workers come from small farms as well as urban areas, and often their work in the grape industry is their first paid employment. The work is physically demanding. It is hot, and the workers are under constant pressure to increase productivity—to prune or harvest faster, for example. Single women, particularly those with children, stay in the industry because they have few alternatives. All of these are circumstances the union has tried to address.

In the 1990s and early 2000s, the STR succeeded in improving working conditions through the collective agreements negotiated with the employers' organization. Through these negotiations, workers secured the right to a two-month paid maternity leave as well as day-care facilities and the right to breastfeed their babies for an hour a day (beyond their lunch breaks). In addition, they now have minimum-wage guarantees and, in response to complaints about sexual harassment on public transport, the workers have company-provided buses as transport to work. As they have become more aware of the STR, workers bring complaints to the union, and some have become union workers. The union leadership encourages the women workers to educate themselves, and has negotiated a clause in the labor agreement that bans compulsory overtime and allows workers to leave the farms by 5 p.m. in order to attend classes. A union lawyer has estimated that literacy levels have increased in the past decade to more than 70 percent.[53]

One of the most significant dimensions of the union's activities, including its support for education, is the emphasis on the skills the workers need to be successful. On large farms, where the highest quality grapes are produced for the Northern Hemisphere, as many as thirty-four different operations characterize the cultivation and harvest cycle. These range from soil analysis and fertilization to pruning and tying branches and shoots at various stages of growth. The union has worked to subvert the stereotype that the tasks women workers undertake (such as tying) reflect their innate ability and manual dexterity. Instead, these are jobs that require training, judgment, and considerable skill. The STR has thus contributed to the workers' increased awareness of their rights and, in turn, a sense of empowerment (see photo 6.3).

Despite these accomplishments, the situation is not static. The grape producers and exporters are under constant competitive pressures in the global economy to reduce costs, improve quality, and increase productivity. Farm managers gradually have changed the gender division of labor to introduce more flexibility in hiring and work assignments. In the view of many managers, training men to undertake the skilled work dominated by women brings greater flexibility in work operations and

Photo 6.3.   STR Salaried Workers' Secretary Addressing Grape Workers. Photo courtesy of Benjamin Selwyn

reduces the social costs associated with women—precisely the benefits that the STR fought to acquire.[54]

India: The Self-Employed Women's Association (SEWA)[55]

By the early twenty-first century, more than 90 percent of female Indian workers were in the informal economy.[56] Female informal economy workers, such as home-based and casual wageworkers, have faced numerous gender-specific hardships. In 1971 a group of workers in Ahmedabad, an Indian city in the state of Gujarat, approached Ela Bhatt, an organizer in a textile workers union, for some help. In response, she formed a trade union called the Self-Employed Women's Association (SEWA). Initially, many people dismissed the idea of a trade union for self-employed women; but SEWA has thrived, growing to encompass both urban and rural women workers, expanding beyond Gujarat, and serving as a model for membership-based organizations of the poor. In 2009, SEWA membership in Gujarat was 631,000; in India as a whole, more than 1.2 million.[57]

SEWA members come from more than eighty occupational groups from three main categories of work: 61 percent are casual day laborers in agriculture or construction, 28 percent are own-account workers (street vendors, rural producers, waste pickers), and 10 percent are industrial outworkers (for garments, hand-rolled cigarettes known as *bidis*, etc.). SEWA members are poor, although they are not the most destitute. SEWA has made a difference in the lives of its members by enabling them to accumulate assets, protect themselves against risks, and acquire strength through collective power. A 2007–2008 study found that SEWA members were more likely than comparable nonmembers to have a savings account and health insurance, they had greater access to credit at lower interest rates, and they exhibited more confidence.[58]

SEWA sees itself as a social movement and a development organization, struggling to advance the interests of poor working women and providing services to promote the economic development of its members. In this way, SEWA combines labor movement and women's movement goals. Ela Bhatt has said that without the inclusion of self-employed women, the labor movement "is no movement worth its name"; and work "is strategically the most effective way of organizing large numbers of women according to issues which are relevant to them."[59]

SEWA combines advocacy efforts at local, state, national, and international levels with development services for its members. It has pushed for a minimum wage for the various groups of casual wageworkers, successfully petitioned the Indian Supreme Court to prevent police and local government harassment of street vendors, negotiated with government officials to improve the situation of industrial outworkers, and successfully lobbied the state government for a pension plan for construction workers. At the international level, SEWA was a central player in successful lobbying of the ILO to get the International Convention on home-based work in 1996. Today, SEWA offers a wide array of business services. Beginning with micro-finance, SEWA formed its own bank in 1975 and promoted savings. It has developed an integrated package of insurance products for its members covering illness, maternity, property loss, and death. It has organized cooperatives and developed a design and marketing program for rural embroiderers. SEWA also offers social services such as child care and adult literacy classes.

A major focus of SEWA activities is the organizing and capacity building of its membership. The organization recruits members into local primary groups (based on occupation and locality), which meet regularly to identify needs and strategies to address them. From these groups, grassroots leaders emerge; they receive training and become paraprofessionals in the organization and/or are elected as representatives to SEWA's governing bodies. SEWA has approximately one elected representative for every two hundred members and considerable diversity in the organization's leadership. For example, in 2006 the president of SEWA was an agricultural laborer, and the general secretary was a college-educated daughter of a tobacco worker who was also a SEWA member.

What Do These Cases Tell Us?

These two case studies show that collective organization can make a difference. Women workers in both Brazil and India have joined together in order to increase their collective agency. In spite of their comparative lack of structural power in the global supply chain or in the overall Indian economy, their unions help them create associational power. In both cases the unions have been responsive to the needs of women workers. At the same time, the location of the women workers in the global economy differs in the two cases, and the trade unions are also different in terms of their history and organization.

In Brazil, the STR had male leadership at the outset, but in the context of a labor force that was in the majority female, transformation was gradual to more women union officials and an agenda addressing the concerns of women workers. The STR negotiated for better wages and working conditions but also imparted a greater sense of agency through education and the idea of skills. The STR subverted the idea of female dexterity—arguing that it is not inherent and is instead an acquired skill that must be acknowledged and paid for.

In contrast, SEWA is a trade union of women workers, so women's leadership has always been central. A trade union of poor workers in the informal economy looks very different from trade unions in factories or agribusiness. Men and women working in the informal economy have set up a variety of local organizations—cooperatives, trade unions, self-help groups using micro-credit as an entry point for organizing, and issue-based associations. SEWA incorporates several of these organizational forms to address the needs of its members.

Trade unions have both facilitated and hampered women's leadership development in work-based organizing around the world. The STR reached out to women and developed a more inclusive leadership and agenda. SEWA also grew out of a trade union, the Textile Labour Association (TLA), where Ela Bhatt had led its women's wing. At first, the TLA was supportive of SEWA; but as SEWA developed, the TLA leadership felt threatened and expelled SEWA in 1981. These two contrasting outcomes can be seen in many other cases of trade unions and women workers.

Some unions have worked together with NGOs in the area of women's leadership training, organizing small study groups to promote self-confidence and skill building in negotiations and labor law.[60] Unions have set up women's directorates to provide a forum for women's voices. In some cases (Indonesia), women gained influence through these measures; but in other cases (Nicaragua), the union leadership, feeling threatened, moved to replace the women leaders because they were seen as too independent.[61]

The workers' collective action strategies to articulate their perspectives in the workplace vary with different settings. The establishment of autonomous women's organizations, as in the case of SEWA, is one approach. Nicaraguan women formed the Working and Unemployed Women's Movement (MEC) that has sought to improve conditions for women working in the *maquilas* as well as for unemployed women. Other examples of autonomous women's organizations include the Korean Women Workers Association, the Chinese Working Women's Network, and the Women's Action Committee in Jamaica.[62] Often incorporated as NGOs, these autonomous organizations have flourished in areas such as China's free trade zones, where traditional independent trade unions are prohibited.

The female Brazilian farm workers are in a very different location in the global economy from the women informal-economy workers in India. Brazil's commitment to neoliberal development strategies linked this region of Brazil to the global supply chain in a new way. In a relatively short period, workers were brought into the global economy. Working conditions were often exploitative, but new opportunities for organizing were created through the clustering of workers, in contrast to their earlier relative isolation on small farms. The importance of the export grape crop in earning foreign exchange for the government initially increased the strategic position of the union. Thus the Brazilian case shows that the government-promoted changes to the structure of the economy in the northeast region altered the structure of the labor force. In the face of these changes, the STR was able to improve its strategic position and negotiating power. Although the corporate employers have developed new strategies to counteract labor militancy and increase worker productivity, these efforts are balanced by government policies to support many worker demands for higher wages and improved working conditions.[63]

The formation of SEWA predates India's adoption of a neoliberal development strategy in the 1990s, and the majority of SEWA members are not part of globalized production networks. They have, on balance, been negatively affected by globalization, which has resulted in a "relative decline in unskilled wages, increased risk and vulnerability, and a declining bargaining power of unskilled labor."[64] SEWA has responded in two ways. First, it has set up programs to increase skills and access to capital and markets among its membership. Second, it has advocated for the interests of poor women workers in policy-making arenas at local, state, national, and global levels.

How do the STR and SEWA cases fit into what is known so far about women workers organizing in the Global South? Some scholars argue that the priorities and strategies of women labor activists are distinctive. Naila Kabeer states that they emphasize "the livelihood security of their membership"; other scholars note that they reflect the "clear continuum between the many areas and arenas of women's lives," such as wage and domestic work and responsibilities as earner, mother, and wife.[65] In addition to wage demands, activists raise issues of transport, sexual harassment, bullying, and child care. They also focus attention on services to promote mutual aid among the members. In some cases they become involved in broader economic campaigns, such as raising the minimum wage.

Most studies find that women workers opt for less confrontational tactics, favoring negotiation over strikes. However, Kabeer points out that what appear to be gender-specific approaches may "reflect modes of organization specific to vulnerable workers of either gender."[66] For example, because STR's workers are central to a global value chain, they may be better positioned than SEWA to use more aggressive bargaining tactics. Similarly, the militancy of women workers in strikes in Chinese foreign-owned factories suggests that greater strategic power and location in integrated production processes may be more important than gender as such in facilitating confrontational strategies.⁶⁷

Both the STR and the SEWA cases demonstrate the importance of multiple levels—from the local to the national to the global. In Brazil, the STR union has fought for farm workers' rights, but another arena for increasing worker wages was the adoption of a national minimum wage law by the Brazilian government. SEWA has been an actor at the levels of state and national government in India to advocate for the rights of female informal economy workers and has lobbied at the global level for an ILO convention on home-based work.

CONCLUSION

The struggle to secure livelihood and gender rights for women workers remains a work in progress. The global economic crisis that began in 2008 has created additional challenges. One positive sign is that gender issues have earned greater visibility in the agendas of the ILO and the global labor movement, primarily through the efforts of union feminists.⁶⁸ Both the international councils of the global labor movement, the International Confederation of Free Trade Unions (ICFTU) and its successor organization, the International Trade Union Confederation (ITUC), as well as other trade union federations, are involved in networking strategies with feminist organizations that push for economic justice. They also support campaigns to increase female membership in unions. The trade unions target women who work in export processing zones and the informal economy, as well as women from ethnic minorities. The 2009 ITUC World Women's Conference, "Decent Work, Decent Life for Women," addressed all of these issues. Recent agricultural collective-bargaining agreements in Africa have included provisions addressing health care and family leave. Gender equality is specifically mentioned in the current ILO Decent Work Agenda. Whether *influencing agendas* at the local, national, and international levels will lead to *substantive policy reform* is still uncertain. The global pattern suggests that collective action has in some instances improved workers' agency in market-based economies, although basic social, cultural, economic, and political structures have seldom been altered.

NOTES

1. David Barboza, "Clues in an iPhone Autopsy," *New York Times*, July 6, 2010. See also Pietra Rivoli, *The Travels of a T-Shirt in the Global Economy: An Economist Examines the Markets, Power and Politics of World Trade* (Hoboken, NJ: John Wiley and Sons, 2005).

2. Leslie T. Chang, *Factory Girls: From Village to City in a Changing China* (New York: Spiegel and Grau, 2009).

3. Kris Holloway, *Monique and the Mango Rains: Two Years with a Midwife in Mali* (Long Grove, IL: Waveland Press, 2007).

4. Nancy Plankey Videla, "Engendering Global Studies of Women and Work," *Feminist Studies* 36, no. 1 (2010): 180–99; and Nancy Caraway, *Assembling Women: The Feminization of Global Manufacturing* (Ithaca, NY: Cornell University Press, 2007).

5. Oxfam, "Trading Away Our Rights; Women Working in Global Supply Chains" (Oxford, UK: Oxfam, 2004); and Jagdish Bhagwati, *In Defense of Globalization* (New York: Oxford University Press, 2004).

6. Videla, "Engendering Global Studies," 197.

7. International Labor Organization, *Key Indicators of the Labor Market 2001–2002* (Geneva: ILO, 2003).

8. Japan Institute of Workers' Evolution, *The Situation of Women in Japan, Women Workers*, 2007, at http://www.jiwe.or.jp/english/situation/working.html (data from Japan Ministry of Labor).

9. World Bank, Food and Agriculture Organization, and International Fund for Agricultural Development, *Gender in Agriculture Sourcebook* (Washington, DC: World Bank, 2009), 1.

10. Tertiary level refers to all types of postsecondary education (not just degree-granting higher educational institutions) and is the way that students are classified in international development statistics. Marit Tjomsland, "Women in Higher Education. A Concern for Development," *Gender, Technology and Development* 13, no. 3 (2009): 411.

11. ILO LABORSTA Internet, Main Statistics by Occupation, 2008, http://laborsta.ilo.org.

12. UNESCO, "Sex-Disaggregated Data: A Brief Analysis of Key Education and Science Indicators since the Beijing Declaration and Platform for Action" (1995). Information Sheet No. 4 (2010), http://www.uis.unesco.org/template/pdf/EducGeneral/Infosheet_No4_Gender_EN.pdf.

13. Available from the World Bank Gender Stats (data not available for all countries).

14. Linda Wirth, *Breaking Through the Glass Ceiling: Women in Management* (Geneva: ILO, 2001), 44.

15. Sheelagh Drudy, "Gender Balance/Gender Bias: The Teaching Profession and the Impact of Feminization," *Gender and Education* 20, no. 4 (July 2008): 310. Drudy's data taken from UNESCO; data not available for South and West Asia.

16. ILO, *Women in Labour Markets: Measuring Progress and Identifying Challenges* (Geneva: ILO, 2010), 54.

17. OECD, "Is Informal Normal? Toward More and Better Jobs," Policy Brief, *OECD Observer*, March 2009, http://www.oecd.org/dataoecd/24/1/42470203.pdf.

18. Martha Chen et al., *Progress of the World's Women 2005* (New York: UNIFEM, United Nations, 2005), 64.

19. ILO, International Labour Conference, 99th Session, 2010, Report IV(1), "Decent Work for Domestic Workers," http://www.ilo.org/wcmsp5/groups/public/@ed_norm/@relconf/documents/meetingdocument/wcms_104700.pdf, 6.

20. Human Rights Watch, *Swept Under the Rug: Abuses Against Domestic Workers Around the World*, July 2006, 3.

21. ILO, "Decent Work for Domestic Workers," 10.

22. Sharit K. Bhowmik, "Street Vendors in Asia: A Review," *Economic and Political Weekly* (May 28–June 4, 2005): 2256–64; Caroline Skinner, "Street Trade in Africa," School of Development Studies, University of Kwazulu-Natal, Working Paper No. 51 (2008); Winnie V. Mitullah, "A Review of Street Trade in Africa," commissioned by Women in Informal Employment: Globalising and Organising (WIEGO), 2004; and Sally Roever, "Street Trade

in Latin America: Demographic Trends, Legal Issues, and Vending Organizations in Six Cities," prepared for the WIEGO Urban Policies Programme, October 6, 2006, http://www.inclusivecities.org/research/other-research.

23. See the UN Fourth World Conference on Women, *Platform for Action*, Women and the Economy (1995), Section IV-F; UN, Department of Economic and Social Affairs, Division for the Advancement of Women, *2009 World Survey on the Role of Women in Development: Women's Control over Economic Resources*; and *Access to Financial Resources, including Microfinance*. UN, Commission on the Status of Women, Economic and Social Council. *Report on the Fifty-fourth Session* (2010), 17–25.

24. V. K. Sapovadia and Maria C. Mattioli, "Laws of Labor: Core Labor Standards and Global Trade," *Harvard International Review* 26, no. 2 (2004): 61.

25. Stephanie Barrientos, *Global Production Systems and Decent Work*, Working Paper No. 77 (Geneva: ILO, May 2007), 1.

26. Paul Garver, "Two More Campus Anti-Sweatshop Movement Victories," *Talking Union. A Project of the DSA Network*, July 28, 2010, http://talkingunion.wordpress.com/2010/07/28/two-more-campus-anti-sweatshop-movement-victories; and Steven Greenhouse, "A Factory Defies Stereotypes, but Can It Thrive?," *New York Times*, July 18, 2010, and "Pressured, Nike to Help Workers in Honduras," *New York Times*, July 27, 2010.

27. Susy Cheston, "State of Global Microfinance: How Public and Private Funds Can Effectively Promote Financial Inclusion for All," Statement to the Committee on House Financial Services, US House of Representatives, January 27, 2010, http://www.house.gov/apps/list/hearing/financialsvcs_dem/cheston_testimony.pdf.

28. Sam Daley-Harris, *State of the Microcredit Summit Campaign Report* (Washington, DC: Microcredit Summit Campaign, 2009).

29. Chen et al., *Progress of the World's Women 2005*; Nandin Azad, "Gender and Equity: Experience of the Working Women's Forum, India," *International Social Science Journal* 48, no. 2 (June 1996): 219–29; and Patrick Develtere and An Huybrechts, "The Impact of Microcredit on the Poor in Bangladesh," *Alternatives: Global, Local, Political* 30, no. 2 (April 2005): 165–89. See references on SEWA below, note 55.

30. Ananya Roy, *Poverty Capital: Microfinance and the Making of Development* (New York: Routledge, 2010), 26.

31. "SKS I.P.O. Ignites Microfinance Debate," *New York Times*, July 29, 2010.

32. Elizabeth Rhyne, "State of Global Microfinance: How Public and Private Funds Can Effectively Promote Financial Inclusion for All," Statement to the Committee on House Financial Services, US House of Representatives, January 27, 2010, http://www.house.gov/apps/list/hearing/financialsvcs_dem/rhyne_testimony.pdf.

33. Neil MacFarquhar, "Banks Making Big Profits from Tiny Loans," *New York Times*, April 13, 2010.

34. Most studies find increases in the level, but not in the diversification, of women's economic activity; no radical change in the gender division of labor; and better nutrition, health care, and education of children, especially girls. Some studies report positive impacts on women's agency, such as an increase in household decision making, accumulation of assets, and a decrease in domestic violence. Other studies find an intensification of workloads, no increase in household decision making, and an increase in domestic violence. More recent studies support the summary of the literature found in Naila Kabeer, "Conflicts over Credit: Re-evaluating the Empowerment Potential of Loans to Women in Rural Bangladesh," *World Development* 29, no. 1 (2000): 63–84.

35. Thomas Dichter, "Too Good to Be True: The Remarkable Resilience of Microfinance," *Harvard International Review* 32, no. 1 (Spring 2010): 19, 21.

36. Hester Eisenstein, "A Dangerous Liaison? Feminism and Corporate Globalization," *Science and Society* 69, no. 3 (July 2005): 487–518; Srilatha Batliwala, "Taking the Power Out of Empowerment: An Experiential Account," *Development in Practice* 17, no. 4–5 (August 2007): 557–65.

37. Linda Mayoux, "Microfinance and Women's Empowerment: Rethinking 'Best Practice,'" *Development Bulletin* 57 (2002): 76–81.

38. Ralph Armbruster-Sandoval, "Workers of the World Unite? The Contemporary Anti-Sweatshop Movement and the Struggle for Social Justice in the Americas," *Work and Occupations* 32, no. 4 (2005): 464–85.

39. Joe Bandy, "Paradoxes of Transnational Civil Societies under Neoliberalism: The Coalition for Justice in the Maquiladoras," *Social Problems* 51, no. 3 (2004): 410–31.

40. Martha Alter Chen, "Women in the Informal Sector: A Global Picture," *SAIS Review* 21, no. 1 (2001): 71–82; also the WIEGO website, http://www.wiego.org.

41. Homeworkers Worldwide, http://www.homeworkersww.org.uk.

42. StreetNet International, http://www.streetnet.org.za.

43. WIEGO, "Informal Workers in Focus: Domestic Workers," http://www.wiego.org/publications/FactSheets/WIEGO_Domestic_Workers.pdf.

44. International Domestic Workers Network, http://www.domesticworkerrights.org; ILO, Decent Work for Domestic Workers; Report IV(1). Fourth Item on the Agenda. Geneva, ILO (2010); ILO, "100th ILO Annual Conference Decides to Bring an Estimated 53 to 100 Million Domestic Workers Worldwide under the Realm of Labour Standards," June 16, 2011, http://www.ilo.org/ilc/ILCSessions/100thSession/media-centre/press-releases/WCMS_157891/lang--en/index.htm.

45. Jennifer N. Fish, "Engendering Democracy: Domestic Labour and Coalition-Building in South Africa," *Journal of Southern African Studies* 32, no. 1 (March 2006): 107–27.

46. Ilda Lindell, "'Glocal' Movements: Place Struggles and Transnational Organizing by Informal Workers," *Geografiska Annaler Series B: Human Geography* 9, no. 2 (2009): 123–36.

47. Chen et al., *Progress of the World's Women* (2005), 75.

48. Mary Margaret Fonow, Suzanne Franzway, and Valentine Moghadam, eds., *Making Globalization Work for Women: States, Trade Unions, and Women's Social Rights* (Albany: SUNY Press, 2011), 10.

49. This case study draws heavily on the work of Ben Selwyn. See "Labour Process and Workers' Bargaining Power in Export Grape Production, North East Brazil," *Journal of Agrarian Change* 7, no. 4 (October 2007): 526–53; "Trade Unions and Women's Empowerment in North-east Brazil," *Gender and Development* 17, no. 2 (July 2009): 189–201; and "Gender Wage Work and Development in North East Brazil," *Bulletin of Latin American Research* 29, no. 1 (2010): 51–70. See also "Gender Issues in Agricultural Labor," *Gender in Agriculture Sourcebook*, 315–59.

50. Stephanie Barrientos, "Gender Flexibility and Global Value Chains," *IDS Bulletin* 32, no. 3 (2001): 83–93.

51. "Oppenheimer to Represent Brazil's Largest Grape Grower," July 7, 2008, from the Oppenheimer group website, http://www.oppyproduce.com. Retrieved August 30, 2010.

52. *Gender in Agriculture Sourcebook*, 321.

53. Selwyn, "Trade Unions and Women's Empowerment in North-east Brazil," 198.

54. Selwyn, "Gender Wage Work," 61–63.

55. This section draws from SEWA organizational materials (http://www.sewa.org) and Martha Alter Chen, "Self-Employed Women: A Profile of SEWA's Membership" (Ahmedabad, India: SEWA, 2006); Martha Chen, "A Spreading Banyan Tree: The Self-Employed Women's Association, India," in *From Clients to Citizens: Communities Changing the Course of Their Own Development*, ed. Alison Mathie and Gordon Cunningham (Rugby, UK: Intermediate Technology Publications Ltd., 2008).

56. UN Research Institute for International Development, *Combating Poverty and Inequality: Structural Change, Social Policy and Politics* (Geneva: UNRISD, 2010), 116.

57. As reported on SEWA's website, http://www.sewa.org/Twenty_Fifth_Issue.asp.

58. Renana Jhabwala et al., "Empowering Women in an Insecure World: Joining SEWA Makes a Difference" (Ahmedabad, India: SEWA, n.d.).

59. Quoted by Chen, "A Spreading Banyan Tree," 28.

60. Mary Beth Mills, "From Nimble Fingers to Raised Fists: Women and Labor Activism in Globalizing Thailand," *Signs: Journal of Women in Culture and Society* 31, no. 1 (Autumn 2005): 117–46.

61. Michele Ford, "Women's Labor Activism in Indonesia," *Signs: Journal of Women in Culture and Society* 3, no. 3 (Spring 2008): 510–14; and Jennifer Bickham Mendez, *From the Revolution to the Maquiladoras: Gender, Labor and Globalization in Nicaragua* (Durham, NC: Duke University Press, 2005).

62. Jennifer Jihye Chun, "The Limits of Labor Exclusion: Redefining the Politics of Split Labor Markets under Globalization," *Critical Sociology* 34, no. 3 (2008): 433–42; Pun Ngai, "China as a World Factory: New Practices and Struggles of Migrant Women Workers," in Martha Chen et al., *Membership-Based Organizations of the Poor* (New York: Routledge, 2007), 83–101; Leith L. Dunn, "Women Organising for Change in the Caribbean Free Trade Zones," in *Confronting State, Capital and Patriarchy*, ed. Amrita Chhachhi and Rene Pittin (New York: St. Martin's Press, 1996), 205–43.

63. Ben Selwyn, "Disciplining Capital: Export Grape Production, the State and Class Dynamics in Northeast Brazil," *Third World Quarterly* 3, no. 3 (2009): 519–34.

64. Renana Jhabvala and Ravi Kanbur, "Globalization and Economic Reform as Seen from the Ground: SEWA's Experience in India," Paper presented to the Indian Economy Conference, Cornell University, April 19–20, 2002, http://www.sewa.org/images/Archive/Pdf/Globalization_Economic_Reform.pdf.

65. Naila Kabeer, "Paid Work, Women's Empowerment, and Gender Justice," *Critical Pathways of Social Change*, no. 3 (2008): 88; and Chhachhi and Pittin, "Introduction," *Confronting State, Capital and Patriarchy*, 11.

66. Kabeer, "Paid Work," 88.

67. Chris King-Chi Chan and Pun Ngai, "The Making of a New Working Class? A Study of the Collective Actions of Migrant Workers in South China," *China Quarterly* 198 (June 2009): 287–303.

68. Mary Margaret Fonow and Suzanne Franzway, "Transnational Union Networks, Feminism and Labour Advocacy," in *Trade Union Responses to Globalization: A Review by the Global Union Research Network*, ed. Verena Schmidt (Geneva: ILO, 2007), 165–75.

7

Debates and Dilemmas: Health

Health, like work, is intensely personal. All of us are concerned about our own health and that of those around us. We understand some of the science surrounding health issues (such as the reality of communicable diseases); we know what epidemics are; and we recognize terms—AIDS being an obvious example—unknown to earlier generations.

In many ways, health issues generate large communities of agreement. Few people disagree about the need to combat malaria or to improve maternal and infant health. In other ways, however, major health controversies affect a wide range of issues: Vaccinations, so-called lifestyle conditions (e.g., diabetes, emphysema, sexually transmitted diseases), and reproductive health are examples of areas where major debates continue over the nature of the problem and the appropriate solutions. Even the areas of substantial consensus generate controversy when the matter of responsibility, the question of who is to pay for treatment, is raised.

STRUCTURE

Some health conditions have scarcely changed over the centuries. Maternal and infant mortality, for example, remain extraordinarily high in some regions of the world, recalling conditions that existed in Europe centuries ago. Water-borne diseases are as common in many areas as they have been since time immemorial. Accidents and diseases associated with certain forms of work (such as mining) continue to be widespread. Despite these realities, the structure of health care has changed as much in the past century as has the nature of work. Three trends stand out: the impact of modern science and technology, the influence of neoliberal capitalism, and the militarization of cultures and social systems.

The most obvious structural impact of modern science has been biomedical research leading to medicines for the prevention and treatment of disease, including antibiotics; immunizations for diseases as varied as rabies, tetanus, and polio; and antiretroviral drugs. The broad changes in science and technology during the twentieth century also led to striking advances in the control of reproduction, including contraceptives and prenatal screening. Access to these medicines and technologies has been uneven, generally determined by a combination of class, information, geography, and sociocultural norms. Even in wealthy countries, people who are poor, uneducated, and geographically isolated often lack access to the best medical options. In some instances, the technologies may be used for purposes unintended by those who developed them and championed their availability. The use of prenatal screening to abort unwanted girls is a well-known example.

Technology, primarily as it has contributed to modern transportation, is an important structural factor facilitating the spread of communicable diseases. For example, the influenza pandemic of 1918–1919, sometimes referred to as the "Spanish flu," killed an estimated twenty to forty million people. The virus spread among troops transported to and from the battlefields of World War I, then followed trade routes around the world. This pandemic was a precursor to numerous other diseases that in later years spread rapidly due to the increasing ease of transportation, including the 2003 severe acute respiratory syndrome (SARS) and AIDS.

The expansion of neoliberal capitalist structures has had multiple, sometimes contradictory, effects on health issues and the policies proposed to address them. During the 1990s, in particular, many governments were under pressure from international institutions to scale back public services in order to save money and improve budgetary prospects. These policies, in turn, sought to make the countries in question better candidates for development loans and international investment. A typical area for curtailed government expenditures was public health, thus reversing a trend begun in Europe during the nineteenth century.

For most of history, providing for health (like education) has been primarily the responsibility of the family. With the advance of industrialization and the consolidation of nation-states, demands increased in western Europe to establish services for the general public. The idea that health or education should be a government responsibility reflected the important structural changes taking place in Europe during this period. Movements for public health, emphasizing sanitation, began in Britain and France in the first half of the nineteenth century; and by the second half of the century, health professionals pressured governments to create community health programs. By the middle of the twentieth century, progress in improving health for individuals, families, and communities had become an accepted measure of development (and an accepted obligation of governments) around the world.

Improved public health programs depend on establishing and maintaining infrastructures for sewage treatment, potable water, rural health facilities, and the prevention of communicable diseases. Government decisions to shrink public health services and infrastructures in the 1990s thus reversed a development pattern that had emerged over the course of the previous two centuries. One of the consequences of this structural shift was to reemphasize families, and particularly women in the family, as the primary (or sole) providers of health services, and to leave poor people vulnerable to communicable—especially water-borne—diseases. By the early part of the twenty-first century, some of the long-term, unintended consequences of the underfunding of public health infrastructures became obvious, and major international organizations began to reconsider this dimension of neoliberal policies.

Finally, militarization reflects a vital structural feature accounting for shifts in the nature of health issues and debates. The term militarization here includes the expanded scope and depth of military conflict, as well as the trade in weapons and the ideologies that sustain weapons and conflicts. As the discussion of the globalization of health issues later in this chapter makes clear, one of the most important consequences of greater militarization was to push gender-based violence to the forefront of feminist organizing. The calculated, systematic use of rape in time of war in the former Yugoslavia (Bosnian War, 1992–1995), the Rwandan civil war (1994), and the Democratic Republic of Congo (2003–present) highlighted the vulnerability of women in ways not seen in earlier conflicts.

It is clear that governments must always make decisions about expenditures, and nothing guarantees that money spent on weapons might otherwise be spent on health care. However, it is equally clear that the interests dedicated to maintaining or expanding military institutions and weapons systems are better organized and represented in budget debates around the world, with the result that social priorities such as health are seldom competitive. To illustrate with the case of the United States, it is not difficult to make the argument that the trillions of dollars committed to the wars in Iraq and Afghanistan in the first decade of the twenty-first century contributed to the budget deficits during the second George W. Bush and the Barack Obama administrations; these deficits, in turn, increased pressure for budget cuts, especially in categories poorly represented by organized interests, such as some health-care services and programs for the poor. A different but very concrete example came to light in Uganda in 2011, when it was revealed that the government was contracting with the Russian Federation to purchase six fighter jets, allegedly for the equivalent of US$740 million. Critics charged that this sum would pay to build and equip seventeen hundred health centers that could handle emergency care and maternity cases in a country with one of the highest maternal mortality rates in the world.[1]

AGENCY

Chapter 1 emphasized not only the importance of the structures within which we operate, but also our ability to influence or change structures through individual and collective efforts. The remainder of this chapter and chapter 8 explore the implications of the structural changes for individual and collective agency identified in the previous section.

The emergence of sophisticated science and technological developments has affected the structure of health in different, often controversial, ways. Those who see their personal agency expanded are typically enthusiastic supporters because the negative repercussions are more removed in time and space. The development of contraceptive technologies, for example, has indisputably benefited those with access to them. Although universal access is still limited by money, information, culture, and family structures, millions of women and families have enjoyed expanded agency in recent decades in terms of their ability to plan for children. Many individuals and families would also argue that prenatal screening, including screening for the purpose of sex selection, has expanded their control over childbearing, and family size and composition. Abortion technologies have been much more controversial, as noted below, with men and women (including feminists) divided over the implications of these technologies.

Other structural changes resulting from science and technology have generally been greeted with similar enthusiasm, despite voices of concern over the ethical or health consequences. For example, most people view immunizations positively, seeing them as a major tool for curtailing, even exterminating, deadly diseases such as smallpox and tuberculosis. Detractors are concerned about their overall effects on health, and, in a few controversial instances, have charged that immunizations are part of a conspiracy to limit family size. In vitro fertilization, a more recent reproductive technology, similarly has both supporters and detractors, with supporters seeing the advances as expanding their agency.

Economic policies associated with neoliberal reforms were the result of strategies determined by international organizations and national governments, and represented a reformulated approach to development beginning in the 1980s. Like with all development strategies, some people benefited more than others. Clearly, some corporations, towns, families, and individuals benefited from these changes as a result of expanded entrepreneurial or trade opportunities. Others, however, saw their business and livelihoods diminished or eliminated. Many rural communities have seen their economic and social bases eroded or erased by cheaper food imports or land conversion to large-scale agribusiness, with negative consequences for individual and family health. An obvious response to these structural changes has been the determination of many individuals to exercise their agency by migrating to urban areas or immigrating to other countries. Migrants, in turn, might find better access to health facilities but also be exposed to negative health conditions more prevalent in urban areas, such as tuberculosis or air pollution.

It is harder to determine who might benefit from increased militarization of economies and cultures. Those who trade in arms or who are the "winners" in military conflicts presumably benefit. Losers are more numerous, primarily because of the reduced scope for agency. On the surface, women arguably suffer more loss of agency than men, because many fewer women are combatants. Those women who are combatants—that is, those who choose to serve in military organizations—

generally think of themselves as enjoying enhanced agency, although when the costs are clearer—through family separations, sexual harassment, or injury and illness—perceived agency may be fleeting.

On a larger scale, agency may be contradictory or depend on one's class and locale, even though the same conditions appear to affect the entire population. A troubling case of this reality is Afghanistan during the first decade of the twenty-first century. The defeat of the Taliban resulted in new or reasserted opportunities for women and girls to go to school or work, for example, and many observers quickly concluded that Afghan women universally enjoyed greater freedom (i.e., agency). However, the opportunities depended on family structures, underlying social norms (which did not necessarily change with the overthrow of the Taliban), and access to facilities such as schools or public transportation. In 2013, Afghanistan ranked 175 out of 186 on the United Nations human development index, with an average life expectancy of forty-nine years and mean years of schooling approximately three. In addition, the ongoing war after the US-led invasion resulted in further deaths and widespread destruction.

LEVELS OF ANALYSIS

The preceding discussion has illustrated the interrelationship of multiple layers of analysis. At the most intimate, localized levels, people try to cope with changes over which they have no control, such as government budgetary priorities or a war. They usually have little knowledge of the underlying causes or decision making that leads to these changes. A new factory may mean jobs—or not. Land "reclaimed" or appropriated, perhaps for a dam, might mean a loss of income and a way of life.

The ability of individuals to cope with these changes depends on what liberal feminists, such as Amartya Sen and Martha Nussbaum, call human capabilities (see chapter 2). These capabilities depend on factors that vary dramatically from one person to another and may be inherent, such as health, intelligence, and imagination. But all of these, as well as others, may be enhanced by structures, including health clinics and schools. Humans endowed with more "native" abilities, enhanced by resources—from family to government support—will be better placed to respond to changes beyond their control and work them to their advantage.

Earlier chapters have emphasized the extent to which individual agency may be enhanced by collective endeavor; that is, collective agency may accomplish what individuals cannot. Collective agency is most desirable when people are confronted with large institutions or issues spread over a large space. In the sections that follow, the importance of collective agency stands out. After an overview of contemporary health issues, the sections on the global politics of health and organizing for women's health issues emphasize the importance of feminist strategies for collective agency.

THE WORLD OF HEALTH

Many health issues affect women and men to approximately the same degree, but a greater number of issues show significant differences by sex.[2] In general, women have a longer life expectancy than men, but the gap is smaller and life expectancies are much lower in low-income countries in comparison with high-income countries. Life expectancy at birth has increased for both men and women since 1990, with a few exceptions such as southern African countries, where the HIV/AIDS epidemic diminished life spans seven years for men and ten years for women from the early 1990s to the late 2000s. Although the number of HIV/AIDS cases appears to be stabilizing, with thirty-four million people estimated to be HIV-positive in 2011, 69 percent of these are in sub-Saharan Africa, and women account for almost 60 percent of these cases.[3]

On a global level, non-communicable diseases, such as cardiovascular disease, diabetes, and cancer, were the most important causes of death. They accounted for 58 percent of male deaths and 63 percent of female deaths in 2004, although causes of death vary considerably across regions. For example, breast cancer and cervical/uterine cancer were the most common forms of cancer for women; and for men, lung and prostate cancer were most common.

As suggested by the statistics for cancer and HIV/AIDS in southern Africa, a number of sex differentials affect health risk factors. Men are more likely to engage in heavy alcohol consumption and tobacco use than women. Women are more likely to be obese than men, and diabetes is more prevalent among women than men. Gender-based violence is another risk factor for women. Violence against women, most often inflicted by intimate partners, affects anywhere between 15 and 71 percent of women, according to a World Health Organization study of eleven countries.[4] Genital cutting has affected an estimated 92.5 million girls and women in Africa.[5] Women are more likely to attempt suicide than men; and in rural China, suicide is the leading cause of death for women. Women are also at risk from their food preparation responsibilities; in poor countries using solid fuels in cooking, death rates for chronic obstructive pulmonary disorder (COPD) from indoor air pollution are 50 percent higher for women than for men.[6] In contrast, men are more likely to die from industrial accidents and murder.

Maternal and Reproductive Health

One of the most striking realities in the global world of health is that reproductive health, notably maternal mortality, remains the Millennium Development Goal where the least progress has been made. Developing countries account for 99 percent of maternal deaths, or more than five hundred million annually.[7] In 2011, the UN Commission on the Status of Women concluded that "unavailable, inaccessible, unaffordable or poor quality care is fundamentally responsible" for the direct causes of maternal mortality and morbidity: "haemorrhage, infection, high blood pressure, unsafe abortion, and obstructed labor" are all contributing factors.[8] Prenatal care improves the outcomes of pregnancy and birth, but levels of prenatal care, as well as percentage of deliveries attended by a skilled attendant and percentage of deliveries in health facilities, vary widely around the world. Table 7.1 shows the percentage of women receiving these services in 2005–2011 across various regions. One of the striking realities to emerge from these statistics is the huge geographical disparity. For example, in Africa, less than half of mothers deliver their babies with the help of a skilled attendant; and only 37 percent get postnatal care, which helps explain why maternal morbidity remains such a huge problem in this region. Widespread adolescent pregnancy, which is associated with increased medical complications and reduced livelihood options, contributes to these high morbidity rates.

In view of the health risks associated with pregnancy and childbirth, access to contraception is an important factor in efforts to reduce maternal morbidity. The United Nations has estimated that contraceptive use is approximately 63 percent among women of reproductive age in marriage or in unions worldwide. In rich countries the most commonly used methods are the pill (18 percent) and the male condom (15 percent), whereas in poor countries, most common are sterilization (22 percent) and the intrauterine device (IUD, 15 percent).[9] Lack of access to contraceptives is most acute in Africa, where only 28 percent of women of childbearing age are using contraceptives and one in four women who would like to limit or delay childbearing is not using any type of contraceptive.[10]

One of the consequences of low contraceptive use is the prevalence of induced abortions. For example, induced abortions in 2008 were estimated at forty-two million, with five out of six taking place in poor countries with limited access to safe abortions; approximately 68,000 women die every year from complications from unsafe abortions.[11] This represents almost 13 percent of all maternal deaths.[12]

Women bear a large responsibility for the health of their children. Mortality for children under five years of age has been falling over the past few decades except in southern Africa (another effect of HIV/AIDS); and although the mortality rate is biologically higher for boys than for girls, important exceptions are notable in Asia, especially in China, India, Pakistan, and Afghanistan. The child mortality and

Table 7.1. Percentage of Women Receiving Childbirth Services (latest available)

Region	Prenatal Care, 2005–2011	Skilled Attendant, 2005–2011	Postnatal Care, 2005–2011
Global	81	69	46
African region	74	48	37
Americas	95	93	—
Southeast Asia region	76	59	48
European region	—	98	—
Eastern Mediterranean region	72	59	42
Western Pacific region	93	91	—

Source: Adapted from World Health Organization, *World Health Statistics 2012.*

Table 7.2.   Adult Sex Ratios in China and India (Males to Females)

	2010–2011	*2000–2001*
China	1000:952	1000:943
India	1000:914	1000:927

Sources: Adapted from *Census of India*, http://censusindia .net (2001 census data and preliminary results of the 2011 census); figures for China from the 2000 census data and summaries of the 2010 census. China and India express their ratios differently; this form was chosen for easier comparison.

morbidity rates in these countries, which are exacerbated by prenatal sex selection, have led to a skewing of the sex ratios. Table 7.2 compares adult sex ratios in the two countries with the largest populations, China and India. These statistics offer only a partial picture of the reality due to regional and age cohort variations. For example, although the adult sex ratio in China at the last census in 2010 showed about 50 females "missing" for every 1,000 males, at birth the discrepancy was much wider, with 118 baby boys for every 100 baby girls born.[13]

THE GLOBAL POLITICS OF HEALTH

The global politics of health over the past sixty years have reflected broad shifts in thinking about development, as well as a dramatic expansion in the number of "players" in international development policies, players ranging from international organizations to national governments, nongovernmental organizations, and private corporations. In 1948, under the auspices of the newly created United Nations, an international health agency, the World Health Organization (WHO), was formally established with priorities to address infectious diseases (malaria, tuberculosis, and venereal disease), maternal and child health, sanitary engineering, and nutrition. Readers may recall that in the 1950s and early 1960s, world leaders were optimistic that advances in science and technology would address most of the water quality and quantity problems confronting poor countries. Similarly, this period saw enormous optimism that modern medicines and equipment would eradicate disease.

The faith in science and technology also contributed to the emphasis on population control in the late 1960s, when birth control pills and IUDs became available. Women were targeted as objects of health programs, but governments and international organizations were particularly concerned to reduce fertility, so separate population control programs were devised as a more effective way to address family planning.

In the 1970s an important Western development approach stressed basic needs and poverty eradication. During this era, health-care policies were inclusive, emphasizing primary health care as the means for providing health care for all people. This approach was spelled out at the 1978 International Conference on Primary Health Care in what was then Alma-Ata, Kazakhstan. The conference was important in that it reflected the thinking about health at the international level before the 1980s, when neoliberal policies and structural adjustment programs became widespread. The Alma-Ata Declaration stated:

> Primary health care is essential health care based on practical, scientifically sound and socially acceptable methods and technology made universally accessible to individuals and families in the community through their full participation and at a cost that the community and country can afford to maintain at every stage of their development in the spirit of selfreliance and self-determination.[14]

In retrospect, the approaches that dominated most of international health policy during the 1960s and 1970s are important today for three reasons. One is the continued importance of scientific and technological thinking in our efforts to address persistent diseases: for example, AIDS. Another is the emphasis on reproductive health in global politics. In an earlier era, reproductive health was interpreted primarily in terms of "family planning" or population control. By the twenty-first century, the scope of debates had expanded to address the implications of new technologies such as prenatal screening, maternal health more generally, and reproductive rights. Although not absent from the earlier discussions about reproductive health, feminists in every country are now fully engaged in the debates. Finally, one should note that the challenge of primary health care has not diminished; in fact, it has expanded to health-care debates in countries such as the United States.

The "Players"

By the 1980s and 1990s, the development philosophy reflected at Alma-Ata was supplanted by the goals of greater efficiency and cost reduction that were central to neoliberal development policies. In 1979, the World Bank established its Health, Nutrition and Population Department and gradually emerged as the most important global actor in health policy.[15] The primary health-care approach formulated in the 1970s was sidelined because it was deemed too expensive and it was replaced by "low-cost, selective interventions as a guaranteed minimum 'basic package' of services."[16] The new focus, exemplified by the kinds of projects the World Bank financed, emphasized greater privatization of health-care services and decentralized responsibility to lower levels of government and to individual families as payers. Bilateral (government-to-government) donors tended to emphasize the same approach in their lending.

According to the economic theory shaping World Bank policy, health-care consumers are rational individuals who will seek medical help when they become sick or injured and will be willing to pay for this service. However, this theory did not work in practice, as poor people did not have the financial resources necessary to access health care. Studies of the impact of these health reforms in developing countries reveal that user fees did not generate much revenue; but they did cause sharp declines in use of health facilities, and privatization and decentralization reduced access of the poor.[17] For women, increases in home deliveries and delays in seeking care led to increases in maternal and infant mortality; women were burdened by more time caring for sick family members, who lacked the financial resources to go to health facilities.[18]

In addition to the World Bank and the World Health Organization, the bilateral development aid program of the United States has enjoyed special influence. For the past half century, the United States has administered the largest bilateral foreign aid program in the world, primarily through the Agency for International Development (USAID). This reality has made the United States one of the most important players in global health policies.

One of the defining characteristics of US foreign health initiatives has been the shifting policies toward funding abortion and reproductive health programs more generally. During the administrations of Presidents Reagan (1981–1989), George H. W. Bush (1989–1993), and George W. Bush (2001–2009), development funding to family planning was cut significantly, and any NGO that dealt with abortion was defunded. This policy became known as the Mexico City policy/Global Gag Rule because of the administrations' prohibition on funding programs that might lead to abortion. Under Presidents Clinton (1993–2001) and Obama (2009–2017), family planning cuts were restored, and the Mexico City policies were suspended. Although President George W. Bush made a substantial commitment to HIV/AIDS funding in the 2003 President's Emergency Plan for AIDS Relief (PEPFAR), many feminists criticized his initiative because of a requirement that 6.7 percent of the funding had to be used for abstinence education.[19]

In the first decade of the twenty-first century, the number of players in global health politics increased. As in the other policy sectors we have examined, the main actors in this multi-stakeholder process include states, international institutions, NGOs, transnational corporations, and transnational social movements. International institutions that have decades of involvement in health issues, notably the World Bank, WHO, and the UN, continue to be significant. Complicating this mix of international actors, pharmaceutical companies[20] assumed greater importance; and private foundations, particularly the Bill and Melinda Gates Foundation, also became prominent.

Old and new international alliances have also become more prominent in global health-policy debates. States and international institutions recognized the importance of health to development in articulating three goals pertaining to health in the eight Millennium Development Goals (reduce child mortality; improve maternal health; and combat HIV/AIDS, malaria, and other diseases). Health issues have become part of the policy agenda of the Group of 8 ("G8"), whose governments make policy pronouncements at their annual meetings.[21] As a result of the call for a more inclusive response to infectious diseases at the 2000 G8 Summit and an agreement reached at the 2001 UN General Assembly Session on AIDS, a new alliance was formed. The Global Fund to Fight AIDS, Tuberculosis, and Malaria made its first round of grants in 2002. During this same period, the Global Alliance for Vaccines and Immunisation (GAVI), a multisectoral, public-private partnership, was established to provide vaccines for children in poor countries.

Some of these collaborative initiatives show the increasing influence in global health politics of the Gates Foundation. The foundation emphasizes investments in science and technology to address diseases that have affected millions of people, especially in Africa and Asia, including AIDS, polio, and malaria. Foundation commitments have resulted "in large amounts of money going directly into mainly biomedical interventions, such as immunization and improved drug supply."[22] Although official government assistance for health, mainly from rich nations, accounted for $10.6 billion in the early 2000s, the fact that the Gates Foundation made global health grants of $2.25 billion, approximately one-fifth the amount of government assistance, testifies to its growth by the early twenty-first century as a major player.[23]

AIDS and the Antiretroviral (ARV) Debate

As suggested above, one of the most critical health issues for global health players has been addressing the treatment and prevention of HIV/AIDS. For transnational social movements, HIV/AIDS advocacy has served to unify diverse groups and provide political momentum. In 2000–2001, a global campaign for access to essential medicines demonstrated the power of social movements acting in a concerted fashion.[24] The campaign focused on the problem of securing antiretroviral (ARV) medicines for people living with HIV/AIDS. For example, the Treatment Action Campaign of South Africa and the US and European branches of the AIDS Coalition to Unleash Power (ACT UP) mounted noisy demonstrations, while allies, such as the NGOs Oxfam and Médecins Sans Frontières (MSF, Doctors without Borders), along with the WHO and the French National AIDS Council, engaged in lobbying.

The campaign around antiretroviral medicines is a key example of the interplay of international organizations and agreements, national governments, social movements, and private corporations in health issues. Antiretroviral medicines came to public attention in the mid-1990s, but they were out of reach financially to millions in poor countries. The movement to expand access to ARV medicines confronted a complex network of international trade, finance, and political structures. The so-called TRIPS Agreement (Trade Related Aspects of International Property Rights) of 1994 had established a minimum global standard of patent and copyright protection that was enforced by the World Trade Organization. The agreement required countries, including poor countries with millions of HIV-positive citizens, to pay the brand-name prices for the ARVs. Although some exceptions to the patent rules applied, only a few countries were in a position to take advantage of them; and when they did, the United States and transnational pharmaceutical companies threatened lawsuits.

The issue came to a head in South Africa with a lawsuit brought by pharmaceutical companies against the government, although the lawsuit was withdrawn after great public agitation. This public pressure contributed to the November 2001 Declaration at the WTO Ministerial Conference in Doha, Qatar, that TRIPS "does not and should not prevent Members from taking measures to protect public health" and the subsequent decisions by pharmaceutical companies to offer "equity" (lower) pricing for ARVs in low-income countries.[25] Since the 2001 Doha Declaration, the balance of power between large pharmaceutical companies demanding high prices for ARVs and other life-saving medicines, and low- and middle-income countries seeking affordable drugs has shifted somewhat against "Big Pharma."[26] For example, Thailand, Brazil, and India manufacture generic versions of ARVs. In retrospect, the ability of social movements to pressure and navigate the structures of the global political economy in order to expand access to antiretroviral drugs for HIV/AIDS patients may be viewed as a successful exercise of collective social and political action.

By the end of the first decade of the twenty-first century, policy makers noted a lack of progress in reaching several of the Millennium Development Goals directly related to health and began to rethink and revise several assumptions of the neoliberal development policies. A broad consensus emerged that some policies contributed to poverty; and "mechanisms such as community-based health insurance, private insurance, and user fees have not proved viable pathways to scaling up coverage and social health protection. As a result, implementation of an incremental shift to public financing that substitutes for out-of-pocket financing, especially for poor and vulnerable groups in society, is crucial."[27]

Starting with the World Bank in 2007, funders developed programs to strengthen health systems in poor countries. In 2008, the WHO announced the resurrection of the primary health-care approach and took the initiative to implement greater coordination in health policies. The result was the establishment of "Health8," a coalition composed of WHO, the World Bank, GAVI, the Global Fund, UNICEF, UNFPA, UNAIDS, and the Gates Foundation. G8 leaders undertook a greater leadership role in global health policy, addressing health issues at their annual summits, creating "a highly personal, visible, and flexible mechanism for addressing global health policy making."[28] However, the global financial crisis of 2008–2010 undermined these initiatives to promote universal coverage.

SEEKING A FEMINIST APPROACH

Abortion, contraception, rape, gender-based violence, and sexuality are all topics in the feminist development discourse and can be seen as components of women's health, broadly conceptualized. This broad characterization of health fits the 1946 World Health Organization (WHO) definition of health: "a state of complete physical, mental and social well-being and not merely the absence of disease or infirmity."[29] Women face many threats to their well-being in the areas of reproduction, sexuality, and violence; and have organized to address these threats. Women's personal experiences of the reproductive body, violated body, caring body, and sexualized body became the bases of feminist political movements in North America and Western Europe beginning in the late 1960s, spreading to many other countries over the 1970s, and subsequently becoming prominent issues in gender and development policies and debates in the 1980s and 1990s.[30]

This section emphasizes the ways in which the female body figures in contemporary debates about health policies and development. The female body is clearly central to traditional understandings of threats to women's health, such as disease and maternal mortality and morbidity. However, the "Second Wave" of feminism in the 1960s and 1970s focused greater attention on the notion that "the personal is political." Feminists argued that topics formerly confined to the private sphere properly belong in the public sphere. Put differently, "personal" issues such as reproduction, sexual autonomy, and violence—customarily hidden in families and considered private matters—should be addressed in public and be subjected to legal and political debates.

Body Politics in American Feminism

The history of the way in which personal issues became part of the political arena in the United States, although unique in many ways, is important in the larger international context. This history also illustrates some important differences that emerged within the feminist movement, differences that continued into the twenty-first century. In the United States, feminists in the 1960s and 1970s sought to reassert control over their bodies, which they viewed as having been taken away by the medical profession.[31] They emphasized self-help and produced their own resources, such as *Our Bodies, Ourselves*, first issued in pamphlet form by the Boston Women's Health Book Collective in 1969 and then published in nine editions between 1971 and 2011 and translated into several languages.[32]

Feminist publications offered women access to reliable information about their own bodies. They charged that some contraceptives, such as Depo-Provera and IUDs, were dangerous, having been released after only limited testing.[33] Before the 1973 *Roe v. Wade* decision, abortion was illegal, and feminists assisted women in finding safe abortions and in some cases performing first-trimester abortions themselves.[34] They created women's crisis centers and "hot lines" to support victims of rape and domestic violence.

Reproductive rights and antiviolence work shaped a feminist ideology of radical feminism based on women's embodied experiences, what we have called difference feminism. Radical feminists were critical of the power of professionals and of the capitalist system, and they created alternative institutions that they hoped would operate on an egalitarian basis. Liberal feminists, in contrast, focused most of their attention on changing laws: for example, laws restricting contraception and prohibiting abortion.

In contrast to the mainstream movements, where both radical and liberal feminist organizational efforts were dominated by middle-class, white women, American women of color expressed frustration that the movements did not address their needs. Whereas radical feminists concentrated on body politics and liberal feminists on legislative reform, women of color raised issues of race and class, articulating a version of diversity feminism. They saw the structural violence of racism and social class as forms of violence against women that undermined their health. Black women, in particular, argued that sterilization abuse, lack of affordable treatment for sexually transmitted diseases (STDs), and high rates of infant mortality were important components of reproductive freedom.[35] Disproportionate numbers of black, Latina, and Native American women had experienced sterilization abuse in the 1960s and 1970s; for example, studies revealed that half of the women sterilized through federally funded programs each year were black.[36] Black women were also critical of what they saw as the "racialization of rape," reminding white feminists that charges of rape had historically been used to control black men.[37]

Internationalizing the Movement

All of these variations of the American feminist health movement were internationalized through the formation of networks and the dissemination of feminist writing. In 1977 European feminists held what became the first International Women's Health Meeting (IWHM) in Rome.[38] The first meetings, held every few years, focused on self-help and legalizing abortion. The focus broadened with the addition of participants from Asia, Africa, and Latin America, who brought up issues of racism and imperialism in population control programs. In a manner similar to women of color in the United States, women from the Global South emphasized diversity feminism in the international feminist health movement. For example, they criticized the neo-Malthusian assumptions that shaped population planning in the 1970s, which they interpreted as blaming underdevelopment on poor people.[39] In contrast, the IWHM perspective emphasized that reproductive rights required material conditions of social justice in order to have any real meaning.

Violence against women was an important issue at the IWHM meetings in the 1980s; and as participants became more diverse, the definition of the scope of violence broadened to encompass religious, militarist, and institutional violence as well as the original focus of interpersonal violence. Women refugees from Latin American military dictatorships told stories of the "disappeared." South Asian Indian women began to talk about police rape and dowry deaths in the late 1970s, and in the 1980s added sex-determination tests leading to "female fetuscide" to the many forms of violence that Indian women experienced. Women from South Korea and the Philippines raised the issue of "comfort women" forced by the Japanese military to be prostitutes during World War II. By 1980, the report of the UN Women's Conference in Copenhagen called for legislation "to prevent domestic and sexual violence

Photo 7.1.   Sri Lankan Poster: "Rural Women Unite Against Violence." Photo courtesy of James W. Boyd

against women"; and violence against women figured even more prominently at the 1985 Nairobi Conference.[40] The Sri Lankan poster highlighting the issue of violence against rural women, which dates from the 1980s, illustrates this international consciousness-raising around the issue of gender-based violence (see photo 7.1).

One of the most difficult issues confronting feminists around the world has been the role of culture in defining "gender-based violence" (GBV) and how to address it. In the 1970s a division between northern and southern activists over gender-based violence was apparent as northern women identified some cultural practices in Africa and Asia, notably genital cutting, as instances of violence against women; and southern activists angrily labeled these claims as "cultural colonialism." The anger reflected a profound disagreement over what was culturally "normal" and acceptable, with defenders of cutting arguing that the practice was intrinsic to important cultural values. In contrast, their opponents claimed that the practice constituted indefensible attacks on girls and women that denigrated their self-worth and placed their health at great risk.

The critics of genital cutting thus reflected the preoccupation with the body politics that had emerged from North American and European feminism, whereas African women, in particular, saw a new form of colonial thinking that denied the value of indigenous practices and failed both to acknowledge the role of local women's groups working to address these cultural practices and the responsibility of northern states in the economic exploitation of the South. By the 1980s, however, movements against GBV had emerged in a number of southern states, and a shared understanding of the wide range of forms that constituted violence had developed among northern and southern feminists. These included genital cutting, honor killings, sex-selective abortions, rape as a weapon of war, as well as the issues first identified by European and American feminist movements: rape and domestic violence.

Collective Agency and International Agenda Setting on Population and Gender-Based Violence (GBV)

In the early 1990s, a group of feminists initiated a campaign to create a uniform feminist stance on reproductive rights to influence the upcoming 1994 UN Conference on Population and Development (ICPD) in Cairo.[41] The resulting "Women's Declaration on Population Policies," supported by women's organizations around the world, called for the recommendations coming from the ICPD to take a reproductive health approach to population planning and to proclaim that "reproductive rights are human rights."[42]

The commitment to reproductive rights that emerged in the Cairo Programme of Action was an enormous achievement for the feminist organizing campaign prior to the 1994 conference, but not all feminist groups agreed with the pragmatist approach that led to the commitment. The feminist debates after Cairo exposed the fault lines between liberal and diversity approaches. Diversity feminists argued, in particular, that the Cairo program did not address the international economic environment created by the widespread dominance of neoliberal policy making. Radical groups, such as the Feminist International Network of Resistance to Reproductive and Genetic Engineering (FINRAGE) and the Committee on Women, Population and the Environment (CWPE), believed that the pragmatists had sold out to the "population establishment" by emphasizing a pragmatic and inclusionary approach rather than a radical, transformative one. Betsy Hartmann charged, "The document accepts the current population paradigm as a given, offering no substantive critique of the 'free market' economic model or its impact on poor women."[43] Rosalind Petchesky, although she supported the ICPD Programme of Action, pointed to an important shortcoming: "the ICPD's failure to address macroeconomic inequities and the inability of the prevailing neoliberal, market-oriented approaches to deliver reproductive and sexual health for the vast majority."[44] One diversity feminist NGO consistently critiquing the neoliberal framework and calling for a comprehensive framework for development was Development Alternatives for Women in a New Era (DAWN), an international feminist organization created in the 1980s.

Violence against women figured prominently in the 1985 UN Women's Conference in Nairobi, and the recommendations made in the Forward Looking Strategies called on governments to increase their assistance to victims and to "increase public awareness of violence against women as a societal problem."[45] The next major push to have violence against women addressed as a global health issue came in the early 1990s, in preparation for the 1993 UN World Conference on Human Rights in Vienna (WCHR). Human rights were conventionally thought of in terms of state harms inflicted on individuals. During the late 1980s, feminist legal scholars began to make the argument that women's human rights rested not only on state action, but also on the actions of (mainly male) community and family members, and that the state had a responsibility to protect women from all of these forms of violence. These efforts reflected the role of liberal feminists working in a variety of institutional contexts.

Feminist leadership for the Vienna conference came from the Center for Women's Global Leadership (CWGL) and its director, Charlotte Bunch, a veteran feminist with a background in civil rights, lesbian feminism, and human rights. The CWGL initiated a global campaign for the incorporation of GBV into the Vienna Programme for Action. CWGL held leadership institutes for southern feminists, launched a global petition drive, and developed a campaign, "16 Days of Action Against Gender-Based Violence," to create a strong base of support for the idea that "women's rights are human rights" and that the elimination of GBV had to be a central plank in the global feminist agenda. During the conference, feminists staged an International Tribunal at which women from twenty-five countries testified on various types of GBV, such as domestic violence, rape, political persecution, and the structural violence that leads to illiteracy.[46]

Feminists were successful in getting GBV recognized as a human rights violation and a crime at the international level. The Vienna Declaration and Programme of Action issued by the WCHR recognized women's human rights and recommended

that the UN General Assembly adopt the Declaration on the Elimination of All
Forms of Violence Against Women, which occurred in late 1993. In 1994 the UN
appointed a special rapporteur on violence against women to the UN Commission
on Human Rights.

In retrospect, the Fourth World Conference on Women (FWCW) in Beijing in
1995 stands as the culmination of feminist organizing and formal international recognition of an expanded definition of women's health rights. The Beijing Platform
for Action reinforced the commitment to women's reproductive rights and freedom
from violence, identified rape as a war crime, and the signatories of the Platform
pledged to end genital cutting, prenatal sex selection, and violence against women.
The Beijing Platform also supported women's right to control their sexuality, although several government delegations objected.[47]

Finally, the UN responded specifically to the gender-based violence that had
emerged in the context of the civil and international wars of the 1980s and 1990s.
The International Criminal Court, established in 1998, included many forms of
GBV as crimes in wartime. The UN Security Council Resolution 1325 in 2000
called for the inclusion of women in peace and security deliberations, and the International Criminal Tribunal for the former Yugoslavia handed down a conviction for
rape and enslavement as crimes against humanity.[48] As a result of these initiatives, by
the early twenty-first century, issues that three decades earlier had been unidentified
or ignored, including domestic violence and rape as a systematic war strategy, were
part of the international discourse on human rights.

In spite of the continued UN attention to gender-based violence, implementation
of recommendations from the Cairo, Vienna, and Beijing conferences disappointed
feminists of nearly every persuasion. The first decade of the twenty-first century
was marked by growing religious fundamentalism hostile to feminist definitions
of women's rights, a conservative US presidential administration under George W.
Bush that once again opposed family planning funding for NGOs, and renewed
neoliberal policies that privatized health services. The UN's institutional clout weakened, whereas the G8, World Bank, IMF, and WTO gained in influence. Although
women's groups did bring up macroeconomic issues at a variety of UN-sponsored
meetings, the official documents issued after these meetings ignored these concerns.
The election of Barack Obama restored family planning funding, but subsequent
attacks within the United States on abortion and funding for contraception raised
doubts about the future of the administration's policy. Moreover, the global economic crisis beginning in 2008 exacerbated unemployment and underemployment
around the world, and governments everywhere were pressured to reduce public debt
by trimming public services.

In retrospect, the debate over the Millennium Development Goals, discussed in
chapter 3, illustrates the long-standing tensions in feminist strategies toward social,
economic, and political change. What can be accomplished through the kinds of
inclusionary strategies advocated by both liberal and difference feminists, especially
in circumstances requiring mobilization of a variety of social groups? The efforts to

mitigate the devastating effects of HIV/AIDS suggest that coalition building across social groups and nation-states can yield progress. Similarly, strategies of elite access to institutional decision making resulted in the modification of MDG 5 to include reproductive health—a long-standing, shared feminist objective. None of these efforts, however, resulted in any major changes in the structures of globalization. Although diversity feminists were quick to point out the defects in government policies and international initiatives such as the MDGs, they lacked the resources to transform those structures.

We assume, therefore, that feminist organizing is unlikely to transform the fundamental power of contemporary neoliberalism in the short term. Consequently, we look for those arenas where feminists may use a combination of inclusive *and* resistance strategies to "work" the existing structures—both those of individual nation-states and those of international systems. In these strategies, agency is contingent on time, place, and political institutions. The two case studies that follow illustrate the variety of circumstances in which collective agency may make a difference in people's lives, even while falling short of transformation.

CASE STUDIES

Since the beginning of the twenty-first century, some successful examples exist of feminist engagement with the state in order to expand women's access to health services and to address issues of reproductive rights and gender-based violence. In this section, we explore two cases of recent feminist collective action in the area of health. The first case depicts the involvement of feminists in health sector reform in Chile. The second case illustrates feminist organizing at the regional level in Africa.

The Politics of Health Care-Reform: Chile

Among states in the Global South, Chile was an early adopter of neoliberal reforms in its system of health care.[49] From the 1930s to the 1970s, for the mainly male formal-sector workforce, both white collar and blue collar, health care was a state-provided right. Most women gained access to health care as female dependents of male workers. General Augusto Pinochet, coming to power through a military coup in 1973, enacted health reforms beginning in 1979 that introduced market principles, eliminated employer contributions, and shifted some of the costs of health care to the individual. Formal-sector workers could purchase health insurance from newly created private providers or rely on state services, which were decentralized to municipalities and regions. A 7 percent mandatory health insurance contribution on earnings was instituted. Low-income individuals received free care in the state system, but were eligible for a limited range of services. The majority of the population relied on state services, and both systems required client co-payments.

In addition to being partially privatized and decentralized, this two-tiered system was also gendered, with women representing about one-third of private insurance beneficiaries in 2001 and women's rates for coverage more than three times higher than men's.[50] Women could purchase slightly less expensive plans (still twice the cost of men's plans) that excluded childbirth ("no-uterus plans"). The influence of the Catholic Church could be seen in the exclusion from coverage of services involving sterilization or treatment for abortion complications. (In Chile and most other Latin American countries, abortion was both illegal and relatively common.)

Chile underwent a democratic transition in 1990, and the coalition government established a government agency for women's issues, the National Women's Service (SERNAM). Chilean feminists were divided over the issue of working with the new government: some did, others took a stance of complete autonomy, and still others recommended "conditional collaboration from an independent base."[51] In 2000, then president Ricardo Lagos initiated a process of health sector "re-reform," and set up working groups and a technical commission to design a new health-care system.[52]

In the broad area of health, most Chilean feminists concentrated on reproductive rights and gender-based violence. Some feminists, along with organizations of nurses and midwives, participated in the working group "Citizenship and Health" and a special commission on gender issues in health-sector reform set up by the health minister, Michelle Bachelet. The special commission issued a report in January 2001, addressing not only reproductive rights and gender-based violence, but also the principles of "financing on the ability to pay rather than risk, and shared responsibility for the costs of social reproduction."[53] The participatory process of working groups ended when Bachelet left the health ministry in early 2002, and a technocratic interministerial commission drafted the new legislation without considering the women's proposals.

A new opportunity to engage with state officials opened for feminists in 2002, when the Pan American Health Organization (PAHO) initiated a "Gender, Equity and Health Reform Project" in Chile. PAHO is an international public health agency and the regional office for the World Health Organization. In Chile, the project resulted in feminist organizations holding four "Parliaments of Women for Health Reform" between 2002 and 2005, demanding greater involvement of civil society in the health-reform process and the commissioning of research on gender and health. The PAHO project included a "mapping exercise," identifying for women's health advocates key entry points for civil-society groups engaging with the state and educating state officials on the unpaid work women contributed in health care.

The Chilean "re-reform," officially called the Plan for Universal Access with Explicit Guarantees or "Plan AUGE," was passed by Chile's legislature in 2004 and came into force in 2005. Plan AUGE provided a universal package of health services for Chilean citizens. Childbirth services were included, ending the "no-uterus" plans.[54] During the implementation phase of Plan AUGE, feminists were able to create allies in the health ministry and SERNAM. An earlier SERNAM minister had declined involvement in the reform process, but a newly appointed minister worked with feminists during the implementation process. Subsequently, Plan AUGE began covering mental health services and the effects of GBV. Through a gender-mainstreaming program, SERNAM was given the authority to evaluate the extent to which government agencies had integrated gender into their policies. In 2004 SERNAM found that the health ministry did not meet the standards of gender integration. The threat of budget cuts led to greater gender responsiveness on the part of the ministry. Gender sensitivity training in the health ministry was carried out through funding from PAHO.

The African Union (AU) Protocol to the African Charter on Human and Peoples' Rights on the Rights of Women in Africa

In addition to transnational and national level organizing, women's networks at the regional level have played an important role in placing women's rights on the political agenda. In Africa, a regional advocacy network composed of regional and national women's organizations formulated a women's rights protocol that addresses GBV and reproductive rights, as well as economic and political rights, such as the right to inherit land. The 1981 African Charter on Human and Peoples' Rights adopted by the Organization of African Unity (OAU) did not address women's rights in a substantial manner, and in 1995 a seminar jointly sponsored by the African Commission on Human and People's Rights and Women in Law and Development in Africa (WiLDAF) discussed "the need to make the African Charter 'more responsive' to women's rights."[55] They pointed out that respect for traditional values the Charter endorsed could be used to justify certain forms of violence against women, such as genital cutting. Over the next eight years, a regional advocacy network of women's organizations developed a draft protocol and lobbied national governments and the OAU/AU.[56] The Women's Rights Protocol was formally approved by the African heads of state in July 2003 and came into force in November 2005. In 2004 the women's network set up a coalition, Solidarity for African Women's Human Rights (SOAWR), to direct the campaign for ratification and implementation of the Women's Protocol.

The Women's Protocol prohibits all forms of violence against women, obliges states to adopt necessary legislation for violence prevention and the punishment of perpetrators, and commits governments to provide the resources necessary to implement these provisions. Specifically prohibited and condemned are harmful practices such as genital cutting, forced marriage, and victimizing women identified as "witches."[57] Reproductive rights are guaranteed by the protocol, including contraception; protection against sexually transmitted diseases, such as HIV/AIDS; and abortion in cases of sexual assault, incest, and under conditions where the pregnancy endangers mental or physical health. The Protocol is legally binding but lacks enforcement provisions. The coalition of women's organizations was unable to gain support from governments for a provision setting restrictions on polygamy but gained acceptance for a statement that "monogamy is the preferred form of marriage."[58] The Protocol requires states to include information on implementation in its biennial reports to the African Commission.

The Women's Protocol has been an important resource for women's rights in African countries. It was referenced in a civil suit brought over a rape of a thirteen-year-old girl by her teacher in Zambia. The judge quoted Article 4 of the Women's Protocol, which stated that the government shall take appropriate and effective measures "to enact and enforce laws that prohibit all forms of violence against women," awarded damages to the girl, and called on the authorities to prosecute the teacher.[59] In several countries, provisions of the Women's Protocol have been translated into songs as an educational tool for women's rights.[60]

Writing in November 2010, Mary Wandia, a cofounder of SOAWR and a member of the African Feminist Forum Working Group, noted that much work is yet to be done in putting into place national legislation to enforce the Women's Protocol provisions. She recommended that feminists form strategic partnerships with professional organizations of lawyers and judges to increase understanding of the Protocol and litigation using it. To that end, SOAWR created "A Guide to Using the Protocol on the Rights of Women in Africa for legal action."[61]

What Do These Cases Tell Us?

At the national level, in the case of health-sector reform in Chile, and at the regional level, in the coalition of African women's groups formalized in SOAWR in 2004, feminists have pursued women's rights goals through inclusionary strategies of policy advocacy. In Chile, the result was improved health-care coverage for women; and in Africa, the result was a formal commitment by African leaders to take action against GBV. In both cases, the policies adopted reflected greater support for feminist values on gender-based violence than on abortion. The African Women's Protocol allowed abortion under limited conditions, and Plan AUGE in Chile did not address abortion, which remained illegal.

The two cases highlight the importance of cooperation between regional and national levels for feminist policy advocacy. In Latin America, PAHO's Gender Equality and Health Reform Project was an important resource for Chilean women activists. In Africa, the regional Women's Protocol was used to enforce women's rights in a Zambian court. In both cases institutional transitions provided a favorable political opportunity structure for women's rights reforms. In Africa, the transition from the OAU to the AU allowed for policy change and greater input for civil-society organizations. In Chile, President Lagos's decision to reform the health sector provided an opportunity for women to lobby for policies meeting women's needs.

The inclusionary strategies pursued in these two cases emphasized relationships between feminist leaders and political elites and de-emphasized relationships between feminist leaders and any kind of mass base of women. Alliances with government leaders were crucial for the success of women activists in Africa; and ties between Michelle Bachelet and feminists, and relationships between feminists and health ministry officials, were important in Chile.

The successes of these examples, however, have been limited by a variety of factors, including insufficient information flows and minimal grassroots organizing. To illustrate, in Chile the Women's Parliaments strongly endorsed reproductive rights and identified unpaid care work as a central gender issue, but those demands went nowhere. Potentially, in Chile women (and men) can claim their rights and file judicial claims against health-care providers who do not provide the health services guaranteed by Plan AUGE, but studies show very few people know this.[62] The potential is similar for the Women's Protocol in Africa. Feminist educational campaigns at grassroots levels, if they involved more systematic two-way communication, could make both Plan AUGE and the Women's Protocol more relevant to urban working-class and rural women. In the end, however, this would require a strategy of greater collective organizing.

Christina Ewig and Jasmine Gideon offer contending feminist perspectives on how to make sense of the agency of women's groups participating in health-sector reform since 2000 in Chile. Ewig argues that the reconfigured neoliberal state offers both limits and opportunities to women's rights groups advocating gender equality in health. She notes that "organized feminists and their allies in the state" were able to "socialize the costs of reproduction, in particular, biological reproduction."[63] In contrast, Jasmine Gideon characterizes the participation of women's groups with the neoliberal state as co-optation, arguing that the participation processes promote neoliberal values and have little impact on state decision making on health care.[64]

The two perspectives are not mutually exclusive; rather, they emphasize lighter and darker shades of gray in assessing the implications of feminist inclusionary strategies with the neoliberal state. We think it is useful to take a "both-and" approach to the perspectives of Ewig and Gideon. We appreciate that inclusionary strategies of participation with and in the state, on the one hand, have the potential to strengthen women's voices and improve outcomes for women in society by engaging with state institutions. On the other hand, inclusionary strategies also have the potential to weaken women's voices and worsen outcomes for women in society because most women are not organized or mobilized at the grassroots level. Without this mobilization, the implementation of gender-sensitive laws and policies is not guaranteed. Additionally, without a mass base of women holding decision makers accountable, a change in political players at the regional or national level may reverse these laws and policies.

The achievements of SOAWR in Africa can be assessed along similar lines. On the one hand, the record on implementing and enforcing the Women's Protocol by the thirty-one states that have ratified it is mixed at best. On the other hand, the existence of the Women's Protocol *is* a resource that feminists in Africa can use in their campaigns for women's rights and empowerment. African governments, through the Women's Protocol, have gone on record in support of women's rights, which has some effect on their actions. For example, in June 2011 African heads of state called on the UN to adopt a resolution banning genital cutting worldwide. For this resolution to be meaningful, however, local collective action campaigns are necessary.

These cases offer illustrations of two different inclusionary strategies of participation. The Chilean case offers an exception to the lack of feminist attention to broad health-care reforms in many countries where neoliberal policies have been adopted. The African case illustrates the potential benefits of regional feminist coalitions in facilitating state buy-ins to feminist positions on violence against women. In both instances, however, as well as in much of the world, aspects of reproductive rights continue to expose deep cleavages in opinion, including among many feminists. In the United States, for example, conservative opposition to gendered aspects of "Obamacare," such as requirements for employers to provide access to contraception, shows the persistence of conflict over reproductive rights.

In summary, we assume that neoliberal globalization is here for the foreseeable future, and we recognize that the preponderance of research suggests negative implications for women, notably in the arena of health. We also note, however, that other dimensions of globalization, such as the transformation of communication technologies and the multiplication of transnational organizations (both intergovernmental and nongovernmental), offer tools and spaces for women to assert collective agency. Likewise, it is clear—particularly in the Chilean case—that it *does* make a difference who is in power, even in a neoliberal world.

CONCLUSION

The history of health debates and policies over the past half century reinforces our understanding of gender and globalization. First, this understanding requires knowledge of the social, political, economic, and ideological structures that set the context for our individual and collective lives. Second, gender inequality is embedded in structures at every level, from the family and household to the global political economy; and this inequality exacerbates health problems, especially for the poor. Third, maternal and reproductive health, along with gender-based violence, have been the most pressing global health issues for women in general. Fourth, despite an unfavorable set of structures, collective action can and has made a difference—for example, in making gender-based violence a public issue, placing reproductive health on international agendas such as the Millennium Development Goals, and expanding the debate on antiretroviral medicines to include the poor.

Feminist movements in many nations have addressed issues of health, broadly defined to include GBV and sexual and reproductive rights.[65] Overall, feminists have achieved substantial legislative success on issues of gender-based violence but not on reproductive or sexual rights. Organized primarily as NGOs with international funding, women's groups have provided legal support, counseling, and shelters to address GBV. In many nations, legislation against domestic violence has been passed.

Coalitions of women's organizations have produced Shadow Reports to the UN Convention on the Elimination of All Forms of Discrimination Against Women (CEDAW), criticizing their governments' records on women's rights. Although legislation criminalizes GBV, serious challenges remain in rectifying the structural factors that contribute to GBV; and women's movements have not, on the whole, emphasized poverty and class inequality.

Feminists have been organizing around women's reproductive, violated, and sexualized bodies for more than forty years. They have built international, regional, and national networks and linked them with local organizations. They were able to secure normative commitments to women's human rights at the international level at UN conferences in the 1990s. They have provided services to women and engaged in a wide variety of advocacy campaigns related to women's health. In advocating for women's rights, feminists have faced strong opposition from conservative and fundamentalist religious groups and some national governments; and in many cases, basic rights have been demolished by civil and international military conflicts. Perhaps the most important contribution feminists have made in health issues broadly conceived has been the articulation of a woman's right to her body. As Brazilian feminist Jacqueline Pitanguy states:

> The struggle around the body is key to women's freedom because women's bodies have always been an occupied territory by the elders, the church, medical establishment, demographic control of her fertility, etc. Throughout history, women have fought for freedom, and the first freedom is over her body. Other factors go along with bodily freedom: economic and social status, legal systems and penal codes, but women's power has also a direct relation to the exercise of sexual and reproductive rights.[66]

NOTES

1. Edris Kiggundu and David Tash Lumu, "Fighter Jet Secrets Out," *The Observer* (Uganda), April 10, 2011, http://www.observer.ug/index.php?option=com_content&view=article&id=12 930:f. See also Celia W. Dugger, "Maternal Deaths Focus Harsh Light on Uganda," *New York Times*, July 30, 2011. Dugger pointed to one of the unintended consequences of foreign aid designed to help African countries fight AIDS and other infectious diseases. Most of the aid recipients have reduced their own share of domestic spending devoted to health.

2. This section draws primarily on the United Nations, Department of Economic and Social Affairs, *The World's Women 2010*, "Health" (New York: UN, 2010), 19–42.

3. The Henry J. Kaiser Family Foundation, "The Global HIV/AIDS Epidemic" Fact Sheet, December 18, 2012, http://kff.org/global-health-policy/fact-sheet/the-global-hivaids-epidemic.

4. World Health Organization, *Women and Health: Today's Evidence, Tomorrow's Agenda* (Geneva: WHO, 2009), 55.

5. World Health Organization, *Women and Health*, 23.

6. World Health Organization, *Women and Health*, 10.

7. UN, Commission on the Status of Women, Fifty-fifth session, February 22–March 4, 2011, "Eliminating Preventable Maternal Mortality and the Empowerment of Women," Panel

Discussion, March 1, 2011, Issues Paper, http://www.un.org/womenwatch/daw/csw/csw55/panels/IssuesPaper-Panel5.pdf.

8. "Eliminating Preventable Maternal Mortality," 2.

9. UN, *The World's Women*, 37–38. The figures are from 2007.

10. UN, *The World's Women*, 37–38; WHO, *Universal Access to Reproductive Health, Accelerated Actions to Enhance Progress on Millennium Development Goal 5 through Advancing Target 5B* (2011), 5, http://whqlibdoc.who.int/hq/2011/WHO_RHR_HRP_11.02_eng.pdf.

11. UN, *The World's Women*, 38.

12. WHO, *Unsafe Abortion: Global and Regional Estimates of the Incidence of Unsafe Abortion and Associated Mortality in 2008*, 6th ed. (Geneva: WHO, 2011), 1. The grounds for legal abortion vary widely across countries; in 98 percent of countries, abortion is legal to save the life of the mother, but in only 28 percent of countries is abortion allowed on request.

13. Figures summarized from the National Population and Family Planning Commission of China, at http://www.npfpc.gov.cn/en.

14. Declaration of Alma-Ata, International Conference on Primary Health Care, Alma-Ata, USSR, September 6–12, 1978, http://www.who.int/publications/almaata_declaration_en.pdf.

15. Howard Stein, *Beyond the World Bank Agenda: An Institutional Approach to Development* (Chicago: University of Chicago Press, 2005).

16. Hilary Standing, "An Overview of Changing Agendas in Health Sector Reforms," *Reproductive Health Matters* 10, no. 20 (2002): 21.

17. Stein, *Beyond the World Bank Agenda*, 227–35.

18. Hilary Standing, "Frameworks for Understanding Health Sector Reform," in *Engendering International Health: The Challenge of Equity*, ed. Gita Sen, Asha George, and Piroska Östlin (Cambridge, MA: MIT Press, 2002), 347–71.

19. PEPFAR Watch Organization, http://www.pepfarwatch.org/the_issues/abstinence_and_fidelity. President Obama subsequently lifted the abstinence stipulation on PEPFAR.

20. Transnational pharmaceutical companies and their lobbying groups, such as IFPMA (the International Federation of Pharmaceutical Manufacturers and Associations), shape drug availability and cost.

21. The Group of 8 is a policy forum comprised of the United States, Russia, the United Kingdom, Japan, Germany, France, Canada, and Italy.

22. Standing, "An Overview of Changing Agendas," 25.

23. People's Health Movement et al., *Global Health Watch: An Alternative Report* (London: Zed Books, 2008), 211. The data are from 2006.

24. Rosaline Petchesky, *Global Prescriptions: Gendering Health and Human Rights* (London: Zed Books, 2003), chap. 3.

25. Quoted in Petchesky, *Global Prescriptions*, 105.

26. Mikhka Glaser and Ann Marie Murphy, "Patients versus Patents: Thailand and the Politics of Access to Pharmaceutical Products," *Journal of Third World Societies* 27, no. 1 (2010): 215–45; Gardiner Harris and Katie Thomas, "Low-Cost Drugs in Poor Nations Get a Lift in Indian Court," *New York Times*, April 1, 2013 (online edition).

27. Ravi P. Rannan-Eliya, "Panel 2: Strengthening Health Financing in Partner Developing Countries," in Michael R. Reich and Keizo Takemi, "G8 and Strengthening of Health Systems: Follow Up to the Tokyo Summit," *Lancet* 373 (2009): 511.

28. Reich and Takemi, "G8 and Strengthening of Health Systems," 512.

29. WHO, Preamble to the Constitution of the World Health Organization as adopted by the International Health Conference, New York, June 19–July 22, 1946; signed on July 22, 1946, by the representatives of sixty-one states (Official Records of the World Health Organization, no. 2, 100), http://www.who.int/suggestions/faq/en/index.html.

30. See Wendy Harcourt, *Body Politics in Development: Critical Debates in Gender and Development* (London: Zed Books, 2009).

31. Estelle Freedman, *No Turning Back: The History of Feminism and the Future of Women* (New York: Ballantine Books, 2002), 216.

32. New York: Simon & Schuster. See "Celebrate Forty Years of Activism," http://www.ourbodiesourselves.org/40thanniversary.asp.

33. Sheryl Burt Ruzek, *The Women's Health Movement: Feminist Alternatives to Medical Control* (New York: Praeger, 1978), 42.

34. Sara M. Evans, *Tidal Wave: How Women Changed America at Century's End* (New York: Free Press, 2003), 47.

35. Jennifer Nelson, "All This That Happened to Me Shouldn't Happen to Nobody Else: Loretta Ross and the Women of Color Reproductive Freedom Movement of the 1980s," *Journal of Women's History* 22, no. 3 (2010): 140.

36. Nelson, "All This That Happened to Me," 141.

37. Kristin Bumiller, *In an Abusive State: How Neoliberalism Appropriated the Feminist Movement against Sexual Violence* (Durham, NC: Duke University Press, 2008), 10.

38. Sylvia Estada-Claudio, "The International Women and Health Meetings: Deploying Multiple Identities for Political Sustainability," in *Solidarities beyond Borders: Transnationalizing Women's Movements*, ed. Pascale Dufour, Dominique Masson, and Dominique Caoutte (Vancouver: University of British Columbia Press, 2010), 108–26.

39. The English scholar Robert Malthus (1766–1834) believed that population would rise faster than the food supply. Neo-Malthusians identified overpopulation as the biggest threat to development. In contrast, feminists and many southern theorists believed that economic development necessary to lower fertility and population control in poor countries was hampered by the governments of rich nations. See Sonia Correa in collaboration with Rebecca Reichman, *Population and Reproductive Rights: Feminist Perspectives from the South* (New Delhi: Kali for Women, 1994), 1.

40. Report of the World Conference of the United Nations Decade for Women: Equality, Development and Peace, held in Copenhagen July 14–30, 1980, A/CONF.94/35, http://www.5wwc.org/conference_background/1980_WCW.html.

41. Martha Alter Chen, "Engendering World Conferences: The International Women's Movement and the United Nations," *Third World Quarterly* 16, no. 3 (September 1995): 477–93.

42. Excerpted in Correa, *Population and Reproductive Rights*, 66.

43. Betsy Hartman, *Reproductive Rights and Wrongs: The Global Politics of Population Control*, rev. ed. (Boston: South End Press, 1995), 153.

44. Petchesky, *Global Prescriptions*, 36.

45. Cited in Jutta Joachim, *Agenda Setting, the UN, and NGOs: Gender Violence and Reproductive Rights* (Washington, DC: Georgetown University Press, 2007), 116.

46. Joachim, *Agenda Setting, the UN, and NGOs*, 127.

47. Conservative delegations forced the deletion of any reference to sexual orientation, but feminists viewed the wording that was adopted in paragraph 96 as offering a foundation for

future efforts to gain explicit recognition for lesbian rights. See Shelagh Day, "Women's Sexual Autonomy: Universality, Sexual Rights and Sexual Orientation at the Beijing Conference," *Canadian Women's Studies* 16, no. 3 (1996): 46–54.

48. Liz Kelly, "'Inside Outsiders': Mainstreaming Violence against Women into Human Rights Discourse and Practice," *International Feminist Journal of Politics* 7, no. 4 (2005): 484.

49. For information on the Chilean case, see Christina Ewig, "Reproduction, Re-reform and the Reconfigured State: Feminists and Neoliberal Health Reforms in Chile," in *Beyond States and Markets: The Challenges of Social Reproduction*, ed. Isabella Bakker and Rachel Silvery (London: Routledge, 2008), 143–58; Jasmine Gideon, "Integrating Gender Interests into Health Policy," *Development and Change* 37, no. 2 (2006): 329–52; Charles Dannreuther and Jasmine Gideon, "Entitled to Health? Social Protection in Chile's Plan AUGE," *Development and Change* 39, no. 5 (2008): 845–64; Jasmine Gideon, "Consultation or Co-option? A Case Study from the Chilean Health Sector," *Progress in Development Studies* 5, no. 3 (2005): 169–81.

50. Ewig, "Reproduction, Re-reform and the Reconfigured State," 148–49.

51. Gideon, "Integrating Gender Interests," 343.

52. "Re-reform" is Ewig's term.

53. Ewig, "Reproduction, Re-reform and the Reconfigured State," 151.

54. Dannreuther and Gideon, "Entitled to Health?," 857.

55. Melinda Adams and Alice Kang, "Regional Advocacy Networks and the Protocol on the Rights of Women in Africa," *Politics and Gender* 3 (2007): 460.

56. In 2002 the African Union (AU) was formed as a successor organization to the Organization of African Unity.

57. Rose Gawaya and Rosemary Semafumu Mukasa, "The African Women's Protocol: A New Dimension for Women's Rights in Africa," *Gender and Development* 13, no. 3 (2005): 42–50. The Women's Protocol is available at http://www.africaunion.org/root/au/Documents/Treaties/Text/Protocol%20on%20the%20Rights%20of%20Women.pdf.

58. Adams and Kang, "Regional Advocacy Networks," 464.

59. Corey Calabrese and Caroline Muthoni Muriithi, "The Next Frontier: Legal Action and the AU Women's Protocol," *Pambazuka News* 507, November 24, 2010, 2.

60. Messain d'Almeida, "African Women's Organizing for the Ratification and Implementation of the Maputo Protocol," AWID Friday File (November 11, 2011), http://awid.org/News-Analysis/Friday-Files/African-Women-s-Organizing-for-the-Ratification-and-Implementation-of-the-Maputo-Protocol.

61. Equality Now, "A Guide to Using the Protocol on the Rights of Women in Africa for Legal Action," 2011, http://www.soawr.org/resources/Manual_on_Protocol_on_Women_Rights_in_Africa.pdf.

62. Dannreuther and Gideon, "Entitled to Health?," 858.

63. Ewig, "Reproduction, Re-reform and the Reconfigured State," 156.

64. Gideon, "Consultation or Co-option?," 169.

65. See the collection of essays in Amrita Basu, ed., *Women's Movements in the Global Era: the Power of Local Feminisms* (Philadelphia: Westview Press, 2010).

66. In Wendy Harcourt, "Empowerment, Women's Bodies and Freedom: In Conversation with Khawar Mumtaz and Jacqueline Pitanguy," *Development* 53, no. 2 (2010): 158.

8

Collective Action, Development, and the Challenges of Globalization

We have argued that "development" simultaneously suggests an intellectual concept, a historical period, and a strategy or project. By the end of the twentieth century, development—in every sense of the term—was inseparable from the forces of globalization. Similarly, gender relations have been immutably influenced by the expectations and realities of development in the new global context.

We have also emphasized that the changes of the late twentieth and early twenty-first centuries have benefited some and disadvantaged others. In general, women have been hurt more than men, with poor women typically the worst off. That this should be the case is a paradox: Global forces have had negative, even disastrous, consequences for millions of women; at the same time, a "global gender equality regime" in governance institutions has emerged in the past half century to champion the cause of women. This equality regime has facilitated connections among women's movements at local, national, and transnational levels: They learn from each other and from a widely shared discourse that helps to legitimize their policies and actions. Chapter 2 explained that the UN-sponsored women's conferences between 1975 and 1995 generated momentum for the growth of women's movements and worldwide government initiatives for women. During this same period and for the early decades of the twenty-first century, collective action strategies, often led by feminists, proliferated. Organizers at every level, from the very local to the international, embarked on development initiatives to improve the well-being of the poor, particularly women. They exploited the new global technologies for information and transportation. At the same time, however, women themselves were exploited by the global currents of consumerism ("sex sells"), neoliberal economics, and militarism.

NAVIGATING GLOBAL STRUCTURES:
NEOLIBERALISM, MILITARISM, AND
THE GLOBAL GENDER EQUALITY REGIME

Neoliberalism

We have noted that neoliberalism refers to the philosophy and practice of favoring market over state development strategies, cutting back state organizations and services, and encouraging the global flow of goods, services, and capital. The majority of feminist activists and researchers have criticized neoliberalism for harming women and children by intensifying the double or triple day (market, family, and community responsibilities) of women, increasing economic inequality, and failing to substantially decrease poverty worldwide.

Although feminist analysis has emphasized the generally detrimental consequences of neoliberal globalization, specific studies have illuminated cases in which certain classes of women enjoy lives that are directly or indirectly improved by the forces of globalization. The decision of the Chinese government to restructure the domestic economy and embrace the global marketplace is one such example. Despite onerous working conditions in export-oriented factories, migrants from rural areas have demonstrated by their moves to coastal factories that they see life in urban manufacturing centers far preferable to farm labor. Moreover, in addition to changing economic structures, demographic trends have, over time, opened windows to collective action. Women generally outnumber men on labor-intensive production lines. Growing labor shortages, a result of slowing rates of population growth and rural-to-urban migration, have led to rising wages and more frequent strikes driven by demands for higher pay and better working conditions. Women have been central to many of these strikes as well as to the subsequent teams of representatives chosen to negotiate with management.[2]

As in the case of the STR in Brazil, shifts in the structure of production—for example, to less labor-intensive manufacturing in China—may work to the disadvantage of collective action by workers, and the tight political control the Chinese government exercises obviously limits the scope for workplace organizing. It is equally plausible, however, that the collective action experience of factory workers may be transferred to new contexts. The dynamic, uneven nature of market economics means that different classes and regions will experience varying opportunities.

Although feminist *analysis* has exposed some of the consequences of neoliberal globalization for women, most international feminist *action* projects have emphasized specific gender issues rather than challenging international economic structures. For example, feminists participated in the UN conferences on the environment in 1992, and on population and development in 1994, where they focused on including gender issues in the conference action plans without explicitly criticizing the neoliberal turn in the global political economy, despite the implications of the latter for both gender relations and development policies.

At the national level, where the context is clearer and the scope of action more focused, a few exceptions break the pattern of emphasizing inclusion rather than structural transformation. The "re-reform" of Chilean health-care policies (chapter 7) is one such instance. In this case, feminists lobbied to ensure that women's health concerns were addressed in the health-care policies being adopted in Chile and that glaring gender inequalities in the existing policies, such as the "no-uterus" plans, were changed.

The Chilean case, whatever its limitations, is important. Although many international and national organizations have claimed that gender concerns have been "mainstreamed" into government, without explicit feminist organizing efforts around economic, social, educational, health, and welfare policies, women's needs are often not recognized or addressed in the legislation. Moreover, even when women's needs *are* addressed, as in the contraceptive coverage mandated in "Obamacare" in the United States, vociferous opposition may arise in the name of cost, religion, or state intrusion into private decisions.

Ironically, one unintended consequence of policies reducing the size of the state, compounded by the innovative dynamism of market economics, has been to open up spaces for the development and growth of NGOs, some of which are explicitly feminist and many of which have challenged what they insist are the negative dimensions of globalization. The explosion of communication technology, including the Internet, cell phones, and social media, has been an important resource for NGOs, enabling them to share information across national boundaries, reach members more easily, and respond to events more quickly. The worldwide reaction to the gang rape in Delhi mentioned at the beginning of this book is one example of this phenomenon. Some of the progressive actions of these NGOs are discussed later in this chapter.

Militarism

National and international militarism constitutes a structural feature of the modern world. Although not an explicit focus of our case studies, military spending and conflict condition the lives of everyone directly or indirectly. Military conflicts in the Balkans in the 1990s, western and southern Africa over the past two decades, and elsewhere created the conditions for organized traffickers to exploit the vulnerability of those displaced by war. Maryam was trafficked by several individuals who were part of an organized crime network operating in east and southeast Europe in the wake of the breakup of communist states and the subsequent conflicts (see chapter 4).

Although precise statistics are elusive, estimates of the level of militarized violence in the world in 2012 included 208 violent conflicts, 18 wars, 25 limited wars, and more intrastate than interstate conflicts.[3] Total world military expenditures in 2012 were estimated to be $1.75 trillion, 2.5 percent of global GDP. US military spending represented 39 percent of the total, the largest share, followed by China and Russia.[4]

At the global level, military spending is roughly similar in size to public education spending.[5] But whereas education spending is arguably central to the development process, violent conflict is "development in reverse": "[w]ars destroy physical and human capital, disrupt service delivery, divert public expenditures to the military, disrupt the efficient functioning of markets and transport infrastructure, and lead to dissaving, capital flight, and the departure of skilled workers."[6]

From a feminist perspective, international war, civil conflict, military spending, and the permeation of cultures by values tolerant of—or glorifying—militarism are issues central to gender analysis. The discussion of health-care policy makes it clear that most, if not all, of the problems of inadequate maternal and child health could be reduced with a reallocation of national resources. In an overview of violent conflict and gender inequalities, Buvinic et al. note that 80 to 90 percent of fatalities in conflicts are men, mostly young men, and about 80 percent of those displaced by war as refugees or internally displaced persons are women and children.[7]

For several decades, feminist scholars have examined the nexus of nationalism, gender, and military conflict. Men at war in defense of their nation-state, as part of their rationale for fighting, use the defense of families and homes—in particular, the integrity of mothers, wives, and daughters. Understanding rape as a frequent by-product, if not a central strategy, of war, governments freely use gendered images to generate patriotism. When families are torn apart and displaced by civil war, women are doubly vulnerable. One response, seen in the case of the ongoing conflict in Afghanistan, may be to further restrict women's freedom in anticipation of what *might* happen. Cynthia Enloe pointed out more than twenty-five years ago that the militarization of Afghanistan "has proved disastrous for women in the rural clan communities waging war." Forced into camps over the border into western Pakistan, their seclusion is more strictly enforced by fathers and husbands. No longer able to work, even in the fields, they are confined to tents and mud huts. "This civil war has been fought in a way that has militarized purdah."[8] Although Enloe was writing in the 1980s, for most women the situation in Afghanistan has not improved.

Christine Sylvester identifies the central ideas of recent feminist research as analyzing war as "a politics of injury," "experienced through the body," and "an emotional experience."[9] The effects of war include widowhood, income and asset loss, gender-based violence, and reduced household income. As a result, women often take over primary responsibility for their children's survival, and if able may undertake increased economic activity and even increased political participation. One dimension of increased activity has been peace movements, long a dimension of women's collective organizing. A century ago, the Women's International League for Peace and Freedom (WILPF) was created in the midst of World War I as an organization dedicated to combating militarism and war. Despite its failure to achieve its central goals, it has proved durable, broadening its focus to include the cultural manifestations of a spectrum of violence from domestic battering to global war. In 2013, for example, WILPF drew attention to an instance of normalizing violence through marketing: a newly released mannequin that represents a potential ex-girlfriend who can be shot as part of target practice.[10]

In 2003 a member of the Swiss National Council, Ruth-Gaby Vermot-Mangold, initiated an effort to raise the visibility of women working for peace by nominating one thousand women across the globe as collective recipients of the 2005 Nobel Peace Prize. The "1000 Peace Women" did not receive the Nobel Prize, but stories about their activities have inspired those who work for peace through a multitude of contexts—from post-conflict situations to grassroots environmental activism—in more than 150 countries. The stories have been compiled in a book, a website, photo exhibits, films, and the global NGO, PeaceWomen Across the Globe.[11]

If the discussions of neoliberalism and militarism have emphasized the negative consequences for too many people, the examples from PeaceWomen show that the structures have not been uncontested. Neoliberalism and militarism are not immutable, and their impact has been uneven, as the case of urban Chinese factory women illustrates. If WILPF has been largely ineffective, collective action strategies have nonetheless been successful in other domains. The establishment of a global gender equality regime is an essential illustration of the efforts of thousands of feminists at all levels and in all cultures who have worked to legitimize the norms of gender equality. These norms have percolated from the grass roots and from the highest levels and, in turn, feminists—despite their frequent disagreements—have deployed them in justifying a wide range of strategies, from inclusionary to transformative.

The Global Gender Equality Regime

It is worth recalling that fifty years ago, no gender equality regime existed. Today it does. The ease of contemporary transportation and communication has been central to the creation of international regimes, which exist both in concert with and in tension with nation-states. The global gender equality regime seeks to establish global governance structures to foster gender equality as an essential component of sustainable development. The discourse of women's human rights provides the language of this gender equality regime.

The previous chapter emphasized the success of women's human rights advocates in enlarging the conception of human rights to encompass violence against women in addition to the more established political, economic, social, and cultural rights. This is one of the key policy areas where equality and difference feminists have largely agreed on their goals. In contrast, diversity feminists have often been more ambivalent, recognizing that many of the human rights norms are rooted in Western historical concepts of development and have been elaborated largely by Western philosophers and activists. As a consequence, these norms reflect the bias toward individualism embedded in Western cultures. The single-subject focus of human rights instruments also reduces their effectiveness. For example, the Convention on the Elimination of Discrimination Against Women (CEDAW) focuses on women's rights; the Convention on the Elimination of All Forms of Racial Discrimination

(CERD), on racial discrimination—but neither addresses issues specific to black women. By definition, the general sweep of the human rights mandates tends to override the particular concerns of communities and even nation-states. This circumstance is also the genesis of the debate over secularism, religion, and the status of women discussed in chapter 3.

The UN occupies the center of the global gender equality regime. The UN Women's Conferences led to the formation of many UN gender-related institutions and processes, such as UNIFEM (UN Development Fund for Women, established in 1976), and INSTRAW (International Research and Training for the Advancement of Women, 1979), but in most years they were understaffed and underfunded. Feminist NGOs campaigned to consolidate, coordinate, and generate more resources for UN gender equality work.[12] The consolidation was accomplished in 2010 with the establishment of UN Women, although neither the UN nor its member governments committed to increased funding. Nonetheless, UN Women typifies the global gender regime that has evolved since the 1970s, and its primary significance has been to provide an administrative center to coordinate and monitor gender issues.

Chapter 2 emphasized the significance of the four United Nations conferences on women and their accompanying NGO conferences between 1975 and 1995. These were followed by the much less successful—in terms of their political impact—"Plus 5," +10, and +15 gatherings that primarily featured high-level officials and activists without the grassroots energy generated by the four global conferences. Between these meetings, and often as a consequence of the connections that they facilitated, feminists lobbied successfully for the drafting and adoption of CEDAW in the late 1970s. As explained below, CEDAW has become an instrument of reporting and, in some instances, government accountability for policies fostering gender equality.

During the 1990s feminist organizations lobbied the Security Council, the branch of the UN formally responsible for international peace and security, to recognize the role of women in peacekeeping and post-conflict reconstruction. As a result of these efforts, in 2000 the Security Council adopted Resolution 1325 on women, peace, and security. During the same period, NGOs, responding to the systematic use of rape in Rwanda and in the Balkans, lobbied the International Court of Justice (ICJ) to prosecute cases of rape when used as a weapon of war. In the 1990s, the ICJ began to examine charges of rape as part of its deliberations on genocide and crimes of war.

Like the UN, the World Bank has instituted a gender equality program to support its analysis of "gender equality as smart economics."[13] The Bank finds significant positive correlations between gender equality, economic growth, and poverty reduction. This is an *instrumental* case for women's empowerment—that is, the rationale is not equity or justice per se, but in the service of the broader objective of economic growth. Nevertheless, the World Bank's rhetorical commitment to gender equality reinforces the global gender equality regime, as do comparable programs in the regional banks.

Taken together, the institutions of the global gender regime are responsible for most of the broad-based research and data-gathering projects that enable international comparisons. Despite their limitations, sources such as *The World's Women*, the annual *Human Development Reports*, data on literacy (the UN Educational, Scientific, and Cultural Organization), employment (the International Labor Organization), and the Millennium Development Goals (the World Bank)—all of which have emerged in the past few decades—are invaluable resources for both researchers and activists.

FEMINIST AGENCY:
USING AND CONTESTING STRUCTURES

The dilemmas of all social activists are *what to change* and *how to change*. In this regard, feminists are no different. We have seen how they struggle with agency in their own lives and seek to enhance agency in broader arenas. Their choices are conditioned by the structures in which they live and their understanding of those structures and their options. We don't know Maryam's long-term fate after her return to Russia, but we do know that Jharna devised a strategy to maximize her agency in Kolkata by eventually becoming her own boss. In their respective water disputes, Maria and Jennifer struggled to provide for their families in hostile structural conditions but used the organizations and institutions (such as courts) that were available to them with some success. In other words, they sought to influence development in ways more responsive to their interests, and they also demonstrated that agency at the grassroots level can challenge, circumvent, even disrupt the forces of globalization.

In these and the other illustrations in the preceding chapters, feminist organizers have wrestled with the inherent tensions in feminist theory: the tension between equality and difference, a gender-exclusive versus gender-plus focus, universalism and diversity, and representing women's interests versus deconstructing gender. Collective action strategies feminists use embody these tensions. For example, we contrasted two opposing feminist antisex trafficking networks, the Coalition Against Trafficking in Women (CATW) and the Global Alliance Against Trafficking in Women (GAATW), which reflect respectively the insights of difference and diversity feminisms. CATW feminists tend to emphasize the gender differences between men and women, and to view the former as criminal perpetrators and the latter as victims of sexual domination. GAATW feminists, in contrast, emphasize the diversity of contexts that structure both prostitution and trafficking. Consequently, they are inclined to view sex work as requiring different policies in order to curtail and eliminate exploitation.

Deconstruction feminisms are less effective in motivating activists, but insights generated through the process of deconstructing language and normative or theoretical assumptions can lead feminists to change their positions. For example, the critical analysis by sex workers of a "rescue" rhetoric—that is, rescuing the victims of prostitution and trafficking—leads some feminists to move from a sexual-domination perspective to a sex-work perspective.

Tensions are also inevitable between feminists who emphasize incremental approaches that seek the inclusion of women into the existing structures of governance and those who are committed to transformative strategies that target structural changes designed to create new frameworks of governance. Equality and difference feminisms usually support inclusionary approaches; diversity feminisms, with their greater appreciation of intersectionality, are more inclined to support transformative strategies, but even these tendencies have exceptions. These distinctions can be seen in the water issue, discussed in chapter 5. Some feminists pursue inclusionary strategies designed to add women to existing decision-making bodies, whereas others call for transformative strategies that would ensure access to clean water for all people. Equality, difference, and diversity feminisms *all* motivate those advocating greater gender equity in water management, whereas diversity feminisms are notable in maintaining the human right to water—a goal to which many equality and difference feminists might also aspire.

In other words, inclusionary and transformative agendas are not necessarily mutually exclusive. The same individuals may be working on both agendas at different times and places. For example, Sara Ahmed participated in the official program of the Fifth World Water Forum and at the alternative conference, simultaneously advocating both the inclusion of women in the existing structures and the transformation of global water politics.

In many cases, a gray middle area lies between inclusion and transformation: in some instances, the inclusion of women will transform institutions; in some, inclusionary strategies will reinforce the existing structures of power; and in other instances, inclusionary strategies will open up power structures in a more egalitarian direction. To illustrate, it is too early to predict the outcomes for women's collective action strategies around labor rights, discussed in chapter 6. The Rural Workers' Union (STR) in Brazil represented both male and female workers, and gradually became more sensitive to the specific conditions confronting female workers. These conditions then became the target of the STR's negotiating strategy. However, even as the STR as an organization became more inclusive of women's interests, the Brazilian government continued to structure its economy in ways that made it more sensitive to global conditions that could suddenly shift in directions hostile to workers' interests. At the same time, growers sought ways to diminish the social costs associated with the female laborers, including training more men to assume niches in the production process formerly dominated by women. The STR is thus a good example of a collective organization trying to respond simultaneously to the needs of its members while operating under the shifting conditions of multinational capitalism and a government development strategy responsive to global supply chains in the grape industry.

Inclusionary agendas typically involve working for change within existing policy and bureaucratic structures. Transformative agendas usually involve actions outside of state structures such as confrontation and contestation through protest actions or self-strengthening activities such as organization or coalition building. Many feminist organizations pursue both types of agendas—often at the same time. For example, like the STR in Brazil and SEWA in India, Sikhula Sonke, a trade union and social movement of women farm workers in South Africa, holds demonstrations and also meets with policy makers in government agencies to get support for fighting unfair labor practices.[14] Women of Zimbabwe Arise (WOZA) marches for social justice but also lobbies the Parliamentary Joint Select Committee on provisions advancing women's empowerment and human rights in the Zimbabwean constitution.[15] The evidence on collective movements thus suggests that to be successful, approaches need to be flexible, multipronged, and multidimensional. For all social movements, the challenge is to do this while not losing sight of basic goals and principles.

In general, elements of equality, difference, and diversity feminism can all be seen in women's participation in labor movements, whether they are included in trade union organizations such as the STR or they are organized separately in autonomous women's organizations. Since its founding, the autonomous Self-Employed Women's Association (SEWA) in India has focused specifically on organizing women, although its earliest roots were in a trade union, the Textile Labour Association. Like the STR, the primary goal of SEWA has been to improve the working conditions of its members. Although SEWA focuses on women in the informal economy and the STR addresses workers in the highly stratified global supply chain economy, both associations have worked within the confines of the structures confronting the workers while endeavoring to alter those structures. In short, many feminist individuals and organizations do not view inclusionary and transformative strategies as incompatible; they are convinced they must respond to the immediate conditions that impact working people even as they try to mold structures in a less hostile fashion.

The Perils and Promises of Institutionalizing Gender

Scholars have documented the wide range of activities that local, national, and transnational movements have undertaken to promote women's rights. The general strategies of these movements have tended to shift from the earlier period of feminist action that demanded transformation to more recent decades when the dominant thrust of women's movements, particularly since the 1990s, has emphasized an inclusionary agenda that creates space for feminist action on the inside.[16] Andrew Merrindahl has contrasted women's movement "protest activity against the state and against dominant norms" in the 1960s and 1970s with their being more recently "partially institutionalized in government and nongovernment bodies, and in policies, practices, and social norms."[17] Sonia Alvarez describes the trend of women's movements undergoing the process of "NGOization," becoming organizations with small professional staffs that depend on foundations and governments to fund their projects.[18] These projects feature gender policy advocacy, from domestic violence legislation to the establishment of legislative quotas and the delivery of services privatized by governments.

The gender equality regime has led to a growing demand for technical knowledge on women and gender within state and global bureaucracies, and university graduates with coursework in women's studies and feminist research credentials have often filled these positions. They become "femocrats" who work with state bureaucracies, serve on government advisory committees, or are hired as consultants. The primary risk in this process is that a process of depoliticization occurs, as the femocrats become gender experts who carry out training of government officials, leaving behind any structural critique of neoliberalism or male domination. For example, although training workshops on sex trafficking for police and judges (conducted by both CATW- and GAATW-affiliated organizations) are essential in the immediate need to mitigate the effects of trafficking, arguably they contribute little to changing the global and domestic structures that generate trafficking opportunities. A CATW prevention workshop, aimed at warning women about deceptive advertising traffickers use, ideally enhances individual capacity to resist trafficking but does little to change the global trafficking dynamics.

Similarly, one might ask whether the widespread efforts to establish training and capacity-building workshops for women primarily reinforce "good citizenship" in the service of institutions that ultimately sustain the negative dimensions of neoliberalism and militarism. Some feminists have pointed out that the goals of many of these workshops are to develop attitudes of self-improvement, self-esteem, and self-responsibility for economic development and political participation in the existing systems.[19]

These types of activities are important because they are manageable in a relatively short time frame and are responsible for most of the incremental progress—such as establishing gender equality regimes—that has occurred in the past half century. But this inclusionary agenda is continually in tension with the more transformative agendas undertaken *consistently* by a few women's organizations and *occasionally* by many women's organizations.

Transformative Agendas

Around the globe, feminists who hew to the assumptions of diversity feminism most frequently drive transformative agendas. Components of the transformative agenda typically include a critique of the state, contestation of state actions, formation of coalitions with other social movements to integrate gender justice with economic justice and ecological values, and a variety of movement-building activities characterized by an identity/solidarity logic.[20] The identity/solidarity logic involves imagining feminist community and the development of feminist identities with the objective of transforming gendered power relations, along with other forms of hierarchical power relations. The participation of feminists in the transnational campaigns for a human right to water is an example of feminist involvement in a transformative agenda.

The main arena for feminist transformative agendas over the past decade has been the World Social Forum (WSF), first held in Porto Alegre, Brazil, in 2001. The WSF is an annual meeting of civil society groups seeking alternatives to neoliberalism, believing that "another world is possible."[21] Even though women have participated in large numbers, receptivity to feminist perspectives at the WSF has been uneven. In recent years, the presence of feminisms at the WSF can be seen in activities of the World March of Women and the Feminist Association Marcosur/Feminist Dialogues.[22]

The World Social Forum operates at the international level with links to national and local social movement initiatives. In some instances, women's movements have linked national and international levels to pursue a transformative agenda. This can be seen in some of the CEDAW Shadow Reports filed with the UN CEDAW Committee, which go beyond a critical analysis of the inadequacies of specific government policies to contest the legitimacy of the state. Examples include the Pakistan women's movement presentation on the "Talibanisation" of the Pakistan state and the critique of Israeli occupation that Palestinian women's organizations presented as an alternative report to the Israel CEDAW Report in 2010.[23]

At the local level, a feminist transformative agenda can be seen in the commitment to change personal interactions in daily life and in struggles "around the specificity of the lived body in a particular place."[24] A feminist NGO in Medellin, Colombia, set out to change power relationships in the lives of women through consciousness-raising (a widespread technique of women's movements in the United States during the 1970s), popular education, participatory organizational processes, and feminist art projects.

Rather than being mutually exclusive, feminist inclusionary and transformative agendas can be understood as points along "a continuum of women's struggles for full citizenship," and in some cases they strengthen each other.[25] In Jinja, Uganda, a local organization, Women's Rights Initiative (WORI), illustrates the way in which local organizations may adopt gender equality and solidarity as a long-term transformative objective while employing incremental steps to inform women of the ways in which they can enhance their individual capacity and agency. Founded in 2007 by three Ugandans, WORI's mission is to educate women and youth to advocate against violence by enhancing awareness of human and women's rights. WORI's activities mirror those of many NGOs around the world: education about gender-based violence, teaching leadership and decision-making skills, providing access to economic resources, instruction about nutrition, sexuality, HIV/AIDS, and so forth.[26] In broad social terms, these activities have limited power to transform all of Ugandan society, but for individuals such as the executive director, Kigere Rose, the results are transformative (see photo 8.1).

DILEMMAS AND TENSIONS IN FEMINIST STRATEGIES

The outcomes for feminist movements pursuing a gender equality agenda in a hostile world climate have been mixed. A major accomplishment has been the engendering of a women's human rights regime in the policies of global and national governments, especially regarding violence against women. In spite of such policies, both

Photo 8.1.   Kigere Rose, Cofounder and Executive Director, Women's Rights Initiative, Jinja, Uganda. Photo courtesy of Katie Leigh Hutt

intergovernmental organizations (IGOs) and national governments have shown high levels of resistance to the implementation and enforcement of these policies. For example, policies on reproductive rights and homosexuality are continually contested in most of the world, with women as well as men challenging the dominant feminist positions. These areas touch on the most intimate cultural values, and diversity feminism would tell us to recognize and honor these values as we address issues of gender equity. To illustrate, the familiar dilemma of an Indian woman agreeing to terminate her pregnancy through sex-selective abortion when she learns she is carrying a female raises difficult questions about the intersection of structure (the primary cultural value placed on boys) and individual agency. These dilemmas have no easy answers, which is why the tensions in feminist theory continue to present challenges for policy makers and activists.

The focus on the individual in most human rights discourse means that claims to group rights—to identity and to organize—will continue to challenge feminists as they navigate global challenges. For example, women's labor rights and women's economic rights (the combination of gender and class) have been relatively neglected in most women's organization agendas. However, this pattern has begun to shift in recent decades, with more gender-sensitive campaigning by labor unions and more class-sensitive strategies by women's organizations. A number of these efforts focusing on work were highlighted in chapter 6.

A very different type of issue—and one of the most difficult to navigate—reminds us of the tension between Western feminist emphasis on sexual autonomy and religious and cultural values. A major chasm in much of the debate over Islam, and particularly the group identity of Muslim women, is expressed through dress. Although some might claim that "Islamic feminism" is an oxymoron, the numerous illustrations of Islamic writers and organizers who have challenged the patriarchal power structures of their societies require that Western non-Muslim feminists continue to engage the debate introduced in chapter 3 regarding the secular, Western bias in development theory and practice. Is the hijab a symbol of all that is repressive? Or is it an expression of freedom of religion and an indication of resistance to Western-dominated culture? Does the effort of the Ukrainian-based organization FEMEN to draw attention to voyeurism and exploitation of the female body by going topless advance feminist agency or reinforce the view of feminism as a northern, white, marginal movement?

Some scholars argue that the inclusionary agenda of women's movements over the past two decades has reinforced the status quo: neoliberalism, class structure, and capitalist values.[27] They point out that micro-credit and attention to gender in economic development policies have integrated women into capitalist markets.[28] Upper-middle-class women with professional credentials have taken paid positions in the "feminism business," circulating between NGOs, government agencies, and IGOs.[29] Working-class women and their organizations have been left out. NGOs compete for funding, and the disciplinary power of funders silences discourse that is critical of the state. Some women's NGO projects can be characterized as instances of "governmentality" where women experts teach women how to be self-sufficient neoliberal citizens through self-management and fund-raising. Anne Runyan points to the "'missionary' model of feminism" implicit in the support by US feminist groups for the Bush administration invasion of Afghanistan based on the justification of women's human rights.[30] This also can be seen in the rescue mode in anti-trafficking initiatives by CATW.

At the same time some elements of the inclusionary agenda can be seen as reinforcing the status quo, other elements of the inclusionary agenda are enabling women activists to change the programs and practices of governance and the realm of possibilities that women citizens imagine. Activists in Kyrgyzstan lobby successfully to insert new language to empower women into government policy documents.[31] In Egypt "the circulation of discourses of 'Muslim women's rights'" reaches village women, bringing new concepts and possibilities into their repertoires.[32]

TAKING STOCK: LEVELS OF ANALYSIS AND ACTION

The debate among feminists about which types of strategies lead to progressive outcomes overall occurs at global, national, and local levels. These levels refer both to the location of the strategies under question and to the vantage points of the feminist scholars and activists. Some examples illustrate these dynamics.

The Global Level: CEDAW

Feminist perspectives on CEDAW and other UN women's rights documents seem to support the old adage that where you stand depends on where you sit.[33] Some feminist academics take a macro top-down perspective. From this vantage point, Western states and Western feminists are in control, and CEDAW mainly functions to sustain this control. Other feminist academics adopt the vantage point of women activists at the nation-state level, engaged in the translation and adaptation of CEDAW to local circumstances. From this vantage point, CEDAW offers both opportunities and dangers. Finally, some feminists working within NGOs are in the midst of ongoing battles at the UN and other international venues between conservative and feminist forces.

This third feminist perspective on CEDAW is advanced by activists engaged in the politics that surrounded the March 2013 UN Commission on the Status of Women Meeting (CSW 57) in New York ("UN Women 2013").[34] This perspective takes a positive stance toward CEDAW and identifies the "hijacking" of religion and culture by fundamentalists as the main obstacle to women's rights and gender equality. The priority theme of CSW 57 was the Elimination and Prevention of All Forms of Violence Against Women and Girls. Within this context, NGOs saw their task as stopping the rollback of women's rights language within international documents that conservative forces, such as the Vatican, a coalition of Muslim-majority states, and Russia, were pushing. In 2012, the CSW was unable to reach agreement regarding "the empowerment of rural women" because of challenges from Russia, the Vatican, Poland, Malta, and Hungary, which objected to proposed language on "reproductive rights, the rights of lesbian and bisexual women and the use of the word 'gender.'"

The Association for Women's Rights in Development (AWID) has taken a leading role in the feminist campaign in CSW 57.[35] AWID acknowledges the diversity within cultures, but foregrounds the current threat to women's rights posed by "diverse anti-rights groups (including States and other non-state actors) [that] are increasingly using arguments based on religion, culture and tradition to justify violence and tradition." AWID identifies the main threat to women as "this coercive tendency of religious fundamentalisms which often leads to violence and other human rights violations"; and argues that fundamentalism is "just one tendency within these religions . . . [which] contradict the fundamental spirit and essence of many faiths and religions, which is love, compassion, inner reflection, and to do right by others."

The danger, according to AWID, is that fundamentalist forces have "positioned themselves as being the authentic representatives of those religions" and have marginalized "more progressive movements and tendencies within all religions." The organization argues, "Women's bodies and rights (and those of people marginalized based on their sexuality, ethnicity, and religion) are particular targets of fundamentalist violence." The response that AWID recommends, under these circumstances, is to support the existing women's rights guarantees in UN Conventions, such as CEDAW, and to oppose strongly the fundamentalist interpretations of religions advanced by conservative states and non-state actors.

AWID's stance is shaped by a survey of sixteen hundred women's rights activists from more than 160 countries, which found that most activists reported a rise in the strength of religious fundamentalism over the past ten years and that these forces had "a negative impact on their work," using "'traditional' and 'moral' values to restrict women's sexual and reproductive health and rights and infringe upon human rights already guaranteed by international law."[36] AWID attributes the growth of fundamentalisms and their increasing strength mainly to factors such as neoliberalism, the growth of relative and absolute poverty, "the failure of states to meet the basic needs of their populations," identity politics, "the loss of certainty and belonging with growing globalization and the onset of modernity, and a concerted backlash to advances in women's rights and sexual diversity."

At the end of CSW 57, states did sign on to the "Agreed Conclusions," condemning violence against women and girls.[37] AWID and the other women's rights organizations were successful in "resisting the backlash against women's human rights" by some states that wanted to roll back previously agreed to international agreements and felt strengthened by their experience at CSW 57, because it "enabled advocates who traversed the political spectrum to work with ally States to advance negotiations, to deal with strong opposition, to monitor the types of arguments and tactics being used, and where possible, to counter and challenge these with rights-based perspectives."[38] In retrospect, the meeting demonstrated the importance of the gender equality regime for feminists defending reproductive rights.

The National Level: Quotas

The 1995 Beijing Platform for Action calls for "measures to ensure women's equal access to and full participation in power structures and decision-making," including "setting specific targets" to achieve equal political representation of women "if necessary through positive action."[39] Although some European states had adopted "quotas" for women's representation in national legislatures as early as the 1960s, a surge in the adoption of quotas occurred following the Beijing Conference.

Three types of electoral gender quotas are used in national legislatures: constitutional or legislative enactment of reserved seats for women, constitutional or legislative enactment of candidate quotas, and voluntary political party quotas. Usually the quota is set at 30 to 40 percent of the candidates for or seats in the legislature.[40] This is higher than the world average for women's representation in national legislatures, which is about 20 percent. However, the proportion of women legislators produced by quotas varies widely across countries. In some countries, some or all of the political parties do not adhere to the voluntary party quotas, resulting in low female representation, such as in Brazil (9 percent). In other countries, strong quota regimes lead to a high level of women's representation in parliament, such as in Rwanda (56 percent) and Sweden (47 percent). Some countries have also instituted quotas at the local level; for example, in India women must constitute one-third of rural and urban council memberships, and some Indian states have increased the requirement to 50 percent.

Two different arguments are put forward for women's quotas in the legislature. One is the "justice" argument: Women constitute half of the population, thus they should be in the legislature in proportion to their numbers in the population. Women's presence in the legislature is called "descriptive representation," meaning that people who are female are in the legislature. In terms of descriptive representation, quotas can be very effective. The second argument for women's quotas is that "women's interests" are better served by women legislators. This "substantive representation" argument assumes that women are better than men in promoting women's interests in the legislature.[41]

The concept of the substantive representation of women has been strongly critiqued, but it remains widely used,[42] although research findings are mixed on the impact of such quotas. American political scientists debate whether electing women at the national level furthers the substantive representation of women or makes little difference. If substantive representation implies support for *feminist* issues, then in the US Congress, where 20 percent of the members are female as of 2013, party affiliation is much more important than gender in shaping support for women's rights legislation. For the most part, the findings are similar in the literature on quotas: Party is more important than gender regarding support for women's rights legislation. But there are some exceptions. In Jana Everett's research at the local level in India, one way women representatives furthered the substantive representation of women is that they were more likely than men to raise issues of violence against women and women's programs.

The research on the effects of women's legislative representation has implications for the feminist strategy of advocating women's presence in decisions on water management, as well as in all governance bodies, from corporate boards to trade union leadership. Feminist scholars argue that we need to adopt a broader perspective on the types of change that might follow from increasing the proportion of women in leadership positions. They point to the effect of women on the social climate of institutions and the nature of political discourse, positing that more women might lead men to become more supportive of women's issues or, in contrast, provoke a backlash among men.[43] In Everett's research on the effects of women's presence in *panchayats* after three five-year election cycles, both male and female representatives, as well as local government officials, thought it had led to changes in the overall social climate and discourse that were favorable to women.[44] A recent study using longitudinal data from Argentina found that the increasing presence of women in the national legislature is associated with more women's rights bills being *introduced* by both women and men—but not with more women's rights bills being *passed*.[45]

The Local Level: Peace Huts and Women's Courts

A different type of inclusionary strategy can be seen in promising efforts to adapt community social-cultural practices to further the cause of gender justice. This can be seen in the creation of peace huts in Liberia and in women's courts in India. Initiated by the Women's Peace Network in Liberia (WIPNET) and funded by UN Women, peace huts are a reinvention of a local Liberian cultural institution for dispute resolution and now address gender-based violence, as well as land and religious disputes.[46] Community members bring their grievances, which are resolved by groups of women in the peace huts. In India, the Mahila Samatkhya organization has established *nari adalats* (women's courts) in several states where a group of local women adjudicate divorce, domestic violence, and property cases brought by women or men.[47] These "courts" are informal and are based on the model of caste *panchayats*, although it is now women and not men who decide the cases.

Some feminist scholars have praised these local-level initiatives; others have criticized them. Strong points recognized in these initiatives are that "social accountability is more effective than mere legal punishment" and that the local-level institutions created become "a pressure group and a force to be reckoned with."[48] Criticisms center on the relative social conservatism of these institutions even though they are innovative in giving a voice to women. For example, Sushma Iyengar notes that the "predominant role" of *nari adalats* "is to protect the rights of a woman within the framework of marriage," and that support is scant for a woman who wants to leave a violent marriage.[49]

Multilevel Strategies

Feminist strategies are not limited to one level of society or governance. Ultimately, they can and must be multilevel strategies to be transformative in the long term. CEDAW is a case in point: It is an international women's convention, and it has often been an awareness-generating agenda at the national and local levels. Feminist strategies are not merely top-down, flowing from the global to the national to the local. In adapting CEDAW to their national contexts, feminists in many countries are also influencing the meaning of CEDAW at the global level; actions at the local level percolate up. A local strategy—peace huts in Liberia—affects Liberian national politics, and can get adopted and adapted in other post-conflict societies after global feminist organizations disseminate information on this process through their websites. Global networks, such as Women in the Informal Economy: Globalizing and Organizing (WIEGO), learn from their local affiliates about strategies that work, and set up exchanges in which activists from one locality travel to other localities to gain know-how and inspiration.

Multilevel strategies do not work well if communication is ineffective both up and down the multiple levels of organizing. Some scholars have noted the negative consequences of certain attempts of global feminist networks to address local in-stances of women's human rights abuses. For example, BAOBAB, a Nigerian wom-en's rights organization, pointed out that protest letters international activists sent regarding a stoning sentence "played into the hands of Islamic political extremists because they contained incorrect information" that harmed BAOBAB's reputation as a credible actor working on the local level to stop the stoning.[50]

When communication from the local to the global levels, and global to local levels, is effective, positive outcomes can occur at both levels. In some cases, local feminist organizations in the global South talk back to northern feminist networks as they adapt and translate feminist practices in their own political, economic, and cultural contexts; and sometimes feminists at the global level listen. Millie Thayer discusses two different ways Brazilian feminist groups exercised agency against the funding practices of north-ern feminist networks: setting up a network of Latin American feminist organizations to critique these practices, and inviting funders to visit them in their rural villages in order to gain an appreciation of the context in which they worked.[51] In another example, the case study of the African Women's Rights Protocol in chapter 7 shows how its promotion by an African regional feminist network provides resources for legal reform that national feminist organizations in Africa can use.

CONCLUDING THOUGHTS:
STRUCTURE AND AGENCY

Throughout our book we have examined the interplay between structure and agency as women around the world negotiate their way forward, seeking different forms of human development. The structures that constrain, channel, and facilitate women's agency range from sociocultural institutions of family, religion, and community to modern institutions of state, neoliberal capitalism, technology, and militarism. Structures of inequality—race, class, gender, religious difference, sexual identity—have ancient roots that are maintained, strengthened, or sometimes weakened by modern forces. In our chapters on sex trafficking, water, work, and health, we have seen how cultural-historical patriarchal structures have evolved under neoliberal globalization in ways that often sustain gender inequality. Thus sexual domination assumes the forms of global sex trafficking and sex tourism. The gender division of labor continues with women assigned housework and child care including the collection of water, and additional responsibilities for income earning and paying for water. Many forms of violence against women continue even as they become increasingly visible and part of public discourse. At the same time, modern structures of state, neoliberal globalization, and technology have undermined some patriarchal structures, creating new options for women—education, paid labor employment, political participation, and communication beyond family and community.

In our chapters we have also explored women's individual and collective agency against injustice and in response to openings created by structural change. We have emphasized instances of women's agency in an emancipatory direction—seeking economic mobility, enhancing women's rights and sexual autonomy. But we also recognize that women exercise agency when they make choices that, from our perspective, appear to be more traditionalist or counterproductive in terms of gender equality—for example, the women in an Egyptian piety movement studied by Saba Mahmoud.[52] Although we cite numerous examples of effective *individual* agency, we also argue that *collective* agency offers greater potential for increased women's empowerment in general. As women engage in agency, they are creating new structures, such as quota systems, legislation establishing minimum wages for domestic workers, comprehensive health-care systems that provide for women's health needs, and international conventions on trafficking.

As students, researchers, and activists, we reflect on how we can use our own agency to promote gender equality. This issue inevitably requires reflection and discussion in the various contexts in which we enact our roles as students, citizens, employees, family members who are single/partnered, gay/straight; of various ethnic/racial heritages, class backgrounds, ages, and locations, rural/urban, rich/middle-income/poor nations. The first step is to educate ourselves on the issues that concern us. A wealth of resources is available on the Internet, some of which are listed in the appendix. For Americans, much is yet to be done in the United States to build awareness and influence policy making in social, economic, and foreign policy. Joining or forming organizations that advocate for women's rights and taking an intersectional approach to a more equal world is another form of agency. For example, the Clean Clothes Campaign (CCC) is a British organization that advocates for improved working conditions and wages in the global garment industry and supports the empowerment of garment workers. The majority of garment workers are female, and CCC challenges the sex discrimination, as well as the exploitative working conditions, women workers experience. After the 2012 factory fire and 2013 factory collapse in Bangladesh, the CCC circulated a petition through its website to demand worker compensation from the Western retail brands that had orders in the factories. Numerous activities of this nature are easily available to us.

With greater energy and resources, we can run for office and campaign for candidates who advocate for social justice. But for a start, we must confront the arena of daily life—how we raise our children, what food we buy and prepare, how much energy we use, what types of transportation we use, what and how many products we buy, and how we talk to and treat the various people we encounter. All of these activities can enhance and/or diminish women's empowerment as well as social justice in general. In the end, we recognize that, for the vast majority of women and men, transformation of structures will come through incremental change.

NOTES

1. The phrase is from Nuket Kardam, "The Emerging Global Gender Equality Regime from Neoliberal and Constructivist Perspectives in International Relations," *International*

Feminist Journal of Politics 6, no. 1 (2004): 86; V. Spike Peterson and Anne Sisson Runyan, *Global Gender Issues in the New Millennium* (Boulder, CO: Westview Press, 2010).

2. "Girl Power," *The Economist*, May 11, 2010, 51–52. See also the postings of the China Labour Bulletin in Hong Kong at its website, www.clb.org.hk.

3. Heidelberg Institute for International Conflict Research, *Conflict Barometer 2012*, http://www.hiik.de/en/konfliktbarometer/pdf/ConflictBarometer_2012.pdf.

4. Stockholm International Peace Research Institute, SIPRI Fact Sheet (2012), http://books.sipri.org/files/FS/SIPRIFS1304.pdf.

5. http://www.worldometers.info/education.

6. Mayra Buvinic et al., "Violent Conflict and Gender Inequality, An Overview," Policy Research Paper 6371 (World Bank, 2013), 8.

7. Buvinic et al., "Violent Conflict and Gender Inequality," 8.

8. Cynthia Enloe, *Bananas, Beaches and Bases: Making Feminist Sense of International Politics* (Berkeley: University of California Press, 1989), 57.

9. Christine Sylvester, *War as Experience: Contributions from International Relations and Feminist Analysis* (New York: Routledge, 2012).

10. See the WILPF website, http://www.wilpfinternational.org/shoot-a-woman-for-99; also the Zombie Industries website, http://zombieindustries.com/shop/alexa-zombie-target.

11. See the website http://www.1000peacewomen.org and the book *Peacewomen Across the Globe* (Zurich: Scalo Verlag, 2006).

12. Anne Sisson Runyan, "Global Feminism," in *Feminism and Women's Rights Worldwide*, ed. Michele A. Paludi (Santa Barbara, CA: ABC-CLIO, 2010), 3.

13. Georgina Waylen, "Transforming Global Governance: Challenges and Opportunities," in *Global Governance Feminist Perspectives*, ed. Shirin Rai and Georgina Waylen (New York: Palgrave Macmillan, 2008), 270. One of the Bank's key statements was *Engendering Development: Through Gender Equality in Rights, Resources, and Voice* (Washington, DC: World Bank, 2001).

14. Fiona White, "Deepening Democracy: A Farm Workers' Movement in Western Cape," *Journal of Southern African Studies* 36, no. 3 (2010): 673–91.

15. WOZA, http://wozazimbabwe.org.

16. Amanda Gouws, "Changing Women's Exclusion from Politics: Examples from Southern Africa," *African and Asian Studies* 7 (2008): 537–63; Shireen Hassim, "Terms of Engagement: South African Challenges," *Feminist Africa* 4 (2005): 10–28.

17. Andrew Merrindahl, "Women's Movement Institutionalization: The Need for New Approaches," *Politics and Gender* 6, no. 4 (2010): 609.

18. Sonia E. Alvarez, "Advocating Feminism: The Latin American Feminist NGO 'Boom,'" *International Feminist Journal of Politics* 1, no. 2 (1999): 181–209.

19. Jennifer Erickson and Caroline Faria, "We Want Empowerment for Our Women: Transnational Feminism, Neoliberal Citizenship, and the Gendering of Women's Political Subjectivity in Postconflict South Sudan," *Signs* 36, no. 3 (Spring 2011): 627–52.

20. Alvarez, "Advocating Feminism."

21. World Social Forum, Charter of Principles, 2001, http://www.forumsocialmundial.org.br/main.php?id_menu=4&cd_language=2.

22. Janet Conway, "Troubling Transnational Feminism(s) at the World Social Forum," in *Solidarities beyond Borders: Transnationalizing Women's Movements*, ed. Pascale Dufour, Dominique Masson, and Dominique Caoutte (Vancouver: University of British Columbia Press, 2010), 149–72.

23. Shirkat Gah-Women's Resource Centre, *Talibanisation and Poor Governance. Undermining CEDAW in Pakistan* (2007); Women's Centre for Legal Aid and Counseling, *Alternative Report for Consideration Regarding Israel's Fifth Periodic Report to CEDAW* (2010).

24. Wendy Harcourt, "The Body Politic in Global Development Discourse," in *Women and the Politics of Place*, ed. Wendy Harcourt and Arturo Escobar (Bloomfield, CT: Kumarian Press, 2005), 45; Donna F. Murdock, *When Women Have Wings: Feminism and Development in Medellín, Colombia* (Ann Arbor: University of Michigan Press, 2008), 35.

25. Hassim, "Terms of Engagement," 3.

26. WORI Uganda, http://woriuganda.wordpress.com.

27. Runyan, "Global Feminism."

28. Christine Keating, Claire Rasmussen, and Pooja Rishi, "The Rationality of Empowerment: Microcredit, Accumulation by Dispossession, and the Gendered Economy," *Signs* 36, no. 1 (Autumn 2010): 153–76.

29. Lila Abu Lughod, "The Active Social Life of Muslim Women's Rights: A Plea for Ethnography Not Polemic with Cases from Egypt and Palestine," *Journal of Middle East Women's Studies* 6, no. 1 (2010): 33.

30. Runyan, "Global Feminism," 7.

31. Marie L. Campbell and Katherine Teghtsoonian, "Aid Effectiveness and Women's Empowerment: Practices of Governance in the Funding of International Development," *Signs* 36, no. 1 (Autumn 2010): 198.

32. Abu Lughod, "The Active Social Life," 33.

33. This section is drawn from a paper presented by Jana Everett, Lucy Brown, Carisa Weaver, and Lindsay Miller at the 2013 Western Social Science Conference, April 10, 2013. Illustrations of these perspectives can be found in Runyan, "Global Feminism"; and Sally Engle Merry, *Human Rights and Gender Violence: Translating International Law into Local Justice* (Chicago: University of Chicago Press, 2006), 8–10.

34. See Association for Women's Rights in Development, "Religion, Culture and Tradition: Strengthening Efforts to Eradicate Violence against Women. AWID Talking Points for CSW 57" (2013), http://www.awid.org/Library/AWID-talking-points-on-religion-culture-and-tradition-for-CSW57; Susan Tolmay, "Will We See Real Progress in Addressing Violence against Women and Girls at the 57th Commission on the Status of Women?" (2013), http://www.awid.org/News-Analysis/Friday-Files/Will-We-See-Real-Progress-In-Addressing-Violence-Against-Women-And-Girls-At-the-57th-Commission-on-the-Status-of-Women; Valerie Costa-Kostritsky, "Beyond a War of Words: Will the UN Agree to Act to End Violence against Women?," *Open Democracy* (March 4, 2013).

35. All the quotes in this and the next paragraph are from AWID, "Religion, Culture, and Tradition."

36. Tolmay, "Will We See Real Progress?"

37. UN Women 2013 Commission on the Status of Women, http://www.un.org/women watch/daw/csw/57sess.htm.

38. Tolmay, "Will We See Real Progress?"

39. UN, Beijing Platform for Action, 80–81, http://www.un.org/womenwatch/daw/beijing/pdf/Beijing%20full%20report%20E.pdf.

40. For a comprehensive examination of quotas, see International IDEA, Quota Project, http://www.quotaproject.org/aboutQuotas.cfm.

41. See Susan Franceschet and Jennifer M. Piscopo, "Gender Quotas and Women's Substantive Representation: Lessons from Argentina," *Politics and Gender* 4 (2008): 393–425.

42. Feminist scholars differ on the meaning of substantive representation and whether or not one can talk about the interests of the category "woman" without addressing issues of intersectionality.

43. "Do Women Represent Women? Rethinking the 'Critical Mass' Debate," *Politics and Gender* 2 (2006): 491–530.

44. Conclusion based on interviews in Pune District in 2005.

45. Mala Htun, Mrina Lacalle, and Juan Pablo Micozzi, "Does Women's Presence Change Legislative Behavior? Evidence from Argentina, 1983–2007," *Journal of Politics in Latin America* 5, no. 1 (2013): 95–125.

46. Women's International League for Peace and Freedom, "Liberia: UN Women Dedicate Peace Huts," *peacewomen*, April 4, 2012.

47. "Women Turn to Nari Adalats for Justice," *Infochange* (October 2002).

48. International Center for Research on Women, "Women-Initiated, Community-Level Responses to Domestic Violence, Summary Report of Three Studies of Domestic Violence in India," Exploring Strategies, Promoting Dialogue (2002), 68, 73.

49. Sushma Iyengar, "A Study of Nari Adalats (Women's Courts) and Caste Panchayats in Gujarat," Asia Pacific Gender Mainstreaming Programme (AGMP), UNDP (2007), 17.

50. Aili Mari Tripp, "Challenges in Transnational Feminist Mobilization," in *The Women, Gender and Development Reader*, 2nd ed., ed. Nalini Visvanathan et al. (London: Zed Books, 2011), 403.

51. Millie Thayer, "Translations and Refusals: Resignifying Meanings as Feminist Political Practice," *Feminist Studies* 36, no. 1 (2010): 200–230.

52. Saba Mahmoud, *Politics of Piety: The Islamic Revival and the Feminist Subject* (Princeton, NJ: Princeton University Press, 2004).

Appendix

Resources on Women, Gender, and Globalization

INTERNET SITES

The Internet offers a wealth of resources on women, gender, and development; many of the topics, institutions, sources, and organizations discussed in the text are easily found by searching for the organization or topic. However, the Web may also be uneven and unstable. In some cases, websites disappear or are reorganized. The usefulness of a site depends on one's purpose. To illustrate, international organizations (IGOs) have worked for several decades to establish consistency in their data gathering. These efforts have not necessarily guaranteed consistency (e.g., in literacy rates) because they generally depend on national sources, but a careful reading of the notes accompanying statistics generally reveals the definitions, criteria, and limitations of the statistics. An example of comparative international data useful to most researchers is the annual *Human Development Report*, including its interactive features on the Internet.

Stable Internet sites also include peer-reviewed research publications. Although it is tempting to overlook or bypass these publications, the fact that they have been reviewed carefully before publication raises their level of reliability as sources of analysis and data.

For those whose interest is not primarily international programs or data, the Internet offers a wide range of other sources that will be familiar to most readers. These range from established media outlets to NGOs around the world, and feminist blogs that may or may not be ephemeral. Often the primary goal of an NGO or blog is not only global information sharing, but also networking or fund-raising. Social media such as Facebook pages, RSS, Twitter feeds, and Tumblr blogs are also widely used.

The following list of organizations is illustrative, not comprehensive, but it includes the organizations whose data and information have been useful in our research, as well as examples of regional and national sites that are accessible in English.

201

International Organizations

The most important IGOs are the United Nations, particularly its site for UN Women; its affiliated agencies, such as the World Health Organization; and the World Bank. All of these may be found easily by typing the name of the organization, then refining a search for specific topics, such as law. For information on women's representation in national legislatures, see the website of the Interparliamentary Union: Women in Parliaments, http://www.ipu.org/wmn-e/world.htm.

Regional Organizations

Notable among the regional organizations are the European Union, the Organization of American States, and the African Union. The regional development banks, such as the Asian Development Bank, also have useful websites. In all cases, search for specific topics—for example, women and gender.

National Governments

National governments, even those in countries where English is not the official language, may maintain websites that are useful—as long as one remembers that the sites reflect the national interests of the government in question. Therefore, certain topics may not be addressed on the site, or some information may be missing or incomplete. Often, however, they are the only resource available—for example, about a country's development policies or "gender machinery." Two illustrations are the Ministry of Women and Child Development for India and the Kenya Ministry of Gender, Children, and Development. In certain cases, census data may be very useful, and many government websites offer these data in English; see, for example, India and Japan.

Organizations Related to Women's Rights

Many global, regional, national, and local feminist organizations are on the Web. Some of the websites of global feminist organizations operate as information directories on news stories, resources, human rights campaigns, and calls for participation related to women (e.g., Association of Women's Rights in Development [AWID], www.awid.org; Women in Informal Employment, Globalizing and Organizing [WIEGO], http://wiego.org/). Global trade union organizations have Web pages related to women's organizing (e.g., International Trade Union Confederation Women, http://www.ituc-csi.org/women). Resources on women's organizations include the Global Women's Network, http://www.global-womens-network.org; Atria Institute for Women's History (Amsterdam), http://www.aletta.nu/aletta/eng; and the Stanford Feminist Resource Site, The Historical Emergence of Feminism, http://ntb.stanford.edu/resources3-5.html.

Resources on Women and ICT

A relatively new area for women, gender, and development resources on the Web is found in online resources in the field of Information and Communication Technologies for Development, ICT4d. Most of the early work in this area found that women were excluded from these new technologies. More recently, women's creative use of these new technologies has been documented. Some of these resources include Global Voices on Line, http://globalvoicesonline.org/2009/12/07/ict4d-for-women-opportunities-and-risks; the Spider Center, Empowering Women Through ICT, http://www.spidercenter.org/sites/default/files/Empowering%20woment%20through%20ICT.pdf; and Girls Globe, http://girlsglobe.org/tag/ict4d.

VIDEOS

Videos are an essential resource for students of women, gender, and globalization. Search university and public libraries for relevant films. YouTube is a useful source for videos, especially on current events gender issues. In addition, a commentary on feminist issues, Feminist Frequency, http://www.feministfrequency.com, is on YouTube. Another valuable resource is Ted Talks, which are eighteen-minute talks on a variety of subjects (e.g., see http://www.ted.com/talks/tags/women). For guides to films, see Films for the Feminist Classroom, http://www.signs.rutgers.edu/ffc_home.html. A variety of documentary films is available through Culture Unplugged, http://www.cultureunplugged.com/documentaries/watch-online/festival/films.php#view=thumb&page=1&listType=entries. To find films, look at film catalogs such as Women Make Movies, http://www.wmm.com/filmcatalog/collect7.shtml; Filmmakers Library, http://www.filmmakers.com; and Bullfrog Films, http://www.bullfrogfilms.com/index.html. TV is another source for films: see Wide Angle, http://www.pbs.org/wnet/wideangle/category/episodes/by-topic/womens-rights-roles; Women, War, and Peace, http://video.pbs.org/program/women-war-and-peace; and check Link TV, HBO, and PBS for films. Documentaries are also available through Amazon, of course.

BOOKS, JOURNAL AND MAGAZINE ARTICLES

Books and journal and magazine articles provide in-depth descriptions and analysis of women, gender, and development issues. Library databases, such as GenderWatch, list research studies and general-interest articles on these topics. WorldCat and PAIS also include books and reports of interest. Novels and short stories about women offer insight into the lives of women in different national, class, religious, and geographic locations. Web resources include Global Women Writers, http://userpages.umbc.edu/~korenman/wmst/global_fiction.html; and Voices from the Gaps, http://voices.cla.umn.edu. For novels about women in a particular country or region, google the name of the country, novels, and women (e.g., women Africa novels); and consider reading some older novels that provide valuable insights. A good example is the classic novel by Kamala Markandaya, *Nectar in a Sieve*. In recent years, perhaps the most compelling book on development and globalization, with abundant insights about gender relations, is Katherine Boo's *Behind the Beautiful Forevers*.

OTHER

Theater is a powerful medium; plays such as *Ruined* and *Nickel and Dimed* are recommended. Speakers from NGOs involved with local, national, and international gender issues can address the question, "What can I do?" Women in leadership positions in business, government, education, and the media can speak about their experiences and ideas for advancing women in their fields. International women students on campus can speak about their backgrounds and plans for the future.

Index

Brazil, 114–15, 193–94; and health, 162, 186; and work, 139–41, 141*f,* 143–44
Bretton Woods Agreement, 60–61
Brundtland Commission, 68n19
Bunch, Charlotte, 167
Bush, George W., 83, 85, 160, 168

Cairo Programme of Action, 166
cancer, 156
capitalism, 48, 59; alternative visions of, 66; and gender, 65; and health, 152; and work, 121
Caraway, Nancy, 126
Cardoso, Fernando, 68n16
care work, 24, 34–35; term, 34. *See also* domestic workers
case studies: on health, 169–74; on sex trafficking, 73–76; on water issues, 98–102; on work, 139–45
CATW. *See* Coalition Against Trafficking in Women
CEDAW. *See* Convention on the Elimination of All Forms of Discrimination Against Women
Center for Women's Global Leadership (CWGL), 167
centralization, and water, 104
childbirth services, access to, 157*t*
child mortality, 157–58, 164
Chile, 169–73
China, 23, 180; and health, 156; sex ratios in, 158, 158*t*; and work, 125–26, 144
Clean Clothes Campaign, 197
climate change: and Peru, 105; and water, 95–96
Clinton, Bill, 160
Coalition Against Trafficking in Women (CATW), 81, 85, 87
Coalition Against Water Privatization, 99, 104
Coalition for Justice in the Maquiladoras, 137
codes of conduct, on labor, 134
coercion: globalization and, 60; sexual domination perspective on, 81
Cold War, 54–55
collective agency, 7–9, 179–200; and health, 155, 166–69

colonialism, 52–53, 166; critiques of, 56–57; decolonization and, 54–55
CoMensha, 74, 90n7
comfort women, 164
Commission on the Status of Women, 36
Committee on Women, Population and the Environment, 167
commodification, of water, 109
Conca, Ken, 109
Consultative Group to Assist the Poor, 135
consumption, 95
contraception, 154, 157–58, 163
Convention on the Elimination of All Forms of Discrimination Against Women (CEDAW), 28, 38–39, 183, 192–93
Convention on the Elimination of All Forms of Racial Discrimination, 183–84
Cook, Judith A., 25
Council of Europe, 84, 84*t*
Creevey, Lucy, 63
criminal justice framework, and sex trafficking, 83–86
culture: and critiques of development, 50–51; and violence against women, 166

dams, opposition to, 106
DAWN network. *See* Development Alternatives for Women in a New Era
decentralization, 62; and water, 98, 103–4, 112
Declaration on the Elimination of Violence Against Women, 28, 168
decolonization, 54–55
deconstruction feminism, 29–31, 185; and work, 138–39
democracy, 48
dependency theory, 55–56
descriptive representation, 194
development, 1–22, 47–70, 179–200; agendas of, 53–58; criticisms of, 49–53; feminist approaches to, 23–46; lineage of, 47–49; term, 3–5, 47, 179
Development Alternatives for Women in a New Era (DAWN), 29, 39*t,* 44n20, 167
Dichter, Thomas, 136

About the Authors

Sue Ellen Charlton specializes in comparative politics and development and gender issues. Her publications have focused on French politics, women in development, and the comparative politics of Asia (India, China, and Japan). She has taught in France, Wales, India, and Japan. She is emeritus professor of political science at Colorado State University.

Jana Everett is a professor of political science at the University of Colorado, Denver. Her publications examine various aspects of gender, politics, and development in India and globally. In 2005, she was a Fulbright research scholar in India studying the impact of reserving one-third of the seats in *panchayats* (rural councils) for women. She teaches courses on gender, globalization, and development; global women's movements; and politics of South Asia.